The Disenchantment of Reason

SUNY Series in Social and Political Thought
Kenneth Baynes, Editor

The Disenchantment of Reason

The Problem of Socrates in Modernity

Paul R. Harrison

State University of New York Press

Published by
State University of New York Press, Albany

© 1994 State University of New York

Printed in the United States of America

For information, address State University of New York
Press, State University Plaza, Albany, N.Y., 12246

Production by E. Moore
Marketing by Fran Keneston

Library of Congress Cataloging-in-Publication Data

Harrison, Paul R., 1955-
    The disenchantment of reason : the problem of Socrates in
modernity / Paul R. Harrison.
        p.   cm. — (SUNY series in social and political thought)
    Includes bibliographical references and index.
    ISBN 0-7914-1837-5 (alk. paper). — ISBN 0-7914-1838-3 (pbk. :
alk. paper)
    1. Socrates. 2. Philosophy, Modern—19th century. 3. Reason.
4. Hegel, Georg Wilhelm Friefrich, 1770-1831—Contributions in
interpretation of Socrates. 5. Kiekegaard, Søren, 1813-1855-
-Contributions in interpretation of Socrates. 6. Nietzsche,
Friedrich Wilhelm, 1844-1900—Contributions in interpretation of
Socrates. I. Title. II. Series.
B317.H37 1994
183'.2—dc20   93-7295
                                                                CIP

10 9 8 7 6 5 4 3 2 1

Contents

Introduction

The Problem of Socrates in Modernity

This book seeks to unravel the fate of reason in the nineteenth century—a century that began in a mood of great intellectual confidence and ended with its finest thinkers already preparing for the polar nights to come. The eighteenth century was one of enlightenment, of *lumière*, of *Aufklärung*, but the twentieth century is one of "icy darkness and hardness." This passage from confidence to despair, from optimism to pessimism, from light to darkness took place in the nineteenth century within a specific cultural context: that of German thought. It took place primarily within German philosophy, but by the twentieth century it had also taken firm hold on German sociology. From German sociology it has now taken firm hold not only of other philosophical traditions that previously remained immune to it and of other human sciences such as anthropology, but also of popular consciousness. This study does not pretend to deal comprehensively with this profound cultural development. It seeks rather to interpret the work of some representative thinkers whose thought most cogently expresses the dilemmas created by this development. In these thinkers the great rationalist narrative undergoes an immanent critique that issues ultimately in either its revision—in a conservative direction; its transcendence—in a religious direction; or, more radically, its total critique. This total critique of reason issues in the counternarrative called "nihilism."[1] Nihilism is the end point of a long process of disenchantment or demagification *(Entzauberung)* of the world that issues logically but self-destructively in the disenchantment of reason itself.

1

I

The disenchantment of reason refers to the loss of meaning *(Sinnverlust)* that reason suffers in modernity with the growing differentiation of cultural value spheres, which results in the sundering of the unity of reason into a number of sphere-specific rationalities. To conduct oneself rationally, henceforth, will only mean to follow the norms and rules specific to that cultural value sphere. This development destroys the magic or charisma of reason, which derives from both its totalistic and universalistic claims, and strips of any ultimate validity the life directed and conducted according to reason. In this study I shall concentrate on the effect that the disenchantment of reason has on knowledge, morals, aesthetics, history, and politics. The most significant question is, however, whether there can be a moral-practical rationality that is capable of providing the meaning for modern man that was lost because of the splintering of reason. In Kantian philosophy this characteristic splintering of reason was first registered with an ambivalence that was to prove premonitory. With regard to the realm of knowledge, the famous Kantian critique of pure reason put paid to what he referred to as the dialectical employment of reason. However, even Kant's eviction of reason from its legislative role with respect to nature, and the consequent dualism that he establishes between nature and freedom, does not so much eliminate the desire for unity that is found in the realm of ideas as it redefines or even displaces it. Hence, in his third *Critique* Kant tries to construct a bridge between the legislation of nature and the concept of freedom. He does this by arguing that between understanding and reason lies judgment, and that judgment can be divided into determinant and reflective judgment. The reflective judgment, which ascends from the particular to the universal, becomes home to ideas of purpose and finality that have been forbidden to determinant judgment, which subsumes objects under the universal. The notion that within either the multiplicity of tastes or the multiplicity of nature there must be contained a finality or purpose is, according to Kant, such a reflective judgment. This same notion of reflective judgment is also alive in the domain of politics and history where it tries to descry hope in the midst of turmoil. Kant's attempted escape from his own dualism is one that will be repeated, in various ways, in the history of post-Kantian philosophy.

The notion of disenchantment is, of course, a Weberian one; however, the other aspect of modernity that Weber focuses on is summed up in the formula of a 'new polytheism'. With this formula he provides an answer to the question of the loss of meaning in modernity within a theoretical framework of great explanatory significance. The formula expresses Weber's belief that one cannot decide with the aid of science, as once one would have with the aid of reason, between the various gods and demons that confront one. These gods and demons are the various value spheres *(Wertordnungen)* that one must choose between. Weber as teacher has nothing to teach on this matter because science must restrict itself to the discussion of the rationality of the means *(Mittel)* chosen to an end, and not the end *(praktischen Stellungnahme)*. This self-renunciation of reason with regard to human self-definition means that modernity and antiquity come to resemble one other as "fate, and certainly not science, holds sway over these gods and their struggles."[2] Hence, the paradox of reason in modernity is that the disenchantment of reason, which results in the reduction of nature to a causal mechanism, leads to the reenchantment of everyday life. This invocation of fate *(Schicksal)* suggests even more pointedly the connection between an antiquity that as yet knows no reason and a modernity that is beyond reason. At two points, however, in "Science As a Vocation" Weber refers to two different cultural forms that are seemingly able to dethrone the prevailing gods and demons: Greek philosophy and occidental Christianity. The Socratic discovery of the concept *(Begriff)* shaped a form of life oriented both to the discovery of true being *(wahres Sein)* and right conduct. Christianity's prophetic legacy was the creation of a "grandiose rationalism of an ethical and methodical conduct of life."[3] Whether it be in a cognitive (reason) or ethical (salvation) direction, both cultural forms contain a principle of unity that annuls the struggle between competing value spheres. It is the possibility of such a principle of unity that has been lost in modernity.

Therefore, modernity involves a process of spheric differentiation, which necessarily leads to the de-centering of society. In Weber's work, the rise of a differentiated system of life orders is invariably linked to the decline of what is for Weber the *'grand narrative' par excellence*—namely, salvationist religion. In his essay "Religious Rejections of the World and Their Directions," Weber shows how salvationist religions cannot be accommodated in the economic, political, and intellectual spheres of modernity. Salvationist religions all presuppose a trans-spheric, substantive form of rationality, which does not tolerate the formal and depersonalized functioning of the modern economy and polity. Such religions cut across the autonomization of life orders and transgress the logic by which they operate. What is of particular importance here, however, is the emergence of art as a rival to salvationist religion in modernity. Weber argues that with the intellectualization of culture and the rationalization of everyday life, art begins to take on a redemptory function; that is, "it provides a *salvation from the routines of everyday life*."[4] Furthermore, Weber argues that the consequent shift from "the moral to the aesthetic evaluation of conduct is a common characteristic of intellectualist epochs," and it was, indeed, a characteristic of the nineteenth century.[5] The neo-Kantian Weber goes beyond Kant himself in denying all universality to aesthetic judgments when he argues that they are beyond appeal. Modernity sees not so much the death of God for Weber, as the cultural displacement of the redemptory function. Once again, the paradox of modernity comes to light: namely, the coexistence of disenchantment and polytheism, rationalization and redemption. Modernity is, for Weber, not so much a dialectic of progress and loss as a dialectic of differentiation and displacement.

The formula of the new polytheism also means that modernity is the hermeneutical age *par excellence*, for it is now up to each individual not only to choose which god to obey, but to create his own god or gods. Modernity is an epoch in which the fetishization of cultural creation and the proliferation of cultural interpretations knows no bounds. Yet all this is accompanied by a curious psychical disinvestment; for as the field of

possible investment widens, the strength of investment simultaneously declines—what could be termed the falling rate of
psychical profit. This characteristic of modernity becomes particularly clear in one line of nineteenth-century thought in the
wake of the breakup of the Hegelian system. Thought becomes
atopic. It multiplies the lines of possible interpretation. It either
resurrects figures, images, and models from the past for further examination or simply invents them. It reinvests in art
and the aesthetic domain as a whole, even when it ultimately
goes beyond this domain. The romantic investment in the
realm of the aesthetic arises to challenge the enlightenment
investment in a certain kind of reason. In the thought of the
nineteenth century, the three targets of what we now identify
as 'the postmodernist critique' first arise: "the global vision of
history as progress or liberation, the strict differentiation of
cultural spheres on the basis of an underlying principle of
rationality or functionality, and the idea of a uniform and universal reason."[6] For some of the major thinkers of the nineteenth century, history is already seen as involving either a
loss of enthusiasm or a loss of relevance to life; the aesthetic is
grasped as a principle of de-differentiation, and reason is either
ceding its place to existence or being subject to a genealogical
destruction. Hence, the postmodern condition is a cultural
interpretation or form of historical consciousness lodged in
modernity itself. The modern condition of thought as a 'field of
tensions' between reason and its other, or between enlightenment and romanticism, first arises in the nineteenth century.

II

In this study I have chosen to examine the disenchantment
of reason in the realm of morals through an analysis of several
nineteenth-century interpretations of the figure of Socrates.
With the progressive disintegration of Christianity in the nineteenth century due to the advent of the new polytheism, or of
what is more commonly called "relativism," there occurs a
new mood of cultural experimentation. The reception of
Socrates takes place within this increasingly nihilistic mood

that the disenchantment of reason creates. The conflict between the old polytheism and the charismatic power of reason that Socrates embodies becomes a hermeneutical key for some nineteenth-century theorists for thinking through the conflict between the new polytheism and the declining power of Christian ethics. With the attack on the ethical rationalism embedded within Christianity, there occurs a renewed attention to the cognitive rationalism embedded in Greek metaphysics. This does not, however, involve any one-sided resurrection of Greek rationalism. It is rather the case that the figure of Socrates becomes an emblem of the fate of reason in a polytheistic universe. He is an embodiment of the unity of the true, the good, and the beautiful in an epoch in which these cultural values split apart into their respective value spheres with their own inherent logic. Socrates is a myth through which the possibility—or, rather, the impossibility—of attributing any charismatic power to reason in modernity is considered. Like any good myth, the figure of Socrates contains the semantic potential for a variety of interpretations; however, at the core of the Socratic myth is the idea of the unity of life-conduct and philosophical practice that Weber deems impossible for science to provide in modernity. This idea expresses itself in the familiar Socratic theme that knowing and doing the good are one and the same thing. Yet even here there is ambivalence: is it the case that knowledge of the good is a product of the negative or dialectical employment of reason in the elimination of falsehood, or is it not also the result of the interdictory power of one's *daimonion*? In the trial of Socrates this unity of life-conduct and philosophical practice comes dramatically to the fore. Does he die as a citizen or does his ironic contempt for his accusers mark him as reason's first martyr, history's first dissident? And what of the accusations themselves: is Socrates pious or impious, educator or corruptor? In sum, even if the brotherly aristocracy of reason can create a trans-spheric unity, whereas the unbrotherly aristocracy of modern science cannot, is it not in fact still an aristocracy that maintains the most tenuous relationship with the culture that surrounds it?

The three most important nineteenth-century interpreters of the figure of Socrates were Hegel, Kierkegaard, and Nietzsche.

Through their respective interpretations all three tried to think through problems peculiar to modernity but that bore striking resemblances in their minds to the situation in antiquity. The attempt either to remain immune from polytheism, to overcome it, or even to welcome it seems to engender a need to reinterpret Socrates. With the Kantian dissolution of the metaphysical concept of reason, thought finds itself in a predicament from which there are three important escape routes. The work of Hegel represents a restorationist attempt to maintain order and unity in the house of reason; it is, of course, a grandiose failure. In the realm of morals the attempt issues in a critique of the impotent formalism of Kantian ethics and an attempt to restore to ethics their influence on life-conduct. The conflict between *Moralität* and *Sittlichkeit* in modernity is read by Hegel back into the context of antiquity as a conflict between the *ethos* of the Athenian *polis* and Socratic moralism. In both the early and late works of Hegel, the power of reason reconciles the conflicting elements; however, as I shall try to show in my chapter on Hegel, his early romanticism is replaced by an increasing conservatism. In the work of Kierkegaard there is a complete rejection of both Hegel's attempt to use reason to resist the new polytheism and Kant's delimitation of a sphere-specific rationality to morals. The notion of the ethical decision in Kierkegaard is both total and beyond reason. In the context of Kierkegaard's theory of stages or spheres, the figure of Socrates develops from an aesthetic figure in the early Kierkegaard to a quasi-religious proponent of the ethical decision for faith in the late Kierkegaard. In the work of Nietzsche there is not only a celebration of the disenchantment of reason, but also a critique of those sphere-specific rationalities that science, art, and morals embody as only the latest and most decadent attempt to resist the new polytheism of forces and drives. At this point the new polytheism links up with the old, and Socrates is seen as the theoretical man whose rationalism destroys Greek tragedy. Even more radically, he is seen as the initiator of that Platonic-Christian tradition that repressed the old polytheism and, in other guises, is forestalling the new. Both elements of what Weber calls the two most potent forces of rationalization in the occident are attacked by Nietzsche.

III

These three writers do not constitute a common tradition; and in treating their writings on Socrates, I am not even trying to suggest some sort of arbitrary and tenuous thematic connection. What I am interested in is their increasingly radical critique of modernity, which is reflected in their widely divergent interpretations of Socrates. Evidence of a romantic reaction against the disenchantment of the world is present in all three writers. The extent to which this reaction may constitute a type of romantic modernism is a question I shall discuss in the conclusion. What I would like to stress here, however, is that the reaction of the various thinkers to the disenchantment of reason in the field of morals can not be reduced one-sidedly to steps in the process of the disintegration of reason.[7] If reason loses its authority in modernity, then every modern thinker is by definition thinking after the disintegration of reason. Hence, we need a new interpretative framework for thinking through these nineteenth-century interpretations of Socrates. This work is, therefore, located in a similar topos as that of Nietzsche's, for in Nietzsche's work, as Ricoeur notes, philosophy becomes the "interpretation of interpretation." Such an interpretative framework must eschew any unilinear reconstruction of the history of ideas as either progress or disintegration, but must be more attuned to the complex tensions both between and within forms of thought and also to the rise of new cultural interpretations. The figure of Socrates is one around which dense clusters of new meaning gather in the nineteenth century. I have tried both to grasp the novelty of these new interpretations in light of the particular thinker's work as a whole and also to locate my reading of why Socrates became a problem in modernity back to a theory of modernity. Such forms of argument, however, do not constitute an explanation as much as an elucidation of contexts.

When Nietzsche wrote his famous chapter "The Problem of Socrates" in the *Twilight of the Idols*, he was, in fact, engaged in such an interpretation of interpretations. In his interpretation of Socrates, which necessarily means the interpretation of interpretations with regard to "the one who does not write," Nietzsche effects a reversal of the Enlightenment depiction of Socrates as the master of the *logos*. What Nietzsche does, in effect, is problematize this interpretation. Behind his problematization of Socrates lies a more far-reaching questioning of the Enlightenment concept of reason itself. Kierkegaard's problematization of Socrates is similarly an interpretation of an interpretation. In Kierkegaard's case, it is the Hegelian interpretation of Socrates as a moralist that is at stake. Yet behind even this lies an attempt to question the relationship between the ironic subject and the world. In the case of Hegel's problematization of Socrates, there is also a questioning of the Enlightenment. However, in this instance, it is Socrates as the discoverer of morality (and not as the master of the logos) that is in question. The elaboration of Socrates as a problem is, in the case of all three thinkers, a process of fabricating new meaning or creating new interpretations. Hence, the rise of 'the problem of Socrates' is not one confined to the texts of Nietzsche. In the problematization of Socrates, and through this emblematic figure, the problematization of the relation between reason and the world in modernity, and between man and world in general, is enacted. What does it mean, more specifically, to turn Socrates into a problem? To answer this question we need to look both at the notion of 'problem' itself and to the question of philosophical interpretation.

I want to look at the notion of 'problem' in two different senses. First, I want to look at it in a disciplinary or tradition-immanent sense. Ever since Aristotle, thinkers have posed their problems with an eye to the history of their past answers. The historical orientation of the nineteenth century sharpens this tendency by radically historicizing the list of possible problems. Thus, the questioning of morals that takes place in the thought of Hegel results in the historicization of the Socratic answers to these questions. There is a turn away from historicism, however, in both Kierkegaard and Nietzsche; and hence, the 'problem of Socrates' constitutes for both a contemporary problem of either existence or theory respectively. Thus, the questions of morals, existence, and theory that troubles Hegel, Kierkegaard, and Nietzsche finds in each particular construction of 'the problem of Socrates' a way of coming to terms with these questions by constructing an imaginary dialogue of question and answer within the tradition. Second, I want to look at the concept of 'problem' in the sense of 'problematization'. In this sense, the problematization of Socrates is also a way of problematizing some fundamental questions of modernity: whether that be the relationship of morals to custom, reason to existence, or theory to life and art. At a deeper, more philosophic-anthropological level, the notion of problematization also refers to the way human beings put into question their relationship to the world. Through the problematization of Socrates, the dissident strand of nineteenth-century thought tries to think through different forms of the relationship between man and world. Although my enterprise is quite different from Foucault's, I endorse his remark that "the task of a history of thought [is] to define the conditions in which human beings 'problematize' what they are, what they do, and the world in which they live."[8]

The choice of Socrates as a way of problematizating both modernity and the relationship between man and world in general is, of course, purely contingent. There is nothing that can be read into the fact that while both Kierkegaard and Nietzsche extensively discuss Socrates, Schopenhauer, who in many respects fits into this tradition, does not. Hence, my choice of Socrates as a key with which to spring open the reality of the nineteenth century and its thought immediately brings forth the broader question of philosophical interpretation and its relation to sociological categories.[9] This book is essentially concerned with the 'interpretation of interpretations' of Socrates. Hence, it is concerned with imaginary creations or imaginary Socrates. Furthermore, it is not concerned with relating each imaginary Socrates back to its referent, as there is no reality freed of interpretation to which these imaginary Socrates could be referred. Yet the problem of Socrates possesses significance and, hence, does have a relationship to reality that is not reducible to propositions. "Equipping something with significance is," as Blumenberg puts it, "the 'charging' of constituent parts of the human world with significance."[10] Therefore, the constitution of Socrates as a problem in modernity is, in effect, the creation of a new vehicle of significance, or a new imaginary signification, that creates and recreates the modern human world in differing ways. This 'equipping' is something that surpasses human subjectivity, yet the problem of Socrates is still capable of individual variation. Work on the problem of Socrates is work on the differing layers of significance that are attached to the figure of Socrates as an entity capable of possessing significance. Every new cultural creation, work of significance, or interpretation, however, arises out of specific sociohistorical contexts, although it must be stressed that these contexts do not *determine* specific cultural interpretations. The task of sociology is, therefore, to provide the concepts to elucidate the context in which new cultural interpretations arise. The main concepts that I have employed are those of modernity and postmodernity. The task of philosophy is to interpret these interpretations themselves. In particular, I want to interpret these interpretations as elements within a 'field of tensions' and to spring open the reality of this field using Socrates as an interpretative key. In this way the *dilemmatic* nature of modern thought and ethics should become clear.

IV

In order to justify such an interpretative approach, a brief look at alternative histories of nineteenth-century thought is necessary. I will look first at Löwith's theory of secularization, then consider the criticism of his approach offered by Blumenberg, and finally discuss Habermas's construction of the *Philosophical Discourse of Modernity*. The two major books of Löwith that I want to discuss here are his more general work on the revolution in nineteenth-century thought entitled *From Hegel to Nietzsche*; and his more specific work on the philosophy of history, which goes far beyond the nineteenth century, entitled *Meaning in History*. *From Hegel to Nietzsche* is a large, sprawling compendium that defies easy analysis, unlike *Meaning in History*, which has an explicit and succinctly argued thesis. Yet the main thesis of the latter book is present in the former—none other than the famous thesis of secularization, which states that the philosophy of history is dependent on the "theological concept of history as a history of fulfillment and salvation."[11] Hence, our modern, western, and secular doctrine of progress toward the better has its roots in theology. In *From Hegel to Marx*, both Hegel and the Young Hegelians are presented as the last bearers of this theological concept. Löwith argues that "this metaphysical historicism of the Hegelian system replaces the vanished doctrine of providence of the Christian religion," and that the Young Hegelians merely replaced Hegel's 'metaphysics of history' with an 'absolute historicism'.[12] As in *Meaning in History*, only Burckhardt is signaled out as an exception. Such a perspective on the nineteenth century results in even Nietzsche being, in part, assimilated into the overdetermined anti-Christianity of the Young Hegelians through the mediation of the figure of Bauer. Hence, nineteenth-century thought tends to be presented as the progressive decomposition of reason in history through the demand that the rational be made real (Marx) or pertinent to existence (Kierkegaard), while at the same time the motif of 'reason in history' is presented as secularized *Heilsgeschichte* that does not cease to have its effect on post-Hegelian thought. The Marxian doctrine of revolution is reduced, as a consequence, to an impoverished version of Jewish messianism. In *Meaning in History*, reason's failure to provide history with meaning, except in the guise of a covert theology, leads Löwith to the post-modern conviction that there can be no "global vision of history" because history is "governed by chance and by fate."[13] This unilinear reading of nineteenth-century thought as leading to the evacuation of meaning in history through the demonstration of the soteriological character of the philosophy of history in both its Hegelian and post-Hegelian forms unduly simplifies the competing tensions in nineteenth-century thought. It is a kind of progress model in reverse in that it leads continually back to the more ancient theological patterns that are said to shape the present. There is, however, a more complex reading of nineteenth-century thought present in Löwith's work that in many ways is more sympathetic to mine. It begins with the contrapuntal introduction with its parallel discussion of Goethe's Primary Phenomena and Hegel's Absolute and the dialogue between Goethe and Hegel over the cross. Yet this contrapuntal introduction soon gives way to a history of the nineteenth century as one driven by a concern with the vicissitudes of the Hegelian Absolute.

The concerns of Blumenberg's work both intersect with mine and go far beyond them because modernity, for Blumenberg, is a process that begins with the second attempt to overcome gnosticism in the late Middle Ages. The solution to the problem of gnosticism was, for Blumenberg, to eliminate the hypothesis of a separate God responsible for the origin of evil, not through the Augustinian solution of making human will the source of evil but through the ascription of infinite power and absolute freedom to God. These attributes were ultimately appropriated by man in modernity. Blumenberg arrives at this conclusion through a reconsideration of the role that theoretical reason, in the form of rational theology, played in the development of human self-assertion with the disappearance of order. Such human self-assertion is, for Blumenberg, intimately bound up with "the immanent self-assertion of reason through the mastery and alteration of reality."[14] Although the modern world is born out of the cognitive matrix of medieval theology, it is not a result of the secularization or 'becoming worldly' of theological concepts. Blumenberg accuses Löwith's secularization theory of both unilinearity and substantialism—that is, of assuming that thought undergoes unilinear progression from unworldy to worldly forms, but that in doing so it merely repeats more primitive motifs of fulfillment and salvation. According to Blumenberg, this theory both underestimates the novelty of modernity and misconstrues its continuity with the past. Hence, Blumenberg speaks of secularization by eschatology, rather than the secularization of eschatology. In other words, the process by which modernity is born is a complex intellectual one in which theoretical spaces or positions once occupied by theology are reoccupied by more secular answer positions. While processes of intellectual revolution are not central to this book, due to the fact that it concerns itself mainly with nineteenth-century thought rather than on any comparison of treatments of the 'problem of Socrates' across an epochal threshold, the more general strictures of Blumenberg against both the dangers of unilinearity and substantialism must be heeded.

While the danger of substantialism is not succumbed to in Habermas's *Philosophical Discourse of Modernity*, the same is not true for the danger of unilinearity.[15] Modernity is, for Habermas, inextricably bound up with the differentiation of the value spheres of science, law, and art. Each sphere has a sphere-specific rationality that replaces the old metaphysico-religious or substantive concept of reason. Hence, Habermas's position is essentially Weberian except for the overformalization of the value spheres along Kantian lines. The danger that haunts modernity in this context is that cultural rationalization will result in the complete impoverishment of the life-world through its colonization by system imperatives. In this context, thought has two ways out of the dilemmatic nature of the modern condition that were intensively explored in the nineteenth and twentieth centuries. The first way out is to revise the concept of reason, and the second is to abandon it. The history of nineteenth- and twentieth-century thought that Habermas presents us with is a history of the victory of the 'abolitionists' over the 'revisionists'. Let me explore these two routes in a little more detail. The first route is, in sum, to complete the project of modernity by recuperating the importance of the normative content of modernity by both anchoring it in the communicative rationality of the life-world and by developing proposals for that form of rationality's further institutionalization. Although Habermas makes a case for some philosophical precursors to what is essentially his own position, the main precursors stem from the sociological tradition. Yet Habermas's problematic is philosophically determined, for it is an attempt to rehabilitate the concept of reason by shifting it from one that is subject centered to one that is communication centered. Hence, the *Philosophical Discourse of Modernity* begins with the first attempt to overcome subject-centered reason in the Hegelian concept of the Absolute. Hegel is, in this sense, the first revisionist, yet the Young Hegelians soon set to work on the desublimation of his absolute spirit. It is the other route, however, that is the central concern of Habermas's book. From Nietzsche onward, according to Habermas, modern thought has developed a radical critique of reason that issues in the elevation of 'the other of reason', the renunciation of the autonomous subject, and the development of a de-differentiated image of society. This tradition of thought does not simply question the incompleteness of the project of modernity, but also questions the very project itself. It constitutes, in sum, a counter-Enlightenment tradition that stems from an overblown concept of the aesthetic. The problem of such a characterization is that it breaks off the two strands of contemporary thought from one other and essentially presents most of the radical strand as a philosophical dead end. I am less confident than Habermas that what he rightly sees as the dilemmatic nature of the modern condition can be adequately grasped from a perspective that is solely in the Enlightenment tradition. Hence, there is a need to articulate a paradigm of intellectual history that is able to grasp the dilemmatic structure of modern thought itself.

V

Modernity is, for Löwith, the secularization of those eternal structures of significance called fulfillment and salvation. For Habermas, on the other hand, modernity is the completion of a project that is embedded in the structure of modern culture itself. Both thinkers operate, therefore, with a closed model of modernity, although the way that this closure is effected differs in each case. In the case of Löwith this closure is effected theologically, whereas in Habermas's case it is effected communicatively; for the prospect of the completion of modernity through the life-world's recovery of its illegitimately colonized territory is prefigured in Habermas's characterization of understanding "as the inherent telos of human speech." His critique of instrumental reason is, therefore, a partial one in that his main objection to this aspect of the Enlightenment project is that it came to characterize the project as a whole and, hence, did not allow for the kind of communicative reason Habermas views as being embedded in human speech. Blumenberg's characterization of modernity in *The Legitimacy of the Modern Age* as involving human self-assertion seems, at first glance, to avoid some of the pitfalls of both Löwith's and Habermas's approach. The notion of self-assertion as an 'existential program' allows for an open-ended relationship between man and world that is not predetermined by theological or linguistic motifs. The notion of self-assertion, however, does contain a cognitivist bias that smacks of a one-sided reduction of modernity to its Enlightenment inheritance. For example, Blumenberg argues modern man now "posits his existence in an historical situation and indicates to himself how he is going to deal with the reality surrounding him and what use he will make of the possibilities that are open to him."[16] Another example is where Blumenberg argues that we must search for the "original motivation" of science and technology in "man's self-interest."[17] Yet there are other elements in Blumenberg's work that point toward a wider conception of modernity. These elements have been taken up in the work of Johann P. Arnason.

In the work of Arnason, the dilemmatic structure of modern thought is conceptualized as an alternative to the concept of a unitary understanding of the modern world, such as that embodied in the idea of modernity as an incomplete project. Rather than either treating romanticism as one element of a modern, differentiated society or exiling it to the role of 'the other' compared to the Enlightenment, Arnason wants to assign romanticism an equal role in what he calls "the self-thematization of modernity."[18] Modern forms of consciousness involve, according to Arnason's various formulations, either "an internal polarization," "a structurally split self-thematization," or, finally, "a constitutive polarity."[19] The two poles constitutive of modern forms of consciousness are, of course, formed around the two discourses of Enlightenment and romanticism. Such a redefinition of the structure of the modern forms of consciousness necessitates "a clearer and more complex definition" of both terms.[20] Both terms constitute, for Arnason, two different ways of linking man and world. In short, they constitute the two sides of the modern form of consciousness that give rise to two very different existential programs. The Enlightenment program embodies a form of rationality that emphasizes "disposability, control and the expansion of power," whereas the romantic program emphasizes the web of meaning or 'significance' that binds the human world to the world as a whole.[21] Modernity is, therefore, conceptualized as a conflict between meaning and meaning-depleting forms of consciousness. "Romanticism in its widest sense" is defined by Arnason, accordingly, as "the defence of significance against its subsumption under the meaning-depleting mechanisms of . . . Enlightenment."[22] Such a wide definition of romanticism does have its disadvantages in that it tends to reduce conservative thought to a form of romanticism and underestimates the romantic element in some elements of liberal thought. More fundamentally, however, it tends to construe romanticism as a defensive form of consciousness, a tendency that underestimates the creative vitality of the romantic form of consciousness. Arnason's reconceptualization of the modern forms of consciousness as a field of tensions *(Spannungsfeld)* between the two constitutive poles of Enlightenment and romanticism is part of a more general project to reconceptualize the basic terms of social theory that lie outside the interests of the present work. I believe, however, that the basic idea of modern thought as a 'field of tensions' can be used, albeit tentatively due to the previously mentioned provisos, in the reconstruction of intellectual history.

It is my intention, therefore, to explore this field of tensions by looking at the conflict of interpretations over the figure of Socrates in several nineteenth-century thinkers. In other words, what I want to look at is the way in which a widened and enlarged definition of the terms *Enlightenment* and *romanticism* can be constructed hermeneutically as the two poles within which modern thought moves in its treatment of the figure of Socrates. This will enable the variety of interpretative positions that have been taken with respect to the figure of Socrates to be reconstructed in terms of their attitude to the problem of Socrates. The problem of Socrates can be seen to lie primarily in his discursive construction of truth in a time when thought undergoes a process of self-relativization. The positions that arise with respect to the problem of Socrates vary according to whether Socrates is seen as an ironical critic of inherited thought or an attempt at a rational reconstruction of inherited thought. In the modern moment these positions can vary from, on the one hand, either a romantic valorization of Socrates' ironical and self-relativizing attitude to inherited thought or a romantic critique of his discursive use of reason to, on the other hand, a rationalist valorization of his discursive employment of reason or an ethical valorization of his moral personality. In the postmodern moment they can vary from, on the one hand, a romantic deconstruction of Socrates' rationalist attempt to reconstruct inherited thought to, on the other hand, a rationalist appreciation of his discursive employment of speech. What is remarkable is the striking degree of continuity within change that occurs through these two moments. In the thought of Hegel, Kierkegaard, and Nietzsche there occurs an increasingly unambiguous reaction against the Enlightenment that can be read through their interpretations of Socrates. In the thought of Apel and Derrida some of the ambiguities are reinstated, but the polarities of the field stand out more starkly. It is remarkable that the constitution of Socrates as a problem in modernity has led to such strikingly different and original interpretations; and it is remarkable, as we shall discuss in the conclusion of this book, that it still does so in contemporary thought. The figure of Socrates continues to be read either as part of the Enlightenment program to deplete the world of meaning due to its emphasis on the discursive nature of speech or as a part of the romantic program to enlarge meaning in the face of either the meaning-depleting nature of formalistic ethics or the meaning-recuperating strategy of logocentric thought. In the romantic program Socrates also appears as the rationalist who threatens meaning, which is identified either with the 'archaic' or with 'writing', through his imposition of an order that is ascribed either to an ontological or to a phonological reductionism. The figure of Socrates still moves between the poles of disenchanted reason and the enchantment of irony, the remedy of the *pharmakon* and the poison of the *pharmakon*, the logocentrism of reason and the atopic nature of thought. It still hovers, in sum, between modernity and postmodernity.

Chapter One

Hegel: Socrates As the Inventor of Morals

In the work of Kant the old metaphysical concept of reason, which sought to order the universe according to certain transcendental ideas produced by pure reason, receives its death blow. Kant achieves this philosophical revolution by refusing to allow to transcendental ideas the possibility of any constitutive employment; that is, they cannot be classed as constitutive of any possible objects of existence. They have a purely ideal existence, and any attempt to transgress this limit, which Kant argues is a quite natural tendency of humankind, leads to the pseudo-rational or dialectical employment of these concepts. It should be clearly noted that in giving up this metaphysical concept of reason Kant does not surrender the notion of reason as such. His aim is merely to assert that the ideas of pure reason cannot supplant experience in the ordering of our physical world. Their realm is, rather, that of the kingdom of ends, which is conceived by Kant as strictly separate from the order of nature. As part of this realm, these ideas have a purely regulative or hypothetical, as opposed to constitutive, employment. Although reason is, therefore, still charged with making sense of the world, it does so in full consciousness of the imaginary, hypothetical, or projected character of any attempt at universality. The task of ordering the objects of possible experience is the rightful task of the understanding or intellect *(Verstand)*. Hence, the critique of pure reason is designed to deny that right to reason *(Vernunft)* by drawing the boundaries of the legitimate use of transcendental ideas. Kant preserves the dignity of reason by teaching it some modesty.

According to Hegel, such a project is equivalent to trying to learn to swim without first throwing oneself in the water. For Hegel cognition is neither an instrument we employ to know things nor a passive medium through which we think things. Thinking is an activity. It is the activity of the spirit (*Geist*) coming to know itself through the simplest forms of cognition (sense-certainty, perception, etc.) to the most complex (self-consciousness, reason, etc.), and through a knowledge of the simplest types of objects (stones, rocks, etc.) to the most complex (cultural objectivations such as artistic works, religious systems, and philosophical texts). It is only when spirit reaches the end of its journey, which is absolute knowing, that the spirit realizes through a kind of recollective reconstruction that the stages of its development are stages in the progression toward the absolute. Having reached this stage, the spirit creates categories that can be examined in their frozen immobility in the Science of Logic. There is, therefore, no simple return to a constitutive employment of the categories of reason in the old metaphysical sense in Hegel; however, through the philosophy of *Geist*, Hegel is able to overcome the duality of *Verstand* and *Vernunft* by making the ordering of reality the paradoxical result of a providentially guided historical process of development. But this historiosophical employment of the concept of reason does not escape the Kantian strictures against any constitutive employment of transcendental ideas. Hence, in this regard Hegel's philosophy falls back to a pre-Kantian position in its attempt to order reality according to the notion of the absolute. Insofar as it takes the notion of the absolute as a result, it directs the attention of philosophy toward history and brings it, as a consequence, into touch with the reality of its own time by forsaking the comfort of a closed conceptual universe.

The greatness of the Hegelian philosophy lies, as Taylor has rightly seen, in its conception of the subject as self-defining rather than as definable in relation to an ontologically structured cosmic order or, I would add, to a closed theological universe.[1] The notion of the self-defining subject is an answer to the question of how the whole or the absolute can be posited as a result rather than as something eternally pregiven. When

Hegel says that "the true is the whole *(das Wahre ist das Ganze),*" he remains faithful to the metaphysical tradition; however, when he adds that "the whole is nothing other than the essence consummating itself through its development *(durch seine Entwicklung sich vollendende Wesen),*" he leaves this tradition in a way that is completely different from Kant's departure.[2] The notion of the substance as subject thrusts the substance into history and sets the subject to work. Hegel further argues that "everything turns on grasping and expressing the true *(Wahre)*, not only as substance *(Substanz)*, but equally as subject *(Subjekt)*."[3] Hence, the true has to be grasped both as activity and as result. Through the process of positing itself as 'simple negativity' *(einfache Negativität)*—that is, by positing itself as something other or by becoming an other to itself—the subject comes to itself.[4] The true is, therefore, a result of the process of development in which what was there potentially is made actual. Only insofar as the rational becomes actual—that is, as the absolute (or God) realizes itself in history—does the actual become rational. In Hegel's philosophy the authority of reason is not denied; it is merely asked to travel through the *via dolorosa* of history and suffer crucifixion before it feels the heavenly light of resurrection.

The historiosophical turn of the concept of reason means that philosophy turns toward the world and, in particular, toward the theorization of its relationship to the world. In modernity this relationship can only be a dynamic and progressive one precisely because the absolute emerges out of negation, out of its collision with being. Hegel realizes the modernity of his own philosophy of *Geist*: "ours is a birth-time and a period of transition to a new era. Spirit *(Geist)* has broken with the world it has hitherto inhabited and imagined *(der bisherigen Welt seines Daseins und Vorstellens)*, and is of a mind to submerge it in the past, and in the labour of its own transformation. Spirit is indeed never at rest but always engaged in moving forward *(in immer fortschreitender Bewegung)*."[5] In his *Lectures on the Philosophy of History* Hegel contrasts this new concept of reason with that which prevailed in antiquity. He argues that the ancient concept of reason as *logos* means that the "in itself and for itself of consciousness only has an ethereal formal existence as language *(ätherische formelle Existenz als Sprache).*"[6] The determination of the concept of reason as absolute spirit means that through the activity of the concept *(Begriff)* itself, spirit strives to overcome the opposition between the "in itself" and the "for itself," between being and thinking; hence, through becoming certain of itself as being all reality, it achieves its rational identity as absolute spirit. The split between thinking and being, which the Hegelian idea of spirit strives to overcome, is what defines the principle of modernity as active self-defining subjectivity. Reality must be grasped by self-consciousness in order for its rational content to be secured. Reason is not simply embedded in the structure of language as such. On the one hand, Hegel is modernist enough to understand the necessity of this split between thinking and being; on the other hand, the idea of reconciliation contained in the notion of spirit already indicates a romantic reaction against this disintegration of an ontological principle of ordering in modernity. The Hegelian concept of reason involves the idea of the redemption of fallen reality (or devalorized being) through the providentially guided journey of spirit in history. This journey is not endless; and the latest stage of the spirit's journey may also be its last, hence, the importance of the contemporary in the thought of Hegel.

Both Foucault and Habermas have recently argued that the philosophical discourse of modernity comes into existence when thought turns toward an analysis of the contemporary world rather than of the eternal problems that have been handed down in the philosophical tradition, and becomes conscious of its relationship to that world. Foucault argues that the inaugurator of this discourse is Kant, the Kant of *Was ist Aufklärung?* and *Der Streit der Fakultäten.* For Habermas, however, it is only with Hegel that the discourse proper gets under way, for only "in his theory does the conceptual constellation between modernity *(Moderne),* time-consciousness and rationality become apparent for the first time."[7] What is central for both Foucault and Habermas is modern thought's recognition of its own historicity. According to Foucault, classical culture could only conceive of modernity in a "longitudinal relation to the ancients," which involved practical questions such as "what model to follow" and questions of value comparison such as "are we in a period of decadence?"[8] With Kant, modern culture poses the question of its modernity in "an 'arrowlike' *(sagital)* relation to its own actuality."[9] Put simply, the philosopher now begins to read his newspaper, which is a creation of *bürgerliche Öffentlichkeit*, for news of those great historical events such as the French Revolution. Foucault cites as evidence for the self-reflexivity of modernity the fact that "the *Aufklärung* has called itself *Aufklärung*," as well as the fact that for Kant it is not the revolution as event that makes it a sign of progress but the revolution as affect; the enthusiasm of those who witnessed it, as did Kant, is a sign of a moral disposition in humanity toward freedom and peace. When Habermas makes Hegel the inaugurator of the discourse of modernity, he does so with the authority of Hegel himself; for the statement of the late Hegel that "philosophy is its own time conceptualized in thought" could stand as the philosophical signature of his whole oeuvre. Again it is the French Revolution that causes philosophy to pose the question of its own historicity. In an earlier essay Habermas notes that Hegel has celebrated the anniversary of the fall of the Bastille every year of his life, but that this celebration is in effect an exorcism.[10] Whereas Kant has not allowed himself to be mesmerized by the terror and judges it from the standpoint of the spectator, Hegel's abhorrence of it leads him to the view that the intellectual foundation of terror lies in the philosophy of the Enlightenment. Hegel's attitude toward the Enlightenment, in both its French and more particularly German form, leads him toward a critique of the formal and abstract character of *Moralität*. Hegel's interpretation of modernity forms a part of the hermeneutical horizon in which he grasps the tragedy of Socrates as a conflict between *Moralität* and *Sittlichkeit* (morality and custom).[11]

If the task of modern thought is to grasp the principle of its own time in thought, then for Hegel that principle is subjectivity. It is important, however, to note that this principle is conceived metaphysically and not critically. Modern thought's recognition of its own historicity ultimately leads to relativism, but this terminus is not reached in Hegel precisely due to his retention and transformation of metaphysical notions such as substance. The idea that substance is subject, as mentioned earlier, is also described by Hegel as the most sublime concept: "That the true is actual only as system, or that Substance is essentially Subject, is expressed in the representation of the Absolute as *Spirit (Geist)*—the most sublime Notion and the one which belongs to the modern age *(neuren Zeit)* and its religion."[12] With this metaphysical notion of the subject Hegel tries to solve "the problem of the self-certainty of modernity" (Habermas); it incorporates those elements of subjectivity that Hegel thinks of positively and lifts up *(aufhebt)* and those that he thinks of negatively. This means that Hegel's discovery of subjectivity as the principle of modernity is, at the same time, a critique of modernity. This principle attempts to conceive both of the nature of the modern world and its crises: "the world of progress and of estranged spirit."[13] Habermas argues that for Hegel the term *Subjectivität* has four connotations: individualism, the right of critique, the autonomy of action, and idealistic philosophy itself.[14] Furthermore, the principle determines, in Habermas's very Kantian reconstruction of Hegel's position, the forms of modern culture: it demagifies nature and liberates the knowing subject for the objectifying sciences; it desubstantializes customary life and elevates the subjective freedom of the individual to *the* principle of morality; and it deplasticizes the art object through the elevation of the principles of absolute inwardness and expressive self-realization in modern art.[15] Hence, there is a threefold separation of the domains of science, ethics, and aesthetics from their entanglement in the net of the life-world. Whereas Habermas tends to accept this separation as the hallmark of modernity, Hegel's philosophy of reconciliation *(Vereinigungsphilosophie)* tries to preserve, through lifting up *(aufhebt)*, what modernity tends to leave behind from the standpoint of the absolutization of the philosophy of the subject itself. Therefore, the philosophy that Hegel is most critical of is the one that most clearly expresses in thought the estranged structure of the modern world: subjective idealism.[16] In Hegel's interpretation of Socrates this separation of ethics from the life-world, which subjective idealism *inter alia* expresses, is read back into antiquity. What I want to argue in this chapter is that the power that subjective idealism still exercises on Hegel's mind, despite the criticisms he makes of it, can be seen in the very Kantian Socrates that he depicts. In the early work of Hegel, Socrates is depicted as the advocate of a purely discursive and thoroughly disenchanted reason in contrast to the figure of Jesus within the Judaeo-Christian tradition. In the late Hegel, the conflict between *Moralität* and *Sittlichkeit* is played out once again in the condemnation of Socrates in a situation in which neither is victor; rather, there occurs a mutual destruction of contending forces. From the standpoint of Hegel's philosophy of history, however, there emerges out of this destruction a new historical principle that will find its actualization only in modernity. Hegel's clear admiration for the discursive rationality of Socrates and for the unwillingness of the latter to accept the merely existent without asserting the right of free subjectivity to question conflicts with his critique of the formalism, abstractness, and impotence of the Kantian ought *(Sollen)* and his attempt to find a place within ethics for the authority of custom *(Sittlichkeit)* as represented by the Greek *polis*. In Hegel's retelling of the fate of Socrates, the *Urgeschichte* of modern rationality within the domain of ethics—the conflict between the individual's right of criticism and the *Sitte des Volkes*—forms the substance of the tragedy.

I

In his early writings, which have been published under the title *Early Theological Writings*, Hegel's thought circles around the attempt to articulate a form of Christianity that, while remaining within the orbit of what he calls in *Faith and Knowledge* the "principles of the north," experiments with the incorporation of elements that both precede and transcend this principle. The principle of the north, which is that of Protestantism, is "subjectivity for which beauty and truth present themselves in feelings and convictions *(Gesinnungen)*, in love and intellect *(Verstand)*. Religion builds its temples and altars in the heart of the individual."[17] Such a definition already goes beyond classic Protestantism in its incorporation of romantic elements; however, for the early Hegel this is no problem, as the real danger to religion is in the tendency toward positivity. The positivity of the Christian religion rests in its dependence on the merely external authority of Christ, as made evident by his miracles, for the validity of its moral laws *(Tugendgesetze)*.[18] In Kierkegaardian terms, Hegel tries to reconcile Religiousness B with Religiousness A to form a religiousness in which elements of Protestantism, Kant, and Rousseau freely intermingle to form a version of Christianity in which there is no conflict between the immanent authority of morality and the transcendental authority of God. If this constitutes the part of the Hegelian experiment that goes beyond pure Protestantism, then what are the elements that precede it that Hegel also experiments with? The short answer is Greek religiousness.

As Taylor has rightly remarked, "Hegel's itinerary" involves an attempt at reconciling the expressivist current of romanticism with the rationalistic current of the Enlightenment—an attempt to reconcile the heart and the intellect *(Verstand)*, love and the law, freedom and reason *(Vernünft)*.[19] Within the expressivist current, however, there circulates images not merely of the 'beautiful soul', but also of an "integrated civilization," to use Lukàcs term. Hence, the concern of the "Fragments on Folk Religion and Christianity" is to develop a form of religion that will respect the claims of the Enlightenment and both strands of the expressivist current of romanticism. Hegel argues that the objective doctrines *(Lehren)* of a *(Volksreligion)* must satisfy three criteria:

1. Its teachings *(Lehren)* must be founded on universal reason.
2. Imagination, the heart, and the senses must not go away empty-handed in the process.
3. It must be so constituted that all of life's needs, including public and official transactions *(die öffentliche Staatshandlungen)*, are bound up with it.[20]

A folk religion is, therefore, not in conflict with a rational religion *(Vernünftreligion)*, as it reconciles the principles of imagination and reason, but is in conflict with a belief in fetishes *(Fetischglauben)*.[21] As a public religion, a folk religion is also in conflict with a private religion *(Privatreligion)*, whose task is merely the cultivation of morality.[22] The critique of fetishism secures the rationality of a folk religion for Hegel, and the critique of privacy its potency. It reconciles the opposition between *Moralität* and *Sittlichkeit* that modernity creates by acknowledging the respective claims of *logos, ethos,* and *pathos.* Hegel pulls these ideas together in quite an elaborate metaphor that centers on the image of milk *(Milch)*. This image returns in his later interpretation of Socrates, where it links religion to custom as mother's milk *(Muttermilch)*. In his early interpretation it is not mother's milk but *Wehmuttermilch* or *Säugammemilch* that concerns Hegel—that is, the milk of the midwife or wet nurse, which is religion, that expresses into its child the warm liquid composed of equal measures of reason, feeling, and love of fate.[23] Hegel writes that

in harmony with these, his wetnurse (i.e. religion) reared this child without fear of the rod or ghosts in the dark *(Finsternis)*, without the bittersweet honey bread of mysticism *(Mystik)*, which the stomach grows tired of, or the fetters of words which would keep him perpetually immature *(Unmündigkeit)*. Instead she had him drink the clear and healthful milk of pure feelings *(lauterer und gesunder Milch reiner Empfindungen)*. . . . Her dominion *(Herrschaft)* holds sway forever, for it is based on the love, the gratitude, the noblest feelings of her ward. She has coaxed their refinement along, she has obeyed his imagination's every whim—yet she has taught him to respect iron necessity *(eiserne Notwendigkeit)*, she has taught him to conform to this inalterable destiny *(Schicksal)* without murmur.[24]

This warm milk is, therefore, still most definitely an agent of *Mündigkeit*. The answer to the question of how mankind can escape from *Unmündigkeit*—the question of Kant's "What Is Enlightenment?"—is not simply the courage, for Hegel, to use one's reason but involves the capacity for pure feelings and a relationship to fate *(Schicksal, moira)*. This redefinition of *Mündigkeit*, which now contains elements both of romanticism and Greek religion, still emphatically retains *Mündigkeit* as a value.

The image of Socrates that Hegel presents in this context is one of an agent of *Mündigkeit*, such as *Wehmuttermilch*. A synonym of *Wehmutter* is *Hebamme*. The maieutic art of bringing youth to maturity is, in the play of metaphor, always a womanly art. Although Hegel stands, therefore, for a folk religion that is both rational and enlightened, he avoids the 'manly' self-assertion of Kant's call for courage through a shift to a maternal metaphor that reconciles reason and fantasy, privacy and publicness, freedom and authority. Hegel draws a portrait of Socrates that harmonizes with this verson of Enlightenment. He begins his reflections with the suggestion that it is only through writing that one can achieve a large-scale effect, for "here the educator *(Belehrer)* stands on an invisible dais *(unsichtbare Kanzel)* before the entire public."[25] Such an educator, however, finds it very easy to berate the public but lacks the courage to address himself to his own circle. Hegel argues, therefore, that if criticism does not begin within the medium of conversation that constitutes a circle *(Kreis)*, then it degenerates into drivel *(Radotage)* and theoretical quackery *(theoretische Quacksalberein)*. Writing needs conversation if it is not to lapse into dogmatism. The distinction that Hegel develops here is between the dialogue that a republican ethos demands and the dogmatism of certain religious ethoses. Only a republican ethos promotes a democratic form of enlightenment. A religious ethos of preaching *(predigen)* and disciples *(Apostel)*, even if it proclaims itself to be in the service of enlightenment as does the ethos of the Masons, rests ultimately on the magical and a dogmatic form of instruction. Hegel illustrates the latter through a contrast between the pedagogical style of Socrates and that of what he calls the national poets of the Jews:

> Socrates, who lived in a republican state where every citizen spoke with every other . . . without didactic tone, without the appearance of wanting to enlighten *(belehren)*, he would start an ordinary conversation, then steer it in the most subtle fashion toward a lesson

(Lehre) that taught itself spontaneously *(die sich von selbst gab)*. The Jews, on the other hand, were long accustomed to being harangued *(haranguiert)* in a far cruder fashion by their national poets. The synagogues had accustomed their ears to direct instruction *(Belehrung)* and moral sermonizing.[26]

Here the opposition between indirect and direct, naive *(unbefangen)* and calculated *(haranguiert)* modes of instruction *(Belehrung)* defines the limit at which enlightenment turns into dogmatism.

In this context, the Jewishness of Christ's disciples is unfavorably compared with the Greekness of Socrates' disciples. For example, the open-ended number of Socrates' students is contrasted with the magically closed circle of twelve apostles. Furthermore, the nullity of these disciples in comparison to Christ is contrasted with the independent greatness of Socrates' students. Socrates is one who needs no disciples; he ascends no mountains and takes no voyages into deserts as Christ does, and he never speaks *ex cathedra*. He is an example of a type of moral individuality that still retains a relationship to beauty, which submission to law denies to the type of moral individuality as defined by Kant. Hegel argues that "he had no mould *(Model)* into which he wanted to pour his own qualities, no rule *(Regel[n])* by which he sought to level out their differences. . . . Each of his own pupils was a master in his own right *(Meister für sich)*."[27] In other words, he respected the moral personality of each of his students and did not want to keep them in a state of *Unmündigkeit* by magical means, such as resurrection. Instead, according to Hegel, he spoke to them of the immortality of the soul through the simple use of reason and imagination. Enlightenment cannot be brought to us, as the good lies within us. It has to be brought out, not drummed in. Hegel argues that

> Socrates left behind no Masonic signs, no mandate *(Befehl)* to proclaim his name, no method for seizing upon the soul and pouring morality *(Moralität)* into it; the agathon is born in us. It is not something that can be drummed into us by preaching. . . . He laid down no

> *ordinem salutis*. . . . Instead he knocked on the right door
> to begin with; dispensing with mediators *(Mittler)*, he
> led the individual only to himself without asking him
> to provide lodging for a guest, i.e. a spirit who was a
> perfect stranger *(wildfremden Gast)* who had arrived
> from some distant land. No, he was asked merely to
> provide better light *(Licht)* for this, his old landlord
> *(alten Hausherrn)*, whom the mob of fiddlers and pipers
> had forced to retreat into an old garret *(Dachkämmer-
> lein)*.[28]

Socrates is neither a prophet with an *ordinem salutis* nor a
sophist who relativizes the idea of the good, for the *agathon* is
indeed this old landlord whom the sophists, those fiddlers and
pipers, have forced into the garret. Socrates, in Hegel's reading,
is the one who wants to return the good to the light and space
of the downstairs rooms. He is not the overbearing guest or
troublesome mediator. In short, he is not the parasite who
interferes with the communication between the individual and
his or her soul.[29]

Despite this almost celebratory tone and despite the critique of the Christian obsession with death, the oriental nature
of its melancholy, and its anxiety-producing effects, which
read almost as an anticipation of the Nietzschean critique,
Hegel is still a Christian philosopher. Hence, if Socrates' students fare better than Jesus' disciples, that does not mean that
Socrates is ultimately raised above Jesus. The importance of
Jesus is world-historical for Hegel, even if his disciples were
mere examples of Jewish culture. If it were not for the divine
nature of Jesus, Hegel argues, he would be no greater exemplar
of moral virtue than Socrates. This is the case even though the
divinity of Jesus means that it costs him but a word to cure
the sick, whereas for Socrates the perfection of moral character
was a lifelong task. We could imitate the Socratic model, Hegel
argues, but never the transcendental model that Jesus offers.
Hence, the argument for Socrates' superiority falls down,
according to Hegel:

> when our understanding *(kalten Verstandes)* coldly pur-
> sues such a line of reasoning, our imagination *(Phan-*

tasie) pays no heed. It is precisely the ad-mixture, the addition of the divine *(der Zusatz des Göttlichen)* that makes the virtuous individual Jesus fit to be an ideal of virtue. Without the divinity of his person we would have only the man; whereas we have truly a superhuman ideal *(übermenschliches Ideal).*[30]

This *übermenschliches Ideal* has been lost through the growing positivity of Christian religiosity. As usual, Hegel's criticism is mordant. Instead of public virtue or inner faith, the masses seek out all the external props to assure themselves of a future life. A 'morality of prudence' or, more accurately, shrewdness anchors such a private religion in contrast to the publicness of a folk religion, which Hegel sees as reconciling intellect and fantasy, the private and the public, *Moralität* and *Sittlichkeit*, the immanently ethical and the *Zusatz der Göttliche.*[31]

Hegel's later theological writings are concerned with the contrast between morality and positivity—that is, with the critique of Christianity and its reconstruction from a moral standpoint. The interest in Socrates, therefore, declines. In the *Positivity of the Christian Religion*, Hegel merely repeats his thoughts on the difference between Jesus' and Socrates' disciples; however, there is an important section concerned with the "difference between Greek phantasy and Christian positive religion."[32] Here positive religion is viewed as having grown out of the collapse of freedom in the ancient world; it is the spiritual correlate of political despotism. Greek and Roman religions were, for Hegel, the religions of free men. The republican ideal was one of self-mastery *(enkrateia)*. The ideal of self-legislation typical of Kantian morality or external direction typical of private religion is foreign to it. This external direction is what links positive religion and political despotism. Late antiquity was not a realm of freedom in any sense. Hegel argues:

As free men the Greeks and Romans obeyed laws laid down by themselves. . . . They neither learned nor taught [a moral system] but evinced by their actions the moral maxims *(übten Tugendmaximen durch Hand-*

lungen aus) which they could call their very own. In public as in private and domestic life, every individual was a free man, one who lived by his own laws.[33]

These maxims of virtue and the importance of the idea of the *polis* for the individual are the two most important value concepts in antiquity. With the breakdown of the *polis* and the decline of this *ethos*, death became a terrifying phenomenon. Hegel argues that faced with the brutality of the contingent, people fled into the magical. The rise of the Church and its accommodation within the Roman Empire is based on the slander that man's nature is essentially corrupt. Religion seeks its legitimation from the miraculous, and the moral teaching of Christ is lost. The solution to this problem in modernity is, however, no longer seen to be a folk religion but a reworking of the notion of *Moralität* so that it loses its Kantian harshness and incorporates more of the expressivist ideal. Instead of founding morality on the domination of inclination *(Neigung)*, Hegel proposes a supplement *(Ausfüllung)* of the law: "an inclination with the law whereby the latter loses its form as law. The correspondence with inclination is the *pleroma* (fulfillment) of the law."[34] He illustrates reconciliation *(Versöhnlichkeit)*, which he calls a modification of love *(Modifikation der Liebe)*, most strikingly in his retelling of the story of Mary Magdalene. With the movement from the attempt to construct a folk religion to a theory of love, Socrates cedes his place in the reflections of Hegel to the figure of Jesus.[35]

For Jesus, virtues were 'modifications of love'. For Kant, virtue was a result of subjecting oneself to one's own law. For Socrates and the Greeks, virtue was a product of self-mastery, a self-mastery achieved not through a submission to law but through the care of the self *(heautou epimelia)*. Love is reconciliation because "in love man had found himself again in another."[36] In the mature Hegel the motif of reconciliation breaks the bonds of mere love, be it either human or divine. It becomes the *telos* of world history itself. World history also presupposes, like love, the overcoming of division *(Trennung)*. The fate of Socrates in Hegel's later work illustrates just such a division.

II

If in modern times philosophy turns toward the contemporary, then what legitimates philosophy's turning toward its own past? The answer is that even if philosophy no longer looks to the past for models with which either to ground or criticize itself, it is nevertheless important for philosophy to search the past for confirmation of its own self-certainty. To put it in psychoanalytical terms, modern philosophy is essentially neurotic; just as the restrained and upright self-certainty of the inauthentic Puritan individual only barely hid a mass of self-doubt and guilt, so also with modern philosophy. The need to conceive of the modern world as the product of a world-historical developmental process links *Zeitdiagnose* and a historical impulse. As Koselleck argues, "Modernity *(Neuzeit)* lends to the whole of the past a world-historical character; . . . diagnosis of modern times and analysis of past epochs belong to one another."[37] Habermas's paraphrase of the latter argument continues: "to which corresponds the new experience of progress and the acceleration of historical events, and the insight into the chronological simultaneity of historically non-simultaneous developments."[38] Thus, although the trial of Socrates precedes the development of Kantian ethics by more than two thousand years, it becomes in Hegel's interpretation a contemporary event because of the difficulties it reveals for any form of ethical rationalism. Through the trial of Socrates, Hegel puts modernity on trial. It is only from this vantage point that the untimely actuality of Socrates, for Hegel, can be grasped.

Hegel's most significant and extended piece of writing on Socrates occurs in his *Lectures on the History of Philosophy*. I shall try to interpret this account of the life of Socrates in light of Hegel's ideas concerning both the nature of antiquity and the 'problems' of modernity. Insofar as they are relevant to this reading, sections of Hegel's other works will also be called on: namely, *Phenomenology of Spirit, Aesthetics,* and *The Philosophy of Right*.

Hegel introduces Socrates as a *"welthistorische* Person" and as a *"*major turning point of the spirit in itself."[39] He is one of the first major portraits in "the gallery of the heroes of *reason's* thinking,"[40] who complete the bringing into consciousness of "the subjectivity of thought *(Denkens)*."[41] In line with his general philosophy of history, the products of absolute spirit are no less a product of their time than any other objectivation. His historicist impulse also informs his reading of Socrates; yet what is no less true of Socrates for Hegel is his ability to go beyond the last shape of reason's thinking. This is the dialectic that forms his reconstruction of the history of Greek philosophy. The two vital elements of Greek thinking that Socrates reconciles, and by that gesture separates himself from the sophists, are the Anaxagorian concept of *nous*, which raised thought to a negative power over all that is determined and existent (the similarity with Hegel's description of *Verstand* in the preface of *Phenomenology* and elsewhere is striking), and the Protagorian concept of the 'I' as a negative unity. Although Protagoras took the concept to be in movement, this movement occurs outside the 'I' as such. Hence, sophistry collapses into relativism when man becomes the measure of all things, whereas with Socrates, according to a striking expression of Hegel's, man "as thinking" *(als Denken)* is the measure of all things. The Socratic 'I' is mediated by the concept and, hence, is "the universal ego *(ich)*," which as self-subsisting consciousness is the good itself. Consciousness may be mediated by thought to produce the good, but the good must be known by me. With this assertion, according to Hegel, "infinite subjectivity, freedom of self-consciousness" has arisen in Socrates.[42] Hegel notes here, significantly from my point of view, that this principle is very much demanded in his own time. This is not quite the self-positing subjectivity of Hegel himself, as that notion reflects a dynamic, progressive, and future-oriented modernity. Here the self does not have to subsist with itself while deploying itself in history; it only has to make its way through the marketplace of Athens. Hegel now introduces the conflict that determines his reading of the fate of Socrates: the conflict between truth posited through thinking and "*die unbefangene Sitte*," which is mistranslated as "untrained morality" and is better rendered as "the unaffected or natural ethical order" or, more simply, "custom." Whereas truth is produced by the thinking of the universal 'I', Sophocles remarked, as Hegel observes, that no one knows where "*die unbefangene Sitte*" comes from. Here we see resumed in a peculiar way the Greek distinction between *nomos* and *physis*, between the self-instituted law that is conventional and yet also generalizable (with regard to the individual, Hegel calls this morality) and the natural or rather pseudonatural character of the already-always instituted customary order, which is for Hegel *Sittlichkeit*.[43] Socrates was at odds with his fellow Athenians because he was a moral man, whereas they were only 'ethical men' (*sittliche Menschen*): "the ethical order (*Sittlichkeit*) is natural (*unbefangen*), the ethical order which is bound together with reflection is morality (*Moralität*)."[44] Hegel notes that this distinction has been made again in recent times by Kant. Socrates is linked to Kant in the thinking of Hegel because both belong to the tradition of moral philosophy. "Morals (*Moral*) mean," according to Hegel, "that the subject posits autonomously (*aus sich*) and freely (*in seine Freiheit*) the determinations of the good, the ethical (*Sittliche*) and the just, and insofar as these determinations are posited autonomously (*aus sich*), any particular autonomously posited determination (*Bestimmung des Aussichsetzens*) is also raised up (*aufhebt*), so that it is eternal. They are being in and for itself (*an und für sich*)."[45]

The fact that these two ethical powers must come into collision constitutes the fate of Socrates. Hegel can argue this even though he also recognizes that in the spirit of the Athenian people one can see "the ethical order transformed into morality" and that Socrates only brought this change to the height of consciousness.[46] Nevertheless, for Hegel both ethical powers had to come into conflict in antiquity, and this conflict determines the fate of Socrates. As I have already suggested at the beginning of this chapter, this conflict between the godly right of the natural ethical order (*Sittlichkeit*) and that of consciousness in its subjective freedom (*Moralität*) can be related to Hegel's conflict with subjective idealism. I would like now to pause to consider the validity of such a thesis in light of Hegel's general construction of the history of philosophy.[47]

I have already pointed out the way Hegel solves the antinomy between relativism and universalism in his philosophy of history. The effect of the twin doctrines that philosophy belongs to its own time and that *Weltgeschichte ist Weltgericht* is that the individual can never escape his or her time because his or her time is but a moment in the world-historical time of spirit. Hegel's judgment as to the fate of Socrates, whom he considers not merely to be an individual but one of reason's great heroes, can easily be inferred from the following: "The individual is a son of his people, of his world. He may give himself airs as he likes but he does not transcend his time."[48] The authoritarian gesture of the world spirit, assured of its own progressive character, dismisses the vanity of the individual as ultimately pointless. The remnant of this philosophical theme within Marxism is what Benjamin wrote so beautifully against in his "Theses on the Philosophy of History." The other consequence of the doctrine is that once the theory of the absolute spirit is given up, as it must be and was in the latter half of the nineteenth century, the historicistic element alone remains, with the consequent inability of the philosophy of that time to explain the historically new and the transhistorical validity of the higher cultural objectivations.[49] But the universalistic element of the doctrine does satisfy, as Habermas rightly points out, modernity's need for self-certainty: to create its own normativity out of itself. This doctrine entails, more specifically, that no philosopher, no philosophical system, and no philosophical epoch can constitute a normative model for modernity. *'Il faut être absolument moderne'*. Consequently, Hegel chides attempts by his contemporaries to revive outmoded philosophies as if they had no idea that in modernity the craving for what is out of date is only the other side of the craving for novelty. Past philosophies are present but not actual. The reason for why they are not actual is that the shape of philosophy has moved on. But why are they still present? Do they represent, in Marx's phrase, the childhood of humanity? Hegel argues that to propose to reawaken older philosophies "by putting back into them the spirit which has developed further, plumbed more of its own depths, would be impossible, just as stupid as for a man to propose to labour to be a youth again, or for a youth to be a boy or a child again, although man, youth and child are one and the same individual."[50] From the standpoint of modern hermeneutics, such statements do indeed stem from the childhood of modernist philosophy, which sought to reduce history to a pseudophysis in order to legitimate its doctrine of progress.

The way in which Hegel ascribes progress to the history of philosophy places limits on my thesis, which asserts that when Hegel discusses Socrates he is also discussing subjective idealism; for Hegel bases his whole project on the strict separation of world-historical epochs. Progress in the history of philosophy is determined by Hegel in line with his basic categorical framework: thought as the merely abstract universal gives way to self-determining thought or the concept, and it in turn gives way to the idea or the self-realization of the concept wherein the latter becomes identical with reality. The Orient is the homeland of thought; but because the oriental consciousness is a religious one, it does not detain Hegel. For him there are only two forms of philosophy: Greek philosophy, which discovered the concept, and Germanic philosophy, which discovered the idea. Two things need to be said about this discovery of the concept. First, it is only possible on the basis of freedom, which Hegel goes on to define further as personal and subjective. Later I will argue that the master-slave dialectic of the *Phenomenology* is a one-sided depiction of the necessary sociopolitical conditions that make possible the birth of the freedom of self-consciousness out of oriental despotism. In my mind this tying together of the birth of philosophy and freedom is forgotten by Hegel in his criticism of Socrates' decision not to go into exile.[51] Second, this discovery of the concept is a development of Attic philosophy; it emerges in Anaxagoras, but is brought to full development by Socrates himself. The Germanic discovery of the idea absolutizes the spirit as subjectivity by making it the self-knowledge of reality. This absolute self-awareness is defined by Hegel as freedom. As in Christianity, man as man has infinite worth; the characteristic of modernity is subjective freedom. As Greek philosophy was earlier described as embodying subjective freedom, wherein lies the difference? Of course, part of the answer lies in the fact that in the Greek world only some were free; that is, all were not yet equal before the sight of God. More importantly,

Hegel argues that the Greeks were naive and saw no beyond—no *mundus intelligibilis*—of the subjective determination by the concept. Hence, Hegel takes the Kantian position and its followers to be the representative position of subjective idealism and warns that "we must hold fast to the different outlooks of Greek and modern philosophy, or otherwise, owing to the similarity of their results, we shall fall into the error of not seeing the specific character of modern subjectivism."[52] Although Hegel is right to suggest that we cannot assimilate Socrates' thought to modern Kantianism,[53] this cannot hide the fact that his critique of both figures is animated by his attempt to replace the empty formalism of the moral standpoint with the standpoint of a reflected, and not naive, *Sittlichkeit*.

III

The next step in Hegel's analysis of Socrates is an outline of the latter's life. This is necessary because Socrates created no system, which for Hegel is the highest form of philosophizing, and because his life practice and his life fate were integral parts of his philosophy. Hegel depicts a Socrates who was a good son of his time, which is to say a good and courageous free citizen of Athens, who also fulfilled all the customary religious obligations, including, as Hegel mentions elsewhere,[54] sacrificing a cock to Asclepius. As well as noting that Socrates was a good son of his time, however, Hegel sees a new principle emerging in Socrates that is to come into conflict with his time: "the becoming-inward of consciousness."[55] The type of subjectivity that Socrates brings into the world is not an abstract and formal one, but one that is still mediated by what is natural and sensuous. Hegel depicts Socrates as one who "stands before us (has lived amongst his fellow citizens) as one of those great plastic natures (individuals) completely of one piece, as we can see them to have lived at that time,—as a complete classical work of art, which has brought itself to this height."[56] Before turning to Hegel's depiction of Socrates' two other characteristics—his moral virtuousness and Attic urbanity—I shall deal firstly with Socrates' plasticity.

As is well known, the three forms of the absolute spirit are, for Hegel, art, religion, and philosophy. In regard to his reconstruction of the history of philosophy, these three forms constitute a developmental sequence. Within Greek philosophy, consciousness is still mediated by a sense of beauty; and the classical artwork itself forms a kind of exemplar that Hegel, only with extreme reluctance, pushes the world spirit beyond. For him late antiquity can scarcely be said to have constructed a philosophy, for its consciousness is entirely mediated by religion. Only in modernity does philosophy *qua* philosophy come into its own and become the absolute master of the household of knowledge. This makes Socrates' plasticity a product of the prevailing form of consciousness in general. As Hegel argues in his introduction to Greek philosophy in his *Lectures on the History of Philosophy*, the Greeks stand between oriental substantiality—wherein there is no split between spirit and nature—and modern, abstract, and formal subjectivity, which sets itself over and above nature. Contrary to the genealogy of the "*Urgeschichte des Subjektivität*" presented in the *Dialektik der Aufklärung*, Greek subjectivity preserves, according to Hegel, a mimetic relation to nature even as it comes to consciousness of itself as consciousness. The many examples of the Greek *kouros* still in existence stand as available witnesses to the superiority of Hegel's judgment. Greek subjectivity is only abstract insofar as it is not the fully developed subjectivity of modernity; as such, it is inhabited by beauty. Hegel characterizes "the stage of Greek consciousness" as "the stage of beauty."[57]

Heidegger has commented on this aspect of Hegel's thought in his lecture entitled "*Hegel und die Griechen*." Here Heidegger clearly sets forth the importance that the history of philosophy, including Greek philosophy, must have for Hegel given his conception of philosophy. Heidegger argues that for Hegel the history of philosophy is "the unitary and therefore necessary process of the progress of spirit to itself"; as philosophy itself is "the development of spirit to absolute knowledge," this means that philosophy and the history of philosophy are identical.[58] As is also well known, Aristotle was the first to write a history of philosophy, but there is no ultimate identity between Aristotle's philosophy itself and his reconstruction of philosophy's history. Here is another mark, therefore, of Hegel's modernity: all past philosophies are constructed from the standpoint of the present as stages in the development of that present. If philosophy and the philosophy of history must have a goal, a completion, then all previous forms of philosophy must belong to the 'not yet'. As Heidegger argues, "Hegel determines 'truth' as the aim of philosophy. This is reached only at the stage of completion (*Vollendung*). The stage of Greek philosophy remains in the 'not yet' (*'Noch nicht'*). It is as the stage of beauty not yet the stage of truth."[59]

The modernity of Hegel's *Aesthetics* is founded on the fact that he is the first philosopher to exclude the beauty of nature totally from this domain; beauty is a product of spirit, and the history of art is divided into the various stages that compose the history of the spirit's coming to itself. These stages are those of symbolic art, classical art, and finally, it seems, romantic art. I say 'it seems' because Hegel almost posits a fourth stage: a post-art (*Nach-Kunst*). The impetus toward a fourth stage is inherent in his very definition of art and the critical relativization of modern art that results from it. Unlike Kant, Hegel does not argue that art mediates reason and sense, inclination and duty, but instead that in art "the beautiful (*Schöne*) has its being in pure appearance (*Schein*)."[60] Art displays the highest reality and therefore qualifies as a part of absolute spirit, but it does so sensuously. In *der schöne Schein*, universality and real particularity are reconciled. In modernity, however, there is a triumph of universal forms and of sheer inwardness at the expense of merely beautiful appearance; the modern artwork becomes overburdened by reflection. The overburdened inwardness of modern subjectivity means that the spirit most adequately satisfies itself in the confines of its own inner self. Hence, there is a post-art not merely because art itself is the most immature and immediate form of the absolute spirit, but because there occurs a growing dissolution of art when beauty "becomes the spiritual beauty of absolute inner life as inherently infinite spiritual subjectivity."[61] This sets up a division between subjective personality and the external material that is not present in classical art, which remains unreconciled. Thus, modern romantic art collapses when the real world is turned into prosaic objectivity over which the subjectivity of the artist arbitrarily rules. Here the contrast with classical art could not be clearer. Classical art has as its element "the untroubled harmony of determinate free individuality in its adequate existence."[62] This is only possible because "the Greeks in their immediate real existence lived in the happy milieu of both self-conscious subjective freedom and the ethical substance."[63] This happy idyll of an "integrated civilisation" (Lukács) comes to a symbolic end in the trial of Socrates. Yet what it does make possible is the sheer plasticity of Socrates' character for which Hegel does not conceal his admiration. Socrates shares this plasticity in common with the classical artwork itself, which, within its perfect unity of less than infinite subjectivity and a harmonious and plastic externality, corresponds better to the Hegelian definition of art as *der schöne Schein* than does romantic art. The plasticity of Socrates' character reflects the classical ideal of beauty that Hegel, because of his adherence to the idea that modernity must construct its own normativity out of itself, refuses to make normative for modernity. Hence, we can admire this personality but not mourn over its present impossibility.

Furthermore, Hegel is not short of good reasons for why we should admire Socrates. He calls him "a model picture of moral virtue *(ein Musterbild moralischer Tugend)*: wisdom, modesty, moderation, restraint, justice, courage, unshakeability, firm uprightness against tyrants and the *demos,* freed from the desire to acquire and to dominate."[64] What is important here, for Hegel, is that Socrates' moderation does not have its basis in any Christian mortification of the flesh but is achieved even through bodily excess. Hegel narrates the story of Socrates' moderation with regard to wine as depicted in Plato's *Symposium* and comments on it as follows: "This is no restraint, *(Massigkeit)* which involves the least pleasure, not an intentional soberness or mortification, but a strength of consciousness, which maintains itself in bodily excesses."[65] And he adds that "we have to think of Socrates not after the fashion of a litany of moral virtues."[66] Here Hegel's love and knowledge of antiquity and his detestation of the moralistic character of modern subjective idealism and its guiding principle of 'chill duty' result in an implicit critique of the latter from the standpoint of another *chrēsis aphrodisiōn*. Basing his argument on evidence concerning the life of Socrates, Foucault argues that "temperance can not take the form of obedience to a system of laws or of a codification of behaviour; it can not also have any validity as a principle concerning the cancellation of pleasures; it is an art, a practice of pleasures, which permits of self-limitation insofar as the 'use' of pleasures is founded upon need."[67] Hence, the assimilation of Socrates to Kant that does surface in Hegel's text, especially in the discussion of self-consciousness and the conflict between *Moralität* and *Sittlichkeit*, is never total. Even in his earliest work, as I have already shown, Hegel makes the distinction between a moral system and maxims of virtue *(Tugendmaximen)* very clear.

The third characteristic of Socrates' character that Hegel discusses is his typicality as "an example of developed Attic urbanity . . . ; movement in the freest relationships, an open talkativeness, which is always thoughtful, and in which there is an inner universality and which, at the same time, always strikes the correct, lively and free relationship to individuals and to the situation wherein it occurs."[68] Such an open, discourse-oriented life meant that his life and philosophy were of one piece; his thinking never congealed into a system, which Hegel usually takes to be necessary for any form of philosophy. It also means that outwardly he appeared to lead an ordinary Attic life, which was one of relative leisure or idleness; yet insofar as this life was one of constant discursive engagement, there was an inner connection between his life and philosophy. The notion that Socrates was an idler *(Mussigänger)* can be profitably contrasted with the modern-day idler *(le flâneur)* as it has been analyzed in Benjamin's interpretation of Baudelaire.[69] The latter, through his lack of a career, sets himself apart to experience alone the chaos of modern city street life in search of profane illumination, an essentially monadological and nondiscursive existence. Socrates' idleness was in tune with his times and made possible by the social structure of the *polis*; the life that it gave rise to was one spent in communication with others and in the discursive testing of the customary validity claims from which arise the 'logical illumination' called truth. This means, furthermore, that Socratic moralizing is quite unlike modern dry moralizing that is mere hectoring or haranguing, as the latter involves "no reciprocally rational relation."[70] In Hegel's depiction of Socrates we can see a discursive theory of truth emerge *avant la lettre*, which is not merely formally determined but presupposes a concrete lifeworld. Hegel argues that "he falls into conversation with everyone with that complete Attic urbanity, which, without instructing the other, wants to impress. Freedom maintains its right completely and is honoured, but everything crude is omitted."[71]

IV

The discursive character of Socrates' philosophizing constitutes his method *(Methode)*, which Hegel describes more as a way or manner *(Weise)*. This remark is perfectly correct, for only in modern philosophy does method become the only road, even the 'royal road', along which the subject must pass to produce truth. In antiquity, the production of *'dire-vrai'* was much more a question of a *'style d'existence'* (Foucault), of which Montaigne was the last exemplar in modern times. Insofar as Socrates has a method to produce the good, however, it is one that rests on conversation *(Konversation)*. The Socratic 'discourse ethics' has two characteristics. First, it wants to lead common people into reflection on their duties by entering into a discourse with them, and second, it wants to lead them from the determinate case to the thought of the universal. The two imperatives are, therefore, "put into question, into discourse all customary norms of action" or "suspend all customary norms of action as the precondition of their discursive testing"; and "develop the universal, which is present in every consciousness, through the particular, concrete case." The first imperative represents a choice for a concrete value (the value preference for an examined instead of an unexamined life), whereas the second imperative is a procedural one. Both have a strongly democratic *parti pris*: all can enter into practical discourse, and the procedure itself starts from the elements of your concrete life-world. The element of existential choice puts Socrates' discourse ethics closer to that of Apel's rather than Habermas's; however, I cannot go into this subject here.[72]

More particularly, according to Hegel, the Socratic method is composed of three moments: irony, midwifery, and confusion. I shall take up each of them in turn. Socratic irony functions to awaken in the other the need to think, to know, to put into question customary ideas *(gewöhnliche Vorstellungen)*. In order to do this, Socrates puts on the appearance of one who knows nothing; and, through this 'method', he brings the other to speech. He asks "with the appearance of naiveté" *("mit dem Scheine der Unbefangenheit")* in order, precisely, to put "naive custom" *("die unbefangene Sitte")* into question.[73] Irony is, therefore, a strategic feint, a bluff designed to induce the other to make the same value choice as Socrates (to examine life itself) without at first being aware of making this step. Hence, at the beginning, there is a fundamental inequality or asymmetry between the discourse partners. For Hegel, however, this aspect marks the Socratic dialectic as inevitably subjective in terms of Hegel's own definition of logic, even though his actual depiction of irony at this stage of the analysis is necessarily intersubjective: "irony is a special mode of behaviour of one person to another *(die Ironie ist besondere Benehmungsweise von Person zu Person)*."[74]

Hegel argues that logical doctrine has three sides: abstract determination, which is a property of the understanding; negative reason, which constitutes the dialectical; and positive reason, which forms the speculative. These three sides form stages through which thinking must pass. The understanding is obsessed with distinction making and dichotomizing; it presents the mind with an "abstract 'either-or'."[75] Dialectics takes these 'finite characterizations' and by demonstrating their very finitude uncovers the law of things that makes them pass over into their opposite. To take Hegel's example: man, according to the understanding, appears to possess both vitality and mortality; yet through dialectics, Hegel believes one can show that life itself as life involves the germ of death. It thus prepares the way for positive reason, which is the affirmative recognition of unity within difference, of the real as rational. What is of interest here is the relationship between the Hegelian dialectic and the Socratic one. Not surprisingly, Hegel is concerned with separating dialectics from skepticism, as mere negation, and from its reputation as an "adventitious art."[76] In other words, Hegel is concerned about taming '*la dialectique sauvage*'. His genealogical reconstruction of dialectics into subjective and objective serves this end. Socrates is, for Hegel, the first proponent of dialectics but only in its subjective form as irony. As such, dialectics overturns both ordinary consciousness and the sophistical by leading the other, through questioning, "to the opposite of what their first impressions had pronounced correct."[77] The objective form of the dialectic, inaugurated by Plato, goes beyond this by making the inversion not the product of discursive questioning but the product of a law that decrees that all the finite concepts of the understanding must pass over into their opposites. Although this idea has other problems,[78] what is important here is the fact that Hegel loses the connection between dialectics and dialogue and expels the *principium individuationis* from thinking and questioning by relegating it to the merely subjective. He forbids dialectics its adventures.

Despite this relativization of Socratic irony, Hegel is still keen to separate this ancient irony from modern romantic irony. As I said before, the so-called subjective dialectic involves an intersubjective relationship, which alone makes dialectical irony possible. When the dialectic turns objective to seek the 'foundation of things' ('*Grunde der Sache*'), all irony becomes impossible as the production of truth becomes an essentially monadological relation. With regard to romantic irony, however, Hegel takes the side of "Greek lightness" against mere "playing with the idea."[79] Romantic irony involves the elevation of the subjective consciousness over and above all existing determinations, which it merely plays or trifles with, and has no sense of the tragic opposition that exists between self-consciousness and the existing ethical order. Hegel argues that Socrates' "tragic irony consists in his opposition of subjective reflection to the existing ethical order,—not a self-consciousness which stands over the latter, but one with the disinterested purpose of leading toward the true good, to the universal idea."[80] Romantic irony reflects the growth of subjective inwardness in modern civil society, which can result in a kind of individual who is both detached from and cynical toward the customs of the people. There is nothing of this in Socratic irony. His questioning is not destructive in this sense, despite the accusation of introducing new gods. Hegel's most extensive treatment of romantic irony, a topic that also obsesses the early Kierkegaard, is found in his *Aesthetics*.

What motivates Hegel's dislike for romantic irony is the same impulse that motivates his critique of dialectics as skepticism or mere adventitiousness: a hostility to the corrosive power of irony on the merely existent in modernity. Both thinking and art become imbued with an egoism that stands over the existing ethical order. Hegel traces back to Fichte the philosophical concept of egoism that informs Schlegel's aesthetic category of irony.[81] According to Hegel, Fichte erects the ego into an abstract and formal absolute principle, where every content is negated and only exists insofar as it has been posited by the ego. This ego itself as living and active individuality is the artist or the artistically formed life. Through his caricature of the artist, Hegel continues his critique of the abstractness of the concept of formal freedom and conducts what is one of the very first trials of the artistic avant-garde from a conservative point of view. From the standpoint of his analysis of Socrates, Hegel's significant point is that whereas Socrates treats his own relationship to the universal as an ironical one, romantic irony treats the universal itself ironically. What the ego posits, it can just as easily negate. Both Socratic and romantic irony trouble the existing order, but Socrates does so in the name of a higher order, which, as Hegel will show, is revealed to him by his *daimonion*. Romantic irony, however, negates the concept of order *tout court*. Hegel's Socrates is a modernist, whereas romantic irony reeks of so-called postmodernism; that is, it represents a relativistic attack on the notion of truth itself. Hegel's description of the morbidly beautiful soul, which longs for truth and substantiality but cannot escape isolation and withdrawal into inwardness, is a transformation of the more positive depiction of a 'religiously' beautiful soul that is found in Goethe's *Willhelm Meister*, where the story of the Moravian sister is given. In any case, for Hegel, this morbidly beautiful soul remains caught in an ironical attitude that is merely trifling and absolutely negative and self-destructive, whereas Socratic irony, even though it leads to Socrates' self-destruction, has an aura of nobility.

The second element of the Socratic 'method' is, according to Hegel, the art of midwifery or the maieutic element *(Hebammenkunft)*. Hegel characterizes this art of bringing thoughts into the world as one that either begins from the concrete, unreflected consciousness in order to produce the universality of the concept or begins from the concept in order to produce the consciousness. What is significant here is the continued portrayal of the Socratic 'method' as a way of conversation. This portrayal means that the type of question and answer found in the Socratic dialogue is, according to Hegel, completely free of the arbitrary element that infects even the best modern dialogues. In the Socratic dialogue, the respondent's replies are to the point and do not merely bring forward another point of view. This is possible because of the plasticity of the youth's character to whom Socrates directs his questions. According to Hegel, this lack of originality in the respondent is not a fault but allows the question to be fully probed rather than broken off in assertion and counterassertion. Hence, even though the respondent's replies are artificial, it is still possible to see the answer escaping the intention of the question in the Socratic dialogue, whereas in a modern, printed dialogue the author's control is absolute. Further and more important, it means that the Socratic method is a kind of education or *Bildung*, for the production of the universal out of the concrete repeats the life history of every individual as he develops from childhood to manhood. Both concern "the formation of self-consciousness" *("die Bildung zum Selbstbwusstsein")*, which as "the development of reason *(Vernunft)* is the consciousness of the universal."[82] This partial assimilation of the Socratic method into the Hegelian concept of culture or *Bildung* must be seen once again as part of Hegel's attempt to construct a critique of modernity in his depiction of Socrates;

the butt of his critical impulse here is the arbitrary and artificial nature of modern philosophical questioning. The third element of the Socratic 'method' is to throw natural consciousness into bewilderment and confusion *(Verwirrung)*. Socrates' questioning leads the respondent into contradiction. This confusion of consciousness causes embarrassment and leads to the suspicion that what was held to be true is not so; it thus stimulates "the need for thinking *(die Bedürfniss nach Denken)*." This is a long way from the kind of reflective, meditative, methodical doubt with which Descartes inaugurates modern philosophy alone and in his heated room. Here contradiction and confusion and, hence, the putting into doubt of the merely received are founded in the intersubjective relation of questioner and respondent. Furthermore, whereas Descartes could not doubt his own self and, therefore, with that gesture exiled madness from the realm of thought, with Socrates madness and truth, as Hegel recognizes, still stand in an intimate relation. This art of throwing people into confusion is a magician's art, and Socrates places a spell on people, as Hegel shows in quoting Plato's *Meno*, which paralyzes their capacity to think. As Meno says of Socrates: "I had earlier, before I knew of you, heard that you live in doubt *(aporeis)*, and bring others also into it. And now you are also bewitching me, so that I am full of embarrassment *(aporeis)*."[83] This bewilderment, which spurs reflection, is the negative side of the Socratic method; but Hegel adds that philosophy as a whole must begin with it, as indeed does *Geist* in the preface to the *Phenomenology of Spirit*. The positive side is the production of the universal concepts of the true, the good, and the beautiful out of the natural consciousness through the process of conversing, knowing, and thinking. Socrates goes beyond the sophists; man is not simply the measure of all things, but "man is the measure" only "as a thinking being."[84]

V

We must now assemble the elements that constitute, for Hegel, the fate of Socrates, which revolve around the conflict between morality and the ethical order. Because it is a conflict between two rights, Hegel has to recognize both the right of morality while acknowledging the abstractness of morality and, hence, the right of the ethical order. Hegel's *Philosophy of Right* is his final statement regarding the reconciliation of the two and as such represents the final stage of his lifelong discussion with Kant. In antiquity, however, the historical stage for the reconciliation of the two principles had not been set, and the resultant falling apart of the two principles takes on an air of inevitability. Yet the significance of Socrates for antiquity is precisely in the fact that he is the "inventor of morals *(Erfinder der Moral)*."[85] He brings to the height of consciousness, as a world-historical individual, this change that is occurring in the Attic people themselves: their change from a customary people to a moral people, which is not accidentally contemporaneous with the development of political democracy. The principle of subjective freedom, which Hegel argues that Socrates discovered, is both the basis of morality and politics. The soul's conversation with itself and the public discussion of the laws are forms of communication that institutionalize reflection on the unexamined, whether in relation to passions *(pathos)* or to custom *(ethos)*. Hegel, however, can only conceive of this return of consciousness to itself—its becoming reflective or theoretical, as Nietzsche would say—as a loss of substantiality of the state itself, as a loss of its immediate validity or authority. Hegel argues, "hence, this return of the individual from the universal into isolation is criminality *(Verbrechen)*. It is taking care of oneself at the expense of the state *(Sorge für sich auf Kosten des Staates)*."[86] The fact that the individual must now take care of his or her own moral conduct goes hand in hand, for Hegel, with the decline of public morality: "no public customs, and morality,—these occur with one another and at the same time."[87] In other words, Socrates brings to consciousness the need of his times: he takes care of his own morality and helps others take care of their own by thinking and reflecting. To him, it is the only way to determine the good as universal at a time when the immediately universal no longer holds any weight. The individual must now make his own determinations; they are no longer present at hand.

The Hegelian notion of criminality is an essentially ambiguous one, for Hegel holds in reserve the normal moral repugnance that one should feel toward a criminal act by erecting criminality itself into a force for moral progress. The notion of criminality is central to Hegel's early philosophy and is extensively treated in his Jena texts, as well as reemerging in his treatment of terrorism in the *Phenomenology of Spirit*.[88] In Axel Honneth's proposed interpretation of these texts, Hegel's philosophy is reconstructed in terms of a critical transformation of modern political philosophy and its guiding concept of the struggle for self-preservation.[89] This notion presupposes the further notion of an atomized subject that prosecutes its struggle for self-preservation by acting in a purposively rational manner. Hegel replaces the notion of a struggle for self-preservation, according to Honneth, with the notion of a struggle for recognition. It places social conflict at the more properly cultural level of a struggle over the societal self-definitions that determine whether a social actor will receive recognition from the other in everyday social interaction. The question, then, becomes one of how an actor changes societal self-definitions in order to win recognition. The answer is through social conflict or struggle that may involve both criminality and terrorism. For Honneth, the Hegelian notion of social struggle overcomes the cognitivist bias of certain theories of development by locating social struggle, and the ethical development that emerges out of social struggles, at an appropriately ethical as well as interactional level of analysis. Criminality emerges within such a framework as an act or series of acts that disrupt previous forms of social integration that leads, or may lead, to higher, more reflective forms of social integration and solidarity. Sometimes, however, criminality or terrorism misfires. Hegel's well-known analysis of the emergence of terrorism in the French Revolution as a result of the formal nature of modern freedom is a case in point. But his analysis of Socrates' actions as criminal because of their destruction of the customary order is both more forgiving and more sympathetic to the formal definition of freedom that Socrates upholds in opposition to the customary nature of the Greek *polis*. The problems that beset the formal notion of freedom when it matures are not present in its infancy. Hence, the late Hegel's analysis of Socrates shows signs of the youthful revolutionary enthusiasms that he progressively set aside as his thought became more conservative. As we shall see later, the trial of Socrates is, for Hegel, not merely the trial of a single individual but that of a historically new moral principle. It is not merely a criminal trial but a world historical trial.

The concept of care that Hegel also raises here is both one of the oldest and newest in the philosophical lexicon. Its history stretches from Greek culture, where it originates, to modern times where it finds an especially prominent place in the work of Heidegger. The fact that Hegel is correct to use this term with respect to Socrates is supported by Foucault, who argues that it received its philosophical consecration in Socrates. In the *Apology*, Foucault argues, Socrates presents himself as the master of the care of the self *(heautou epimelia)*.[90] Hence, although for Foucault this care of the self does not become a veritable culture of the self until Roman antiquity, it is still present, in a more plastic form, in Greek antiquity. It is present in the relationship that the moral subject has to himself or herself in the choice of pleasures *(chrēsis aphrodisiōn)*. It takes on a more plastic form because the subject does not subject itself to a moral code that defines the permitted and the prohibited but constructs a relation to himself or herself as a subject of moral conduct in the form of a style or aesthetic of existence. As we have already seen, Hegel recognizes the plasticity of Greek culture and the inseparability of Socrates' life and his philosophy. Furthermore, for Foucault, the Socratian principle concerning the inseparability of knowing the good and doing the good, although philosophically arguable, reflects the fact that "one cannot constitute oneself as a moral subject in the choice of pleasures without constituting oneself at the same time as a knowing subject."[91]

According to Hegel, Socrates makes the determination of the good in the field of human action dependent, in the final instance, on what he somewhat anachronistically calls subjectivity, a Latin-derived concept that embraces a less plastic and more lawful relationship of the self to itself and to the external world. Notwithstanding, Hegel recognizes in Socrates the beginning of the intimate relation between the individual and the good, which must be mediated by knowledge that constitutes, for him, what is once again perhaps anachronistically labeled as morality. Hegel argues that "human beings shall know what is right and do it with this consciousness. This is called morality *(Moralität)*, which is distinguished from the ethical order *(Sittlichkeit)*, in which human beings do what is right unknowingly."[92] Here begins Hegel's critique of Socrates, for he refuses to accept the Socratic equation of knowing the good with doing the good. He argues that Socrates has not yet arrived at the opposition of the good or knowledge of the good and the subject as chooser of the good. For Hegel, in pursuing his critique through an analysis of Aristotle, the choice of the good is not a purely rational one but has its subjective actuality in the law of the heart. This does not mean, of course, that Hegel simply abandons the reflective determinations of morality but rather that they are not separable from the subject who makes them. In this way, Hegel can develop a critique of the moralistic uprightness of the moral consciousness and its abstractness and formality vis-à-vis actual existence, which he argues is defined as an equally abstract sensuousness. He applies this diagnosis both to the time of Socrates and *mutatis mutandis* to his own modern times. The Socratic return of consciousness to itself leaves behind what has disappeared in reality—the spirit of the people—and, hence, what determines virtue is only the subjectivity of opinion "without the reality of the ethical order."[93] Hence, in criticizing Socrates, Hegel is never far away from criticizing Kant; however, even as he argues against the overrationalistic bias of Socrates' position, he still recognizes the arational source of reflective judgment in Socrates—his *daimonion*—which partly mitigates against any naive rapprochement between Socrates and the moderns.

Before we turn to a discussion of this latter concept, we must linger a while on the dark side of the dialectic—that is, on what Hegel sees as the positive and, more importantly, negative side of the Socratic dialectic of the universal. This involves first and foremost the question of the freedom of self-consciousness and the sociopolitical conditions of its formation; it also involves the sociopolitical consequences on the society in which it comes into existence. Hegel's most famous discussion on self-consciousness occurs in his *Phenomenology of Spirit* in the discussion of mastery *(Herrschaft)* and slavery *(Knechtschaft)*, which immediately precedes the discussion of stoicism, skepticism, and the unhappy consciousness that goes under the title of the freedom of self-consciousness. The section on mastery and slavery is, therefore, the *Bildungsroman* of the struggle of the spirit to self-consciousness. While in the text itself no historical context is specified, there are some indications that it is in Greek antiquity in general and in Socrates in particular that Hegel sees this principle arising. This speculation is confirmed by the text itself because what immediately follows is a discussion of postclassical, Hellenistic philosophies. A possible reading of the dialectic of recognition and work is that it is the philosophical representation of the Solonic revolution: the cancellation of the forfeiture of one's person in case of default on debt repayments. Taken by itself, however, the text could be just as easily referring to a feudal context or a philosophical fiction made out of diverse historical materials. Yet there are some arguments that suggest a weaker linkage of this section to Greek antiquity. The fact that self-consciousness only exists insofar as it is recognized presupposes, from the standpoint of Hegel's *Philosophy of History*, a transition from the Oriental to the Greek world.

In general terms, Hegel's philosophy of history is a story of the progressive development of freedom, from the freedom of one in the Oriental world, the freedom of some in the Greek world, and the recognition of freedom as universal in modernity. In accord with Montesquieu, Hegel presents the Oriental world as one ruled by fear and despotism, where "either a man stands in fear, is afraid, or he rules by fear, and so is either servant or master."[94] This is akin to the situation in the *Phenomenology*, where the life-and-death struggle between two self-consciousnesses is negated by the fact that the immediate self-consciousness recognizes that life is essential to it and, therefore, becomes consciousness in the form of thinghood which, as being for the other, is called dependent consciousness or servitude/slavery, as opposed to the pure being for itself of independent consciousness or lordship/mastery. The

Solonic revolution de-Orientalized the Greek world; by eliminating the possibility of enslavement through debt bondage, it eliminated the possibility of slavery within the category of free citizens. Furthermore, the Hegelian reversal of the status of the dependent and independent consciousness is effected through the former's ability to become a being-for-self through work while the latter, in its passivity, becomes the dependent consciousness whose desire, unchecked through work, leaves it enmeshed in the natural order. Here once again, a possible parallel with the Greek world consists in the fact that the free citizens were producers, unlike the Roman plebeians after the second century B.C.; and their victory against plutocracy established the sociopolitical preconditions of their freedom in a society of small-scale production, rather than, for example, in a society of latifundia. Against this argument, however, stands the following criticism: namely, that the servile consciousnesses turning of its own fear against the master through its drive to work unduly naturalizes the process of mutual recognition. This should turn around a purely intersubjective relation rather than the monological relation typical of work.[95] In the context of Greek antiquity it turns around the politically binding decision of the *polis* to refuse the enslavement of its citizenry.

There are hints at such an alternative account in Hegel's introduction to the *Lectures on the History of Philosophy*. Here Hegel argues that the birth of philosophy and political freedom go hand in hand. He does not surrender in this text the importance of a nonimmediate relation to nature and explicitly argues that philosophy, as thought that has become reflexive, can only emerge when thought sunders its immediate unity with nature. In the *Phenomenology*, however, before the servant gains self-consciousness in his relationship to the object that is mediated by work that tempers desire, the lord can no longer find any recognition in a consciousness that is still at such a servile level. Hegel never adequately solves the master's need for recognition, although the servant finds it in work. In this text the need for the mutual recognition of each other's self-consciousness is rightly referred to the level of the institutions of political freedom themselves. Hence, Hegel determines the emergence of the freedom of self-consciousness in Greece as *the* simultaneously individual and social event in the birth of philosophy. As free self-consciousness, the individual elevates himself in his very particularity to the level of the universal and knows himself in his being to be 'a universal within the universal', a relation in which the individual does not have his essence in the other, as does the servant in the master, but feels at home with himself. At the same time, the individual can only feel at home with himself if he knows that others feel the same and that all recognize and respect his freedom. Hegel argues that "I am free only inasmuch as I allow the freedom of others and am recognized as free by them. Real freedom presupposes the freedom of many; only amongst several people is freedom actual and existent. Thus is the relation of free men to free men established and thereby the laws of ethical life and justice."[96] Of course, he goes on to add that the Germanic world has invented a higher freedom than that of the Greeks, which is still very greatly restricted. This higher freedom is, for Hegel, a product of that world-historical development called Christianity.

As the trial of Socrates shows, this mutual recognition of each other's freedom is a precarious achievement, which is only to be expected in a society where political and state institutions are based on laws that are, from our vantage point, neither abstract nor formal enough. Hence, the extent to which differing opinions and values are respected is a shifting and variable quantity. This influence of the always already-instituted ethical order upon the city-state ultimately sets limits to the Socratic dialectic of the universal as its critical potential becomes evident. The power of the concept makes this order waver and deprives it of its holiness, which is an accusation that Nietzsche also makes, for it demonstrates the limitations and deficiencies of every particular determination. Nothing can be taken naively as a value; everything must be subject to thinking. Nothing is fixed; everything becomes wavering. Such is the consequence of "the formation of reflective consciousness."[97] According to Hegel, *The Clouds* of Aristophanes must be read as a prefiguration of what would happen to Socrates when the one-sidedness and the negativity of his dialectic were generally recognized. The reaction against the subject, against the conscience, against freedom, against the universal, and for the truth of 'unformed spirit' (*'ungebildeten Geistes'*) has set in, according to the increasingly critical and ethically conservative reading of Hegel. The unformed spirit becomes the true spirit of the people, which unconsciously corrects its own limitations and deficiencies and is held to be the real universal spirit.

Yet true to his own philosophy of history, Hegel does not so much oppose the principles of Socrates but their very prematurity. Against the universal as such, Hegel counterpoises the acting individual who decides for himself what is to be taken as universal. In opposition to the *Sitte des Volkes*, Socrates prefigures the claim of conscience, which as pure, deciding individuality is the knowledge of what is right. Against the very modernity of Socrates, Hegel posits the archaic nature of the Socratic conscience and its proximity to the ancient oracle and to the dubious sciences of magnetism and mesmerism of his own day. Socrates' *daimonion* stands outside of its time but is not yet the completely modern form of the conscience. Instead of being the "representation of universal consciousness," it is something "without consciousness; Socrates is driven."[98] The Socratian conscience is more Freudian than Hegel would like, whereas the modern conscience possesses the element of subjective freedom, which means that we moderns "want to stand for what we do."[99] In short, Socrates is the middle point of an entire world-historical shift. As Hegel puts it, "the *daimonion* is therefore in the middle, between the externality of the oracle and pure inwardness of the spirit. It is something inward, but in a way that distinguishes it from the human will. It has its own genius, which is not that of human intelligence and arbitrariness."[100] Given Socrates' untimeliness, his conflict with his contemporaries, in which he upheld the right of his own *daimonion* against *die Sitte*, became inevitable.

VI

In the context of Hegel's *Philosophy of History*, not only Socrates but also the whole of Greek antiquity stands at a midpoint in world history between the Asiatic principle of the 'selflessness of human beings' and the modern Germanic principle of 'infinite subjectivity'. The Greek principle is that of 'beautiful individuality'; and despite Socrates' status as the 'inventor of morals *(Erfinder der Moral)'*, his character and activity remain determined by the general character of antiquity even as he participates in the decay of its general presuppositions. As mentioned previously, the transition from the Greek to the modern world is the transition from the stage of beauty to that of truth; this means that the principle of subjective freedom can only bring about the ruin and decay *(Verderben)* of the city-state as it undermines its ethos *(sittliche Gesinnung)*. The immediate connection of thought and life that custom constitutes is burst asunder by the revolutionary principles that the Attic enlightenment brings into the world: that of 'freely becoming inwardness' and pure thinking as 'disinterested play'. Socrates taught that "human beings have to find and to recognize in themselves what is right and good and that this right and good is, according to its own nature, universal."[101] The revolutionary character of Socrates' project makes his dialectic always negative as he brings everything under question in his conversations with his fellow citizens. This results in the objective determination of Socrates' behavior from the standpoint of the city-state as criminality *(Verbrechen)*. In condemning him to death as its "absolute enemy", Hegel argues, the city-state could not hide its complicity in his fate, as the principle of discursive rationality that he embodied had taken firm root in it. Hegel ends his remarks on the Attic state by arguing that Socrates' punishment goes hand in hand with its decay; however, even in the period of their decay, brought about in part by their rejection of Socrates' new principle, the Greeks retained something of their plasticity of beauty and form.[102]

In the trial of Socrates, the right to reflection, to discursive testing of customary values and norms, to the freedom of self-consciousness, to moral freedom, which in being exercised leads to the de-absolutization of "that which is valid in and for itself," faces the right of the always already-instituted world of customary norms and values that permits no gap between being and doing in which thinking can emerge. Socrates' fate rests on the result of this struggle between *Moralität* and *Sittlichkeit*, and the determiners of his fate are none other than the Athenian people themselves. The trial of Socrates is composed, according to Hegel, of two parts: the charges themselves or Socrates' condemnation through law and Socrates' relation to the people whose sovereignty he ultimately denies. I shall turn first to Hegel's characterization of the charges laid against Socrates, charges that Hegel takes to be legitimately laid and upheld. Both charges, of course, concern alleged breaches of custom. The first charge was, as is well known, that Socrates did not believe in the old gods and that he introduced new ones. The new god that Socrates introduced is, according to Hegel, his *daimonion*, which is nothing other than the "human being's own self-consciousness."[103] In other words, in answer to the question 'how do I know what is right or wrong?' Socrates relied on a form of knowledge that depended on his own willing and deciding individuality. In Greece up until that time, Hegel suggests, such knowledge was a function of either purely accidental occurrences to do with the behavior of birds or was the officially and religiously sanctioned Delphic oracle to whom all could go to seek advice from a universal knowledge that represented the customs and values of Greek life itself. From a historiosophical standpoint, the source of moral and ethical judgment shifts from being shaped by the community to being shaped by the individual; that is, 'it is my will that decides right'. Once again Socrates stands as a midpoint in this evolution; for with him, although consciousness becomes inward, it seems as if it is still represented by an actual voice. That is to say, it is still encased in a degree of materiality that the increasing spiritualization of self-consciousness must ultimately cast aside. Hegel argues that "with Socrates, however, these external laws had entered into consciousness, as with us and yet still not completely, for it was to him still the voice which stems from being *(die seiende Stimme)* and not the voice of individuality as such."[104] Even so, what lies contained within his *daimonion* is nothing less than a 'revolution' (*'Umwälzung'*) that makes Socrates the philosophical hero of the birth of self-consciousness itself. It also makes him, for Hegel, undoubtedly guilty of the accusation of impiety.

The second charge made against Socrates was that of misleading the youth of Athens, particularly in the case of Antytus's son. For Hegel, Socrates' interference constitutes a breach of the familial unity that should exist between parents and children, as there can be no "moral interference of a third party in the absolute relationship between parents and children."[105] This unity and trust between them is "the mother's milk of the ethical order *(die Muttermilch der Sittlichkeit)*."[106] He also adds the following political wisdom: anyone who touches or attacks the basic ethical principles, such as parental obedience (familial piety) and religious obedience (piety in general), is a danger that the state must take seriously. There is a limit to the freedom of thought and speech beyond which it must not go, for the state is a "spiritual kingdom *(geistiges Reich)*" and hence any such attacks could wound it mortally. On both counts Socrates was guilty of destroying the *Geist* of Athenian laws. Is it any wonder, Hegel asks himself, that Socrates was found guilty: "it must be so *(er musste es werden)*."[107]

Yet if it is true that the criminal must be punished, it is not necessarily the case that the punishment must be death. It did not have to be, but Socrates chose it. He could have chosen to go into exile as was customary, but he refused to take this option. In doing so, he refused to submit himself to the just punishment of the people because he refused to recognize the sovereignty of the people with regard to his own conscience. Socrates once again violated custom and in this last act of choosing death remained true to his basic principle of the freedom of self-consciousness. Hegel argues that "we wonder at this moral independence and his consciousness of what is right, which consists in his ability never to be moved either to act in any other way or to recognize what is not right. He exposes himself, therefore, to death."[108] Socrates' placement of the tribunal of his conscience above that of the state does not meet with Hegel's approval, for "the first principle of a state in general is that there is no higher reason, certainty, uprightness, which we all want, than what the city-state *(Stadt)* recognizes as right."[109] Despite this, however, Socrates remains a hero of the new right of morality, which, given the stage of development of the Attic state, necessarily had to come into collision with the old right of *Sittlichkeit*. Furthermore, despite the fact that the individual is annihilated by punishment, the principle is, if anything, strengthened through it. Socrates' fame is posthumous, for his principle will *mutatis mutandis* be the principle of a higher stage of development when truth more properly comes into its own. Hence, the question must be asked as to whether Hegel's historiosophical relativization of the fate of Socrates and his acceptance of the authority of the state over that of the individual is not another case of Hegel's siding with the universal. To answer this question we must first look at the conflict in modernity, as Hegel sees it, between *Moralität* and *Sittlichkeit* and how he proposes to solve it.

The actuality of this conflict is evident from the beginnings of modernity to the present day. It can be summed up as follows: take as given the decline of traditional society and its unproblematic reproduction of its own premises, both at the level of society as a whole and at the level of the individual, precisely through the existence of the already always-existent ethical order of norms, values, customs, and real concrete institutions such as the Church, the guilds, the various estates, and the state itself, which binds the whole, and the consequent rise of individualism, which deprives this order of its ethical validity by reducing it to the sphere of positive law or by making it problematic through natural law theory (the realm of right). The result is that the individual is increasingly no longer determined in his or her conduct by concrete norms or virtues that constitute an intersubjectively shared 'second nature', but by abstract and universalizable norms of conduct by which the individual rationally determines his or her conduct (the realm of morality). The Kantian position is, for Hegel, focused on the questions of right and morality at the expense of that of ethical life itself. As Habermas amusingly puts it, Kant focuses on the input side of practical discourse—the question of the discursive grounding of norms—whereas Hegel focuses on the output side—on the effective realization of moral views.[110] The result of such an emphasis is, according to Hegel, that the Kantian ought remains powerless in the face of reality; and that reality itself is conceived abstractly as the key social institutions of social life that are the bearers of *Sittlichkeit,* such as the family, civil society and the state, are neglected.

The *Phenomenology of Spirit* traces the education of the spirit until it becomes fit for absolute knowing and, hence, enters the realm of science, which is conceived as a system of knowledge. The realm of what is called in the *Phenomenology* spirit, and what will later be known *mutatis mutandis* as objective spirit, is the realm in which spirit emerges from the ethical order into the self-alienated world of culture until it finally becomes certain of itself in morality. In a very real sense, what Hegel is writing in this section of the *Phenomenology* in particular is the history of humanity from the pre-Socratic to the postrevolutionary period in terms of its moral development. Looked at from this perspective, the customary or ethical order *(Sittlichkeit)* seems to be something that is left behind rather than part of our own actuality; however, as any reading of *The Philosophy of Right* would show, this is, in fact, not the case. Hegel's project in that work could be defined as an attempt to show that although inwardness and subjectivity are the basic principles of the modern world and, hence, that the Kantian split between morality and right is absolutely correct, we can nevertheless go beyond this split by demonstrating the rationality of ethical life as the solution to the output problem mentioned previously. The weakness of the project, however, rests on the fact that the reconciliation remains forced, and hence, the motivation behind it remains suspect. The problem has been well put by Ritter, who cannot be accused of *parti pris* as he does not accept the interpretation himself: "Hegel's sublation *(Aufhebung)* of morality in and through objective institutions, habits, and laws must appear as a negation and challenge to the moral authority of the individual in the hidden motivation of his action; the concept of ethical being may seem to remain outside the horizon of ethics or else to be suspected of being the instrument of a philosophical 'Machiavellianism,' which Hegel uses to assert political power and force as something higher than moral selfhood, to allow them to triumph over the impotence of the individual."[111] Within Hegel's philosophy the question is, in short, whether *Moralität* and *Sit-*

tlichkeit must be construed as antinomical and morality favored as the more historically progressive or whether morality can, in effect, be dialectically preserved and not merely negated in a modern version of the ancient ethical community.

The dissonances in modernity that constitute the Hegelian dialectic of enlightenment are, in part, found in the period of Attic enlightenment itself. The analyses of ethical order, culture, and morality in the *Phenomenology* could apply to the developments within Greek antiquity and not simply to the history of the West as a whole. The central conflict of modernity—that between *Moralität* and *Sittlichkeit*—is also central within antiquity. The sophists as *Aufklärer* and Socrates as Kant are plausible parallels in Hegel's mind, for the critique of subjective idealism that informs his work leads to a reappreciation of the ethical validity of customary order *(Sittlichkeit)* against which both Socrates and Kant, in very different ways, are opposed. Hegel, however, is still a modernist in terms of his philosophy of history, which means that once morality appears its truth cannot be denied; hence, his attempt at a dialectical mediation of the two principles in *The Philosophy of Right*. In antiquity the time is not yet right for such a mediation; here the two principles must enter into a fatal collision, despite the fact that Socrates himself and the transition toward morality of which he is the hero is a real tendency of Greek antiquity. Hegel separates antiquity from modernity according to the oppositions between external beauty and inner truth, *Sittlichkeit* and *Moralität*. Hence, despite Hegel's recognition of the untimely actuality of Socrates as the inventor of morals, there is still something too beautiful about his individuality that makes him not quite modern. Hegel's strategy, therefore, becomes one of stressing antiquity as a midpoint and Socrates as a mid-point. This argument is more successful when dealing with Socrates' character than with his fate, for here the trial of morality strikes one as having great actuality given Hegel's own critique of modernity. The principle of subjectivity, of the right to freedom and reflection that comes into conflict with the ethical order, is the principle and the matter of conflict in modernity as well. In antiquity this conflict takes on a fateful air that it does not have in modernity. In *The Philosophy of Right*,

Hegel hopes to have secured for modernity a happier *dénouement*. Yet in his interpretation of Socrates, Hegel also hopes to have secured a happy *dénouement* for antiquity: Socrates must die and the principle of subjective freedom turn inward as the *polis* form stagnates. So wherein lies the happy ending? It is provided by world history, of course, which declares Socrates a hero. The characteristic of heroes is that "through them new worlds arise."[112] Socrates' victory is posthumous; hence, once again his actuality is ironically untimely.

In this argument concerning untimeliness Hegel provides himself with a position that avoids taking a definite stance either for Socrates or for his accusers, for *Moralität* or *Sittlichkeit*. Socratic morality can be acknowledged while at the same time being declared premature. In this way Hegel can displace the central tension in his work into the domain of world history itself. I define this tension as one that exists between his admiration for morality, for progress, for an economically conceived civil society, for both individual and political freedom—in sum, for modernity—which pushes him in a direction that could be called liberal-progressive, and between his fears concerning the divisiveness and negativity of thinking and enlightenment—in sum, a critic of modernity—which pushes him in a conservative direction. Hegel's reading of Socrates stands within the force field created by this tension.

Chapter Two

Kierkegaard: Socrates As Existential Thinker

In the creation of an oeuvre, the act of foundation is often a part of its prehistory rather than its history, and its prehistory often takes a long time to be uncovered, as Marx's oeuvre testifies. This is not the case with Kierkegaard who, notwithstanding his copious private writings, lays before the reader nearly every act in the foundation of his position as thinker and writer. This transparency of oeuvre, its explicitly thought-autobiographical character, as well as the very rapidity of its unfolding suggest a mind in the process of formation and positions not yet fully taken. From the thesis on Socrates in 1841, through the so-called pseudonymous aesthetic writings, until the final revelation of his authorship in his greatest work, the *Concluding Unscientific Postscript*, Kierkegaard presents to the reader a whole series of positions and personnae and invites him or her to choose. These choices are not doctrinal but existential. The authenticity of one form of existence over another can no longer be taken for granted; it must be argued for, and decided upon, by every individual. It is the choice, however, that is "beyond reason," for it decides for us "what is to count for us as reason."[1] Kierkegaard breaks from modernity's drive for self-certainty, for rational self-grounding, with his assertion that such an *archē* is linked not so much to rational discourse as to existential choice, to a leap. With this he also breaks out of that branch of Western theology that attempts to reconcile faith *and* reason and joins up with that other branch, for which it is a question of *either* faith *or* reason. This conflict appears in Kierkegaard's philosophical work *mutatis mutandis* as one between Hegel and the romantics. Besides the existential choice between the aesthetic and the ethical, another existential choice that Kierkegaard presents us is the choice between the ethical and the religious. The two great representatives of these spheres are Socrates and Christ, whose similarity exists in their dissimilarity according to an early formulation from his thesis. Even though his choice between the two is clear, so also is his continual attraction to both. The concept of the ethical that attracts Kierkegaard to Socrates is very different from the Christian concept that MacIntyre discovers in his reading of *Either/Or*. Socratic ignorance, rather than those concrete values of Protestant Christianity susceptible to universalization, fascinates Kierkegaard. How, therefore, can Kierkegaard reconcile his admiration for Socrates the rationalist with his belief in the notion of paradox in Christianity—his belief that faith is still possible even after the prospect of its rational foundation is given up? The solution to this riddle lies in the concept of reason that Kierkegaard eschews, the Hegelian one, which he views as one that reduces the role of the individual in moral choice to a reflection of the ethical spirit of his or her time. The individual cannot do or decide anything à rebours. The discursive employment of reason that Socrates embodies enjoys a chronic indeterminancy vis-à-vis what is universalizable, beyond the imperative of universalizability itself. The ontological employment of reason that Hegel embodies represents a chronic pre- and overdetermination of what is universalizable. With regard to Christianity, Kierkegaard's Socratic discursiveness and Socratic insistence on the right of the individual to choose the ethical over the aesthetic mode of existence, and even the religious over the ethical mode of existence, comes up against the limits of discursiveness and judgment that any revealed religion contains. As Castoriadis has once again reminded us, "the very idea of judgment and of choice are greco-occidental," whereas "a true Christian has nothing to either judge or choose; he has only to believe and love, for it is written: 'Judge not, that ye be not judged' (Matthew 7,1)."[2] For a true Christian, faith could not appear paradoxical; it is only for a person like Kierkegaard, who was deeply influenced by these greco-occidental ideas that were mediated to him through the figure of Socrates, that the paradox could be so. These ideas, which reemerge in modernity from the seventeenth century onward in various guises and in conjunction with totally new ideas, put into question the Christian world view, which already by Kierkegaard's time was in a state of advanced decomposition. In this context, if Kierkegaard's aim was restorationist, then his thought would be of little contemporary interest. Rather, his radical subjectivization and de-totalization of religious belief subjects religion to the impulses of modernity from within its very structures. The paradox is that Kierkegaard's modernization of religion prepares the ground for its demolition, which is a task undertaken by Nietzsche.

Hence, rather than there being any *tertium datur* that reconciles Kierkegaard's Socratic and Christian impulses, his oeuvre stands within the performative contradiction generated by these radically different strands of thought. His early reading of Socrates, which is what mainly concerns us here, is the product of two different sources of his thought: first, his appropriation and critique of the Hegelian philosophy, and second, his indebtedness to romanticism in his construction of the aesthetic in general and in his reading of Socratic irony in particular. As we shall see in this chapter, these sources give rise to a reading of Socrates as an aesthetic figure who deploys irony as a way of dismantling inherited thought. But Kierkegaard's later reading of Socrates is more powerfully determined by his reinterpretation of Christianity, which gives rise to a reading of Socrates as an 'existing thinker' for whom thought as a form of existence has a specificially ethical content. The romantic rather than rationalist portrayal of Socrates as the ironic destroyer of inherited meaning gives way to a more post-romantic, rather than Kantian, portrayal of Socrates as fashioning a new ethically charged 'stylistics of existence'. As such, it is a stylistics of existence second only to the religious. It remains an anti-Kantian portrayal insofar as the Hegelian assimilation of Socrates to the modern problematic of subjective freedom is resisted because of the attempt to define subjectivity in less formal and more existential terms. Kierkegaard's Socrates is never assimilable to the very Kantian Judge William of

Either/Or. Before I begin a discussion of Kierkegaard's earliest works, however, some general remarks about his theory of existence-spheres, as contained in "Epistle to the Reader" from Frater Taciturnus in *Stages on Life's Way,* will serve as a general introduction to the structure of Kierkegaard's thought.

I

With due deference to Nietzsche, one could almost say that Kierkegaard's thinking is contained in the slogan "Don Juan versus the Crucified"; however, like Nietzsche, Kierkegaard fights his intellectual wars on many fronts. The conflict between the immediate erotic and the religious is only one. The first conflict that has direct implications on the formulation of the theory of existence-spheres is that between the religious and the increasingly evident atheistical tendency of modern philosophy, implicit in Hegel, as well as that between existence itself and the logical abstractness of Hegelian philosophy. Of course, Kierkegaard shares the latter reservation against Hegelianism with his contemporary—Karl Marx. But Marx's acceptance of the Feuerbachian critique of Hegel directs his concern with existence in an increasingly materialist and atheistical direction. Kierkegaard's concern is elsewhere, but he shares with Marx, and in line with modern romanticism as a whole, the notion that man is not simply an *animal rationale.* This notion necessitates a turning away from metaphysics. Kierkegaard argues that "the metaphysical is abstraction, there is no man that exists metaphysically."[3] This turning of the philosophical agenda toward existence is in line with Marx's eleventh thesis yet is both more complex and more fecund than Marx's *coup de main.* It is more complex because it does not result in a one-sided emphasis on man as *homo faber* or even as *animal laborans,* which more complex versions of the philosophy of praxis try to avoid by becoming increasingly unfaithful to Marx. It is more fecund because much of modern philosophy from phenomenology on has taken key Kierkegaardian categories into account. For example, connections have been made between Kierkegaard's account of religiousness A and the Heideggerian doctrine of authenticity.[4] The authors who make this connection are quick to point out that Heidegger takes up a secularized version of religiousness A, which Kierkegaard sees as an antidote to nihilism. This indicates that Kierkegaard's renewed emphasis on the religious does not withstand the increasingly atheistical tendencies already mentioned; however, his theory of the religious also contains elements of psychological and sociological profundity that will be examined later.

Taylor argues, as I have already mentioned, that a distinction must be made between the premodern view of the subject, which places it in relation to the cosmic order, and the modern view of the essentially self-defining subject.[5] If the Kierkegaardian subject retreats from world history as the *topos* for its self-definition into a more private realm, then this retreat does not in any way lessen its modernity. In *Sickness Unto Death* Kierkegaard argues that "man is spirit. But what is Spirit? Spirit is the self. But what is the self? The self is a relation which relates itself to its own self."[6] But if this were the case, then one could only despair at not willing to be one's own self, for a dialectic of human self-constitution and self-estrangement such as one finds in Hegel and Marx would be all that Kierkegaard intends in his definition of the self. Although a modernist, Kierkegaard is not an atheist. Hence, the self as the relation that relates itself to its own self is constituted by another. The 'Power' which constitutes the whole relationship deepens despair; it is not simply despair at not willing to be one's own self but despair at willing to be oneself. Kierkegaard argues that "this formula [i.e., that the self is constituted by another] is the expression for the total dependence of the relation (the self namely), the expression for the fact that the self cannot of itself attain and remain in equilibrium and rest by itself, but only by relating itself to that Power which constituted the whole relation."[7] Kierkegaard's interpretation of Abraham's predicament would not be possible without such a theory of the self, for a totally self-defining subject would need to submit only to ethical regulation and not to divine commandment. Hence, while not simply jettisoning the theory of the self-defining subject for a static view of the self's role in the divine order, Kierkegaard tries to preserve the God-rela-tionship by transforming it into an internal and dynamic aspect of the self. In place of the glorious *hybris* of the self-defining subject enters the comic performance of the *heauton-timorumenos* (self-tormentor).

Outside of the God-relationship, however, the self is 'not yet'. Kierkegaard argues that "man is a synthesis of the infinite and the finite, of the temporal and the eternal, of freedom and necessity, in short it is a synthesis. A synthesis is a relation between two factors. So regarded man is not yet a self."[8] The possibilities with which this incomplete self imaginatively experiments are the subject matter of Kierkegaard's pseudony-mous production. The stenographic expression of these possi-bilities is the theory of existence-spheres, of which there are three: the aesthetic, the ethical, and the religious. The aesthetic is the sphere of the immediate and the outward. It can be fur-ther divided into two forms: that of the immediate aesthetic where enjoyment is paramount and that of the reflective aes-thetic where enjoyment is transferred to the imagination.[9] One example of an individual that lived an immediate aesthetic existence is Don Juan, whom Kierkegaard depicts as an erotic-sensuous genius who necessarily had to find his correct aes-thetic expression in music; that medium exists, like speech, only in being performed and, hence, is more capable of expressing the momentary nature of desire. Another example is the Roman emperor Nero, whose melancholic spirit ensues from being unable to emerge from immediacy. With regard to the reflective aesthetics, the 'rotation method' is the self's instrument for alternating its desires, while never leaving the security of its own imagination. An example of a reflective aes-thetic type is A, the putative author of the papers in part 1 of *Either/Or*, who is described by Judge William in part 2 as being in a "despair in thought"; although A recognizes the nullity of immediate existence and its pleasures, he cannot escape the intoxication that is despair.[10] The self is still 'not yet' unless it passes over into that sphere of existence that Judge William recommends to A: the ethical, or desire versus law, or "Don Juan versus the Königsbergian."

The ethical is qualified by Kierkegaard as only a "transitional sphere" between the immediacy of the aesthetic and the fulfillment of the religious. It has "repentance as a negative action" as its highest expression and as such makes possible "infinite room" for the individual's entry into religious fulfillment.[11] Kierkegaard's further characterization of it as the sphere of infinite requirement, wherein the individual always goes bankrupt, brings out more clearly not only the Kantian inspiration behind his depiction of this sphere but also the extent to which the stages theory is ultimately at variance with Kant's conception. The exact nature of ethical repentance is spelled out earlier in the second volume of *Either/Or* where its spokesman is Judge William. The latter repeats, with a little annoyance, "that choosing oneself is identical with repenting oneself."[12] The specific target here is the mystic who "repents himself out of himself, not into himself."[13] The more general distinction that is being made here is, to use categories derived from Hegel, the distinction between concrete and abstract individuality. The concrete individual sees choosing himself or herself as a definite individual in definite surroundings as a task that he or she assumes responsibility for, whereas the abstract individual sees no tasks but only the 'bad infinity' of possibilities that come from without and are never acted on. Just as Kierkegaard shares Hegel's critique of romanticism's concept of the aesthetic, however, he also shares Hegel's reservations concerning the Kantian concept of practical reason. Judge William argues that "the fact that the individual sees possibility as his task expresses precisely his sovereignty over himself, which he never relinquishes, even though he can find no pleasure in the very embarrassing sovereignty which characterizes a King without a country."[14] Yet Judge William stresses the assurance rather than the isolation that this sense of inwardness brings to the ethical individual, for Judge William embodies the highest possibilities of the ethical form of life. This life centers on four fundamental concepts: duty, the universal, a conception of man as a *homo duplex*, and a stress on rules.

The sense of assurance stems from the fact that duty suggests for Judge William not an outward relation but an inward relation. It is not an imposition but is encumbent on the individual; and as his or her duties are self-imposed rather than externally dictated, the ethical individual avoids the despair of the aesthetic individual who is reliant on the outward for direction. It also stems from the fact that "the ethical is the universal" and as such contains only prohibitions and not positive commands.[15] The notion of positive commands already smacks, according to Judge William, of the aesthetical that he, as ever, sharply differentiates from the ethical purity of the law. The man who possesses the universal as conscience is the universal man. To become universal, the individual must labor to remove accidentality and reach the universal. This means, for example, that he or she will not love adventitiously but only in a way that realizes the universal: that is, through marriage. The ethical life is one of work, the work of choosing oneself and not simply of knowing oneself. The distinction that Judge William makes here reflects the rejection of the contemplative conception of the self in favor of the more dynamic and ethically oriented conception typical of modernity. The self develops out of the creative tension that exists within each individual between the universal within (the ideal self) and the individual as particularity (the actual self). Thus, man is a *homo duplex*, forever becoming what he or she is. The notion of rule also reflects the modernity of Judge William's approach to the ethical. Here he makes a parallel between his respect for the grammatical rule and his disdain for the exception, learnt significantly enough through the purely intellectual process of mastering a Latin grammar, and his respect for moral rules and his disdain for an aesthetic life devoted to the cultivation of the exceptional. Hence, instead of a life led in conformity with received customs and values *(Sittlichkeit)*, for which a linguistic parallel would be the acquisition of a *mother* tongue *(Muttersprache)*, Judge William opts for a life led in conformity with rules in a society where these customs and values, and even the language itself, have been debased. The aesthetical life is the expression of this disintegration. The aesthetical man is the polyglot of desire.

The opposition of desire and law expresses the opposition between the aesthetical and ethical stages. The religious stage is not only differentiated from the metaphysical, aesthetical, and ethical stages but is also internally differentiated into religiousness A and religiousness B. In *Stages on Life's Way*, however, Kierkegaard's main concern is to distinguish the religious from the aesthetical. The religious individual suffers from within, whereas the aesthetic individual suffers from without. In the aesthetic individual there is some proportion between his suffering and his strength; hence, the possibility of conquering defines the aesthetic hero. In the religious individual there is no such proportion, for it is basically an inward relationship; hence, religious self-torment appears comic when viewed aesthetically. The religious self-tormentor is unable to press through to joy, to the truly religious type of fulfillment. Here one can see the emergence of an internal differentiation of the religious, which receives its most mature statement in the *Concluding Unscientific Postscript*. This differentiation, however, must be viewed in the totality of Kierkegaard's thinking, which is based on two preliminary oppositions: that between the understanding or intellect *(Verstand)* and faith, and that between reason *(Vernunft)* and faith. These two secular versions of immanence are complemented by a form of religious faith that is also immanent (religiousness A), which is also further characterized as normal Christian ethico-religiosity. Opposed to it is a form of faith that is transcendent (religiousness B), where faith becomes something dependent on the outward, on the intervention of Christ in history, and, hence, is paradoxically reminiscent of the aesthetical and a move away from the immanent justification of ethico-religious norms and values typical of religiousness A.

Kierkegaard argues, therefore, that religiousness A could exist in paganism and that only religiousness B is Christian in character. Religiousness B involves, therefore, a type of faith that adjures the Christian to believe against the understanding, to believe against reason, and to believe against immanence. Kierkegaard begins *The Concept of Dread*, as always, with a motto, this time from Hamann: "For Socrates was great in 'that he distinguished between what he understood and what he did not understand.'" This obviously refers to the celebrated Socratic ignorance that involves, on the one hand, a recognition of the immanent limits to reason's employment as the self-criticism of the intellect and, on the other hand, a recognition of the transcendent origin (the *daimonion*) of reason's edicts. Later I shall discuss in detail how this makes Socratic philosophy, according to Kierkegaard, "an analogue to faith," but what I want to point out here is the similarity of argumentative strategy that underlies his reconstruction of religiousness B. What Kierkegaard wants is a type of faith where the believer believes against the understanding and accepts the fact that his or her faith is dependent on the paradoxical appearance of the eternal in time; only this external occurrence, and no immanent ethico-religious justification, can command faith. The critique of immanence goes hand in hand with an appeal to something transcendent, which appears as paradoxical, just as it does *mutatis mutandis* in the case of Socratic ignorance. Religiousness B or paradoxical *(para doxa)* religiousness is what Kierkegaard calls "the dialectical in the second instance," not a purely immanent dialectic, but a "stepping out of dialectics" (Adorno). Kierkegaard argues that "the dialectical in the second instance" does "posit conditions, of such a sort that they are not merely deeper dialectical apprehensions of inwardness, but are a definite something which defines more closely the eternal happiness," but only does so by thrusting "a man down into the pathos of the absurd."[16] The absurd is Christianity; and Christianity as an existence-communication and not merely a doctrine plunges the individual, by virtue of its paradoxical nature, into believing against the understanding. The paradox differentiates the immanent nature of religiousness A, which is more fully explored in Kierkegaard's *Edifying Discourses*, from the transcendent nature of religiousness B. As Kierkegaard argues:

> In religiousness B the edifying is something outside of the individual, the individual does not find edification by finding the God-relationship within himself, but relates himself to something outside himself to find edification. The paradox consists in the fact that this apparently aesthetic relationship (the individual being related to something outside of himself) is nevertheless the right relationship; for in immanence God is nei-

ther a something (He being all and infinitely all), nor is He outside the individual, since edification consists precisely in the fact that He is in the individual. The paradoxical edification corresponds therefore to the determination of God in time as the individual man; for if such be the case, the individual is related to something outside of himself. The fact that it is not possible to think this, is precisely the paradox.[17]

The paradoxical proximity of the aesthetical and religiousness B further emphasizes the transitional character of the ethical stage as a stage of pure inwardness and immanent rationality. John Powell Clayton has argued that there is a close parallel between Nietzsche's parable concerning the three metamorphoses, which he also contends forms the structure of *Thus Spake Zarathustra*, and Kierkegaard's stage theory.[18] The spirit's transformation from a camel to a lion and then to a child parallels respectively the stages of the religious, the ethical, and the aesthetic. Hence, Nietzsche's parallel also involves a critical inversion in which only one term maintains its place: the transitional stage of the ethical. Powell concludes, therefore, that Nietzsche's main concern centers on the question of "Dionysius versus the Crucified"; and raises the further question as to whether Kierkegaard's main concern was not also the contrast between the aesthetic and the religious. Such a parallel ignores the extent to which there is, in Nietzsche, a systematic attempt to reduce ethical systems and even concrete forms of life either to quasi-biological drives and needs or to pallid and decadent descendants of once great religio-metaphysical systems. Kierkegaard's thought lacks any such quasi-biological theory of power and takes more seriously the independence of modern ethical and speculative thought. Hence, the ethical stage in Kierkegaard is not merely transitional. From *Either/Or* to *Fear and Trembling*, it is the existence sphere that Kierkegaard views as the greatest rival to the religious.

Mark C. Taylor has argued that these stages must be seen as stages in the development of selfhood, which unfolds dialectically, hence, it is only in this sense that one can see the ethical as a middle term.[19] This approach leads him to reconstruct the

Kierkegaardian theory of the self in typically Hegelian terms as the free unfolding of the self driven by the internal splitting of the latter into a series of oppositions summarized by the terms "actuality" and "possibility." This leads him to see the merit in Stephen Crites's suggestion that Kierkegaard's pseudonymous works represent a new *Phenomenology*, wherein the world-historical process sketched in the old *Phenomenology* is played out in what Hegel would have called the realm of subjective spirit. This results in an untenable psychologization of Kierkegaard's thinking that even Taylor recognizes when he argues that he will try to combine such an approach with one that sees the various stages as "ideal representations of various life views."[20] Even though he notices the proximity of this conception to Husserl's notion of 'significance structure' and Heidegger's notion of 'world', Taylor is still tempted to psychologize the stages as "ideal personality types."[21] This is not to deny that psychology is relevant to Kierkegaard's oeuvre in a way that it cannot be with Hegel's, but to assert merely that the 'worldly' structure of existence spheres has a philosophical rather than a psychological validity. Therefore, I argue that Kierkegaard's construction of the aesthetic must be read in terms of a critique of romanticism, his construction of the ethical in terms of a critique of human self-definition that relies on a theory of the religious that sets aside radically, as we have seen, the metaphysical sphere as one lacking in existence.

II

For Hegel, Socrates has most importance with regard to a part, albeit important, of his philosophy: to the question of the relation between *Moralität* and *Sittlichkeit* both in antiquity and modernity. For Kierkegaard, the figure of Socrates stamps his entire oeuvre. This is a strange result, as I have already remarked, for a thinker who also reveres Christ. The position of Christ in the work of Kierkegaard is unproblematical, however, because the stage theory culminates in religiousness B, which is his own distinctive interpretation of Christianity. This is not the case with Socrates. To which stage does Kierkegaard confine him? The answer is to none. Socrates is relevant to all but at home in none. This extraterritoriality of Socrates vis-à-vis the stages or existence-spheres is due, to some extent, to the antiquity of Socrates' thought and the modernity of Kierkegaard's categories. They force Kierkegaard to treat Socrates first as an ironist, then as an ethicist, and finally as a quasi-religious thinker, even as he recognizes that Socrates cannot be confined to any category. Socrates as an ancient ethicist cannot escape the intermingling of the ethical and the aesthetical typical of the times that is embodied in the understanding of virtue as *kalokagathia* rather than in the modern definition of virtue as submission to law.[22] Nor can Socrates as an ancient ethicist escape the intermingling of the ethical and the metaphysical typical of the times that results in his twin ideas of sin as ignorance and knowledge as recollection rather than the more modern and more Christian definition of sin as guilt and knowledge as involving faith in the paradox.[23] Hence, Socrates' very extraterritoriality makes him a constant point of reference. He is relevant to Kierkegaard's theorization of the aesthetic stage insofar as his position is characterized as irony and counterpoised as such to the very different characteristics of romantic irony. He is relevant to Kierkegaard's theorization of the ethical insofar as it is identified with immanence but counterpoised at the same time with abstract ethics. He is relevant to Kierkegaard's theorization of the religious insofar as he provides a parallel and counterpoint to Kierkegaard's attempt to radicalize Christianity. At the most simple and obvious level the parallel resides in the exceptional character of both Socrates and Christ; they are both single individuals who seek, either immanently or paradoxically, to think the truth of existence; they are both existential thinkers. At the most simple and obvious level the difference resides in the fact that one is an ethical exception for whom irony is central, whereas the other is a religious exception for whom humor is central. These two categories—irony and humor—are essential to the way in which Kierkegaard understands the transition between the aesthetical and ethical stages and the ethical and the religious stages respectively.

There is always a temptation when speaking of

Kierkegaard's theory of stages or existence-spheres to over-look the fragmentary and incomplete nature of his oeuvre and to treat it as a system. This is, of course, a kind of infidelity toward a thinker who always tries to focus on problems of concrete existence and eschews *l'esprit de systeme*. Hence, if I had divided my analysis of Kierkegaard's interpretation of Socrates into three, following Malantschuk, I would have been faced with the problem that Kierkegaard's treatment of the relation between Socratic and modern ethics is not as devel-oped as his treatment of Socrates in relation both to irony and the religious.[24] Even if ethics is not simply transitional in Kierkegaard, it is nonetheless true that he is at his most original in his treatment of problems of the aesthetic (and the critique of romanticism) and of the religious (and the critique of meta-physics). The question of Socratic irony is most obviously treated in detail in the book entitled *The Concept of Irony*, but the problem complex of the aesthetic as a whole necessitates consideration of *Stages on Life's Way* and, especially, of one of Kierkegaard's two masterpieces, *Either/Or*. The second part of *Either/Or* is relevant to the question of Socratic ethics as is, in a much broader context, *De omnibus dubitandum est* and also, more directly, *The Concept of Dread*. It is obvious, however, that it is the parallels that Kierkegaard draws between the Socratic philosophy and faith, which are explored in the *Philosophical Fragments* and the *Concluding Unscientific Postscript*, are piv-otal to any treatment of Kierkegaard's interpretation of Socrates. Both *Fear and Trembling* and *The Sickness Unto Death*, however, need to be considered for the ways in which they draw the boundaries between the ethical and the religious. My discussion will end by analyzing Kierkegaard's critique of modernity, both in relation to his interpretation of Socrates and his theory of religiousness B.

III

According to Heidegger, we live in the era of the end or completion of philosophy and stand before the question of the task of thinking.[25] This 'completion' entails both the overturning of metaphysics, which Heidegger argues is Platonic, and the flight of the modern sciences. His identification of metaphysics with Platonism is both significant and in accord with Nietzsche's judgment, whereas his identification of Marx as the one who accomplishes this overturning leaves unmentioned the contribution of Kierkegaard. The fact that Heidegger's theses were presented to a UNESCO colloquium on Kierkegaard means that although Kierkegaard's contribution was left unstated, it was not unimplied. Furthermore, the identification of metaphysics with a Platonism that exhausted itself with Hegel is completely in sympathy with the rejection of system-philosophical thinking in Kierkegaard. In one of his earliest unpublished works, entitled *Johannes Climacus or De omnibus dubitandum est*,[26] he tries to dispute the fact that modern philosophy must begin in doubt on the basis that knowledge produced by such reflective thinking can have no relationship to our interest or consciousness. Disinterested knowledge cannot be produced by doubt, because doubt itself is due to interest. He argues that the Greek skeptics were more correct in their way of surmounting doubt; they realized that because doubt implies interest in removing doubt, one must transform interest into apathy. One cannot remove doubt methodically via the system but only existentially via a change of disposition. Of course, even in Descartes's inaugurating myth such a moment is retained, but it has only autobiographical significance; for Kierkegaard, however, the abandonment of speculative thinking leads to the standpoint that thinking is irredeemably bound up with existence.

The dethroning of metaphysics leaves thought in the same situation as before its coronation. The type of thinking invented by Socrates returns to haunt post-Hegelian thinking as an emblem of paradoxical thinking—hence, the importance of the question of irony and the need to differentiate Socratic from romantic irony. This is a task Kierkegaard set himself in his M.A. thesis, *The Concept of Irony*, a work that still stands under the sway of Hegel both in terms of its conceptual apparatus and its substantive argumentation, even as it distances itself from Hegel. This distance from Hegel is tersely formulated in Kierkegaard's fifteenth thesis, which is the last of the theses that accompanies his main work. It reads, "As philosophy begins with doubt, so also that life which may be called worthy of man begins with irony."[27] The thesis implies a distance from philosophy, an unwillingness to move through doubt to systemic philosophy, an attempt to live a life that begins with irony and, perhaps, may end with irony. According to Kierkegaard's own interpretation in *Point of View of My Work as an Author*, where he presents, surely ironically, his "report to history," he asserts that he was from the first till the last a religious thinker.[28] This, of course, raises the question of the status of the aesthetic or pseudonymous works, which he began to publish immediately after his dissertation. His reply is that these works were "deceptions"; their function was to act as instruments for the unmasking of illusion and, hence, for the indirect communication of truth. They were, therefore, conceived Socratically and neither metaphysically nor dogmatically. As Kierkegaard argues, "What then does it mean, to 'deceive'? It means that one does not begin *directly* with the matter one wants to communicate, but begins by accepting the other man's illusion as good money."[29] Hence, he asserts the importance of dialectical irony, for the indirect communication of truth makes Socrates his teacher with, perhaps, even more influence over his thinking than Kierkegaard, the believer in Christ, would like to admit.

For Kierkegaard, therefore, Socrates is an antisystemic thinker, the kind of thinker Kierkegaard himself sets out to be. As such a thinker, his main weapon is irony, which raises a claim to knowledge that is self-refuting. Kierkegaard's attempt to put dialectical irony in the service of theology reflects the latter's very weakness even as he struggles against it. If theology is left off stage, then what stands at the center of Kierkegaard's attention in *The Concept of Irony* is, as I mentioned earlier, the question of his relationship both to Hegel and to German romanticism. The first part of that work considers the historical sources of our knowledge of Socrates in order to arrive at a conception of his standpoint as irony rather than subjectivity, inwardness, and morality as in the Hegelian interpretation. Hence, Kierkegaard's initial picture of Socrates is more negative than Hegel's who wishes to stress, as I have shown, the positive and negative sides of Socratic dialectics. In order to prove his interpretation Kierkegaard relies more heavily on Aristophanes' depiction of Socrates than on Hegel's. In the second part of the work Kierkegaard puts romantic irony on the dissection table and comes to some findings remarkably similar to Hegel's; however, their strategies remain distinct. Hegel contrasts the yearning of the 'beautiful soul' with the abstract and formal character of duty in order to demonstrate their reconciliation in that actual 'I' or dual 'I' that has "the universal knowledge of *itself* in its absolute opposite": this 'I' is God.[30] This purely immanent conception of religion is one that, as we have seen, Kierkegaard rejects. Evidence of this rejection appears in *Irony* even though the conception of irony as a 'mastered moment' only approaches the idea of the religious proper. The parallels he draws between poetic and religious illumination, however, point toward a more transcendent conception, and hence, to another lingering romantic strain in Kierkegaard's thought.

The notion of dialectical irony as deception or indirect communication, which Kierkegaard operates with in his report to history, is what he refers to as executive or dramatic irony in his book on irony. He counterpoises such a notion with the more metaphysical concept of irony as theoretical or contemplative, which involves not simply dissembling, cutting loose, or being hypocritical but a kind of purposiveness without purpose in which the freedom of the ironist lies. Whereas executive irony has a purpose external to itself, which in Kierkegaard's self-interpretation is the indirect communication of the higher truth of Christianity, theoretical irony possesses only an immanent purpose. Hence, if Socratic irony is more theoretical than executive, as is the case, then Kierkegaard's interpretation of his own aesthetic works as Socratic is a misinterpretation. Socratic dialectic aims at the elimination of falsehood and not at the indirect communication of truth. It is true, of course, that with the concept of irony as a mastered moment Kierkegaard tries to take his distance from Socrates, even in this work; nevertheless, Kierkegaard's fascination with the figure of Socrates is always deeper than he would like to admit. Kierkegaard is a figure who always remains attached to the 'higher madness' of dialectical irony and never truly finds in Christianity the anchorage he seeks. His use of irony is not merely a dissemblance, a contrivance for the indirect communication of truth, but embodies the negativity that is attached to its Socratic employment. Kierkegaard begins his interpretation of *The Concept of Irony* with this observation: "What Socrates valued so highly, namely, to stand still and come to himself, i.e. silence, this is what his whole life is in relation to world history."[31] Thus, what makes a conception of Socrates possible is that Xenophon, Plato, and Aristophanes have indirectly communicated the words of the master of indirect communication. Unlike some philosophers, Kierkegaard argues, "wherein the very lecture itself constitutes the presence of the idea," for Socrates there was always a difference between what he said and what he meant, between the outer and the inner, between expression and indication.[32] Socrates, as Kierkegaard later remarks, had a *bifrons* character. Thus, any interpretation of Socrates is doubly deferred: because his voice is silent, we are relayed from his own words to that of his interpreters; and because his own communication incessantly postpones its meaning—it conceives of the idea as a limit and not as a presence—any interpretation that does not recognize this fact inadequately grasps the Socratic standpoint of irony. Socratic irony, when read from the standpoint of German romanticism, becomes the true intellectual progenitor of deconstructionism because meaning is always deferred and delayed. It goes beyond deconstructionism because its negativity is not only directed toward the tradition of Western metaphysical discourse, a purely professorial attitude, but also because Socrates was a citizen of a city-state in a time of political and intellectual turbulence, it was also directed at the customs and practices of his fellow citizens. 'Irony as a negative concept' is the hermeneutical key through which Kierkegaard hopes to surmount all partial conceptions of Socrates and to arrive at a new 'integral calculation'.

This key determines Kierkegaard's attitude toward the three historical sources of our conception of Socrates. Although Kierkegaard has played the third against each of them (that is, he has counterpoised their conception to another stand-point—irony—and, hence, does not concur entirely with any), it is clear that it is the early Plato and Aristophanes come closest to a depiction of the Socratic standpoint as irony. Xenophon, according to Kierkegaard, remains purely at the level of the immediate and the external in his depiction of Socrates and has not captured the way irony undermines existence. His Socrates is more of a sophist, which is to say something of a chatterbox, whereas the power of irony lies in its silence. These silences are the "secret trap doors" through which the sophist falls into "the infinite nothingness of irony."[33] These silences are not 'pure silences' but refer rather to the plainness or meagerness of expression that characterizes the ironist and links his art to the rhetorical figure known as "litotes."[34] Irony is to sophistry what litotes is to *alazoneia* (paucity versus boastfulness of expression). The meagerness of expression consists in saying more, and saying it more conclusively, but with less. There is always something evasive in this underemphasis; it is a type of saying without appearing to understand. Cicero referred to it as *dissimulato urbano*.[35] This feigned naïveté hides a cunningness of reason that operates through speech, but never directly. Xenophon's Socrates is a crass and vulgar figure whose speech hides nothing. Kierkegaard cites as evidence for such a conclusion a reference in Xenophon's *Memorabilia*, where the latter has Socrates boasting of the fact that he has love potions that attract young boys to him. Hence, the ironical inversion implied in the phrase "to love young boys according to the love of wisdom" *(paederastein meta philosophias)"* becomes merely a crass boastfulness *(alazoneia)*.

In relation to Xenophon's Socrates, Kierkegaard tries to save Socrates from sophistry; whereas in relation to Plato's Socrates, Kierkegaard tries to save irony from the speculative idea. What separates Socrates from sophistry is that he converses and not discourses; that is, he holds fast to the object under discussion instead of turning expression itself into an object of beauty. This is the familiar Socratic separation of the search for truth from the snare of rhetoric, which has determined the whole history of philosophical thinking even though the latter has remained unfaithful to the Socratic art of questioning as a whole. This art, according to Kierkegaard, separates Socrates from Plato. Due to the fact that the Platonic philosophy presupposes the immediate unity of thought and being, thinking becomes a kind of questioning that occurs within the thinking subject and is imposed on the object rather than a kind of questioning that arises out of the nature of the object itself. The latter style of thinking links Hegel's concept of the negative to Socratic irony and results in thought actualizing itself "in an alternating (alterno pede) gait, a hobbling from side to side."[36] The literary form that corresponds to such a style of thinking is the dialogue, which is structured according to the principle of duality—question and answer—and not that of trilogy—question, answer and content. Kierkegaard resumes his argument thus:

> one may ask a question for the purpose of obtaining the desired content, so that the more one questions, the deeper and more meaningful becomes the answer; or one may ask a question, not in the interest of obtaining an answer, but to suck out the apparent content with a question and leave only an emptiness remaining. The first method naturally presupposes a content, the second an emptiness; the first is the speculative, the second the ironic. Now it was the latter method which was especially practised by Socrates.[37]

To question, therefore, is to dispel the illusions of knowledge. The task is not methodological, as doubt is for the Cartesian philosophy; that is, the task is not a propaedeutic to the true knowledge but one that involves a whole stylistics of existence.

If irony finds its most appropriate literary expression in the dialogue, then a sure way of separating the Socratic Plato from the Platonic Socrates is to look for changes in the literary form of the Platonic dialogues. Kierkegaard follows Schleiermacher in claiming that one can make a clear line of demarcation between the dialogical dialogues and the constructive dialogues of Plato, with the former employing an irony that resists argumentative closure or resolution and the latter employing a more systematic and closed deployment of concepts. From Socrates to Plato there is a move from a general to a restrictive economy, which Kierkegaard interprets as a shift from an existential to a speculative mode of thought.[38] Hence, he separates the early dialogues of Plato up to and including the first part of the *Republic* from the later constructive dialogues and considers only the former because they alone embody Socrates as ironist and not merely as *nomen appelativum*. The *Symposium* shows love as not positive but negative: as lack and as desire it has an 'immanent negativity' that contrasts sharply with the Christian idea of love as 'fullness'. In the same way that the ironist has the idea as a limit and not as a presence, love appears here as negatively determined, as the incitement to love. This characterization of irony leads Kierkegaard to compare the ironist to a vampire who sucks the blood out of her *(sic)* lover or to the counterfeiter who always appears to be dealing in valueless currency. Kierkegaard sees the irony of the *Protagoras* as resting primarily in its 'ironic design'; it is a dialogue without a result. Irony is compared to an old witch who begins by devouring everything around her and in the end devours her own stomach. In the *Phaedo*, dying is presented not as a victory, as it is in Christianity, but as something negative that is encapsulated, according to Kierkegaard, in the following epitaph: "Nor in the end could he be bothered with living."[39] In contrast to Christianity, Kierkegaard argues, which conceives of dying from a moral point of view and therefore does not tarry on the negative due to its myth of resurrection, the Greek conception of death is purely intellectual and therefore more detached and ironical. What characterizes Socrates' stance in the face of death is neither rejoicing over rebirth nor enthusiasm about death but rather a jesting attitude. Such a form of irony is, according to Kierkegaard, "the abstract criterion whereby it levels everything, whereby it masters every excessive emotion, and hence does not set the pathos of enthusiasm against the fear of death, but finds it a most curious experiment to become nothing at all."[40] Again, of course, the notion of experiment indicates both the intellectual nature of irony and something of its playful nature in comparison with the moral seriousness involved in the adoption of a Christian attitude to life. One also senses the profound ambivalence that rests in this constant comparison between a Socratic or Greek ethos and the Christian ethos. For a man who, from a biographical point of view, had already chosen the Christian ethos, this ambivalence demonstrates a hidden 'either-or', a question asked in Kierkegaard's work as well.

This either-or is not the Socratic '*aut-aut*'. Kierkegaard keeps the terms of his choice clearly separate, and of course, the choice is different. For Socrates, intellectual irony performs the trick that Shakespeare later attributes to gold: of soldering "close impossibilities" and making them kiss. It performs the trick with counterfeit currency, however, for irony is not interested in windfall profit but in debasing the established coinage. "Socrates," Kierkegaard argues, "relishes the play of light and shadow entailed in a syllogistic *aut-aut*, when almost at the same instant appear the noontide of day and the pitch black of night, the infinitely real and infinite nothingness."[41] He refers to the Socratic view of immortality, which is one, according to Kierkegaard, where a foreground characterized by a Socrates clinging onto life melts into a background characterized by the "infinite possibility of death." But the real irony of the *Apology* lies, for Kierkegaard, in the fact that the *Apology* contains none; that is, Socrates turns his back on the accusations when, with one gesture, he turns down the defense written for him that would have probably refuted the charges adequately. Instead, he takes a stance that asserts that he could not possibly have set up any new doctrines, for he is a man who has never claimed to have known anything. This ironical Socrates of Plato's early dialogues is, however, about to disappear; Kierkegaard argues that after book 1 of the *Republic* Plato enters into the constructive phase of his thinking in which there is no longer any place for irony. Kierkegaard says of book 1:

> The individual expressions of irony are here not in the service of the Idea, not its emissary gathering the scattered parts together in a whole; for they do not consolidate but disperse, and every new beginning is not the consummation of anything preceding, not an approxi-

mation to the Idea, but without any deeper connection with what went before and without any relation to the Idea.[42]

In other words, the ironical moment of Socratic thinking is lost in the later Plato as the existential thinker gives way to the speculative thinker. The existential thinker requires a dialogical mode of existence, whereas the speculative thinker's mode of existence is monological. A dialogical mode of existence is a peripatetic one as, indeed, was Kierkegaard's inclination, for he also roamed the streets of Copenhagen in search of interlocutors among the common people. Kierkegaard, however, had this difference: although the Attic people took Socrates to be a fool, as he is portrayed in Aristophanes' comedy, they also took him seriously, as his trial and execution amply proves; for the people of Copenhagen Kierkegaard was "pure fool, pure poet" and the only execution he suffered was the self-inflicted one of a merely literary execution at the hands of the *Corsair*. In the age of positivity the people preferred real gold to intellectual counterfeit. With regard to Kierkegaard, there is also a literary embodiment of the difference between a dialogical and monological mode of existence: the difference in literary form between the aesthetical works, which, while *in strictu sensu* are not dialogical, have a dialogical intent that is expressed very nicely in the expression 'either-or', and the edifying discourses, which take the literary form of a sermon that he never gives for he is not, as he constantly stresses, theologically qualified.

Hegel, as we have seen, tries to preserve what is positive in the dialectic of Socrates and for that reason describes the standpoint of Socrates as one of subjectivity and inwardness. In order to do so, Hegel must argue against the more negative image of Socrates found in Aristophanes, which he does by redeeming from the Socratic moment its world-historical significance. Kierkegaard's standpoint is, as we have seen, completely different. His image of Socrates as an ironical figure leaves him more fully at home in the Attic world. It emphasizes what Hegel relativizes: his negativity, which enters in an even more radical guise in romantic irony. Kierkegaard emphasizes Socrates' negativity vis-à-vis Plato by distinguishing two forms of irony and two forms of dialectic in the work of Plato. Only the first is the genuinely Socratic: it involves a form of irony that is "a goad for thought" and a form of dialectic in which the problem that is kept hovering is left unresolved. The other is Platonic: here irony is both "agent and terminus," and dialectic is the way reality is constructed "by means of the Idea."[43] The Socratic dialectic, as conceived of by Kierkegaard, resembles the 'negative dialectic' of Adorno in its antisystematic impulse, a resemblance that is probably not coincidental when one recognizes that Adorno devoted his *Habilitationshrift* to the Danish thinker. The words that Kierkegaard uses to describe Socrates could just as well be said of Adorno. Both represent "irony in its total striving, and dialectic in its negative, emancipating activity."[44] Not only is Adorno's *Negative Dialectic* a philosophical manifesto predicated on the latter principle, but also his *Minima Moralia* is constructed according to the principle of ironical inversion; it is this principle that provides "a goad for thought." But similarities in the thought of both Kierkegaard and Adorno must ultimately be traced back to the common inheritance of German romanticism, and such a project can not be attempted here.

What is of immediate interest here is the favorable reception of Aristophanes found in Kierkegaard's thesis, for it stands in opposition to the Hegelian reserve toward Aristophanes' depiction of Socrates. For Kierkegaard, the ironist is "lighthearted about the idea," for "the absolute is nothingness"; therefore, it is completely apposite that Aristophanes' should depict Socrates suspended in a basket in the thoughtery.[45] As the idea is kept hovering in dialectical irony, so, too, is Socrates kept hovering in his basket. Hence, according to Kierkegaard, Aristophanes has achieved the perfect theatrical representation of the Socratic principle: philosophy dramatized. If the Socratic principle had been one of subjectivity or inwardness, then Socrates should have been represented, according to Kierkegaard, as "infinitely vanishing," as something unable to be kept sight of. Furthermore, Kierkegaard argues, the fact that Aristophanes has Socrates call upon the clouds illustrates "perfectly the directionless movement of thought" that allows nothing to endure, to become established.[46] Socrates is in an *intermundia*: hovering above the ground in order to preserve his fragile subjectivity *(he phrontis leptē)*, he still feels the need to cry, "Give me a place to stand *(dos moi pou sto)*."[47]

Like Hegel, Kierkegaard conceives of the *daimonion* as warning rather than counseling—that is, the voice of interdictions. In this, too, he follows Plato and eschews Xenophon. Any other view would be incompatible with the Socratic standpoint of irony. The principle of conscience enters into the world in conflict with the existing state and its customs; however, Kierkegaard is unwilling to label the event as tragedy. It is easy to see why, for once the notion of *daimonion* is placed back into the context of irony and not merely that of subjectivity, inwardness, or morality, it then becomes extraordinarily difficult to construe the fate of such a jester, such a buffoon for whom living and dying can be made to meet through a bit of dialectical inversion as that of a tragic hero on a par with Oedipus and Antigone. It follows from Kierkegaard's general position that Aristophanes got it right: Socrates is the stuff that comedies are made of, not tragedies. Perhaps I have gone a little far, however, for Kierkegaard does speak of Plato as capturing the tragic ideality and Aristophanes the comic.[48]

Kierkegaard's view of the charges and execution of Socrates is clear, yet he prefers to leave for himself a degree of detachment and join neither the lamentations nor the celebrations. With regard to the charge that Socrates did not accept the gods of the state and that he introduced new ones, it follows from Kierkegaard's depiction that Socrates' negative standpoint of irony, in effect, is ignorance; therefore, he cannot introduce something that would require true knowledge, such as new gods. For the very same reason he cannot help but have a negative relationship to the actually existing gods. The ironical negativity embodied in the protestation of ignorance is a challenge to the authority and the customs of the state. Kierkegaard interprets the famous phrase "know thyself" here as "separate yourself from the 'other.'"[49] Socrates brought, therefore, the individual under the force of his dialectical vacuum pump, deprived him of the atmospheric air in which he was accustomed to breathe, and abandoned him. For such individuals everything was now lost, except insofar as they were able to breathe in an ether. Yet Socrates no longer concerned himself with them, but hastened on to new experiments.[50]

The callousness of intellectual experimentation vis-à-vis the 'other', vis-à-vis existing customs and authorities makes Socrates a bloodsucker, a revolutionary in and for his times not so much in terms of what he did do but what he failed to do. According to Kierkegaard, even a modern state that leaves more room for subjectivity would feel uneasy with such an individual. It is clear, to put it mildly, that Kierkegaard does not belong to those who see Socrates as the first dissident in human history but rather to those who accuse the intellectual of treason.

In response to the second charge against Socrates—that he corrupted the youth—Kierkegaard's judgment is equally clear and even more condemnatory than Hegel's. Not only the state but also the family had no validity for this "eroticist"; he was a "seducer"—albeit a reflective one. He was, for Kierkegaard, a kind of intellectual Don Juan.

> An eroticist he certainly was to the fullest extent; the enthusiasm for knowledge was his on an extraordinary scale; in short, he possessed all the seductive gifts of the spirit. But communicate, fill, enrich, this he could not do. In this sense one might possibly call him a seducer, for he deceived the youth and awakened longings which he never satisfied, allowed them to become inflamed by the subtle pleasures of anticipation yet never gave them solid and nourishing food. He deceived them all in the same way he deceived Alcibiades, who, as previously mentioned, observes that instead of the lover, Socrates became the beloved.[51]

A in *Either/Or*, as I have already mentioned, is a reflective seducer; however, A is a product of romantic irony rather than of Socratic irony. An "ironic observer," the "*accoucheur*" who takes no responsibility for the youth whom he influences are some of the accusations that Kierkegaard hurls against Socrates. They are the judgments that the court itself directs against Socrates: that of "*apragmosynē* or indifferentism."[52] The negativity of irony is the principle that gives rise to this indifferentism, and it is an ironic fate rather than a tragic fate that Socrates suffers when he is asked to choose his own punishment. Once again Kierkegaard sees nothing but pure comedy in the situation, for Socrates and the state are no longer congruent. They do not, to use an apparent anachronism, share the same paradigm: Socrates rejects the kind of objective determination that the state by its very nature must embody. The two talk past each other. In the face of impending death, Socrates plays the buffoon again and demands to be partially kept at the public expense. Kierkegaard argues:

> It would indeed be comical to see Socrates attempt to conjugate his life according to the paradigm of the state, since his life was wholly irregular; but the situation becomes still more comical by the *dira necessitas* which under pain of death bids him find a similarity in this dissimilarity. It is always comical when one conjoins two things which can have no possible agreement. But it becomes even more comical when it is said: make no mistake about it, unless you discover an agreement you must die.[53]

Here we are very far from Hegel's reading, where an immature world-historical principle has to surrender its right to the right of prevailing custom and authority. We are once again closer to Aristophanes' than to Plato's Socrates, although, of course, Kierkegaard's reading is based on the Platonic sources. Socratic irony is, however, the world-historical preamble to another principle, which Kierkegaard refers to as even more dangerous: that is, of course, the principle of romantic irony. Here, if anywhere, is the connection between Socrates and A. As Kierkegaard would say, it is a similarity in a dissimilarity. The similarity and the danger lie in the claims of subjectivity and infinite negativity, which having been discovered by Socrates, lie dormant like rats before their new and more dangerous reemergence. The dissimilarity lies in the fact that in antiquity Socrates could only arrive at the idea of *kalokagathia* as a limit— that is, as ideal infinity in the form of possibility and not of actuality.[54] Before I discuss romantic irony, however, I would like to turn to Kierkegaard's squaring of accounts with Hegel.

Kierkegaard, like Hegel, sees Socrates arising out of his times—that is, out of the general decay of Hellenism that reaches its philosophical expression in sophism. Even more so than Hegel, Kierkegaard likes to emphasize what historicism finds difficult to explain—the new, the 'divine gift' that was Socrates. Even more paradoxical, Kierkegaard's main charge against the Hegelian interpretation is that it misreads the role and function that Socrates has to play for his time. Here again, it is the negativity of irony that Kierkegaard wants to stress; therefore, he is completely at odds with any attempt to make of Socrates something positive—namely, a founder of morality *(Moralität)*. For Kierkegaard such a view, first of all, misunderstands the polemical nature of the relationship that Socrates has with the sophists. The sophists, above all else, had set in motion the decline of the Greek substantial ethic of *Sittlichkeit* with their peripatetic teaching; and they represent for Kierkegaard, as they did for Hegel, the "evil principle" that is "the arbitrary freedom of finite subjectivity."[55] Yet the importance of the sophists for Socrates is, according to Kierkegaard, that they try to introduce a new positive teaching, summarized in the famous Protagorean teaching that "man is the measure of all things" *(panton chrēmaton anthropon einai)*," toward which Socrates can have nothing but a negative attitude. As Kierkegaard continually asserts, Socrates has the idea of the infinite as a limit and not as a manifestation. Hence, he is good at destroying all claims to positivity, be they that of the city-state or those of the sophist. The metaphor that Kierkegaard employs to describe his activity vis-à-vis the teaching of the sophists is that of "cannibalism." Socrates is a devourer of concepts. The negativity of the metaphor is in line with the whole series of such metaphors that Kierkegaard employs in the book. His attraction to such a position is clear, yet he always guards his distance. "What he [Socrates] lacked," Kierkegaard argues, "was the objectivity wherein subjectivity is free in itself, the objectivity which is not the constricting but the expanding limit of subjectivity."[56] Kierkegaard's Christianity, his anti-Socratic impulse, is on display here, as it is at the end of the book when he speaks of irony as a mastered moment.

Socratic irony's negativity is something that Hegel fully realizes; however, his attempt to secure a positive content for Socrates' activity falls foul of Kierkegaard's point: as Socrates only has the idea of the good as a limit, he can have no positive teaching. Socrates is not the founder of morality for Kierkegaard, for he only has the idea of the good as a task and not as an acquisition. To Kierkegaard, Socrates is a "divine missionary," but the metaphor that is employed to illustrate his activity comes from the very pagan world or underworld of Hades:

> As Charon ferried men over from the fullness of life to the sombre land of the underworld, and in order that his shallow barque might not be overburdened made the voyagers divest themselves of all the manifold determinations of a concrete life: titles, honours, purples, great speeches, sorrows, and tribulations, etc., so that only the pure man remained, so also Socrates ferried the individual from reality over to ideality, and ideal infinity, as infinite negativity, became the nothingness into which he made the whole manifold of reality disappear.[57]

By stressing the negativity of Socratic irony, Kierkegaard brings out the danger it shares with romantic irony, whereas the Hegelian interpretation secures for Socrates a more positive evaluation in comparison with the particularly harsh judgment that Hegel levies against romantic irony. This does not mean that Kierkegaard conflates Socratic and romantic irony. Rather, by distinguishing them properly he more accurately establishes the similarity in dissimilarity. Within the romantic movement proper the themes of infinity and nothingness give rise to a new, more potent, and more dangerous form of irony. For Kierkegaard, Hegel's abhorrence of this form of irony has unduly colored his attitude to the truth of irony. Hegel's attempt to rescue a positive evaluation of Socrates is due, therefore, to a misreading, which paradoxically modernizes and, hence, disqualifies the Socratic standpoint as irony. Instead of adequately distinguishing the two concepts of irony, Hegel conflates them. Kierkegaard distinguishes them thus: "it was not actuality altogether that he [Socrates] negated, but the given actuality of a certain age, of substantiality as embodied in Hellas."[58] For romanticism, finitude as such is nothingness, whereas what Socratic irony negates has a real existence. This negation is an act of the ironic subject not of a prophetic hero or of a tragic hero, the other means via which the new can make its appearance in the world. Socrates as an ironic subject does not face death as does a tragic hero. Death has no weight for him; he can hover above the state and his fate. "The tragic hero," Kierkegaard argues,

> does not fear death, to be sure, but he knows it as a suffering, as a hard and difficult way, and to this extent it has validity when he is condemned to death. But Socrates knows nothing at all, and to this this extent it is an irony over the state when it deprives him of life and thinks by his death to have inflicted a punishment upon him.[59]

For Kierkegaard, the Hegelian reading of Socrates' fate as a result of an irony of world history misses the point; the ironical moment resides in the state's inability to punish the ironic subject. The state does not execute the judgment of world history. It is a victim of the buffoonery of the ironic subject. Post-history is the epoch of the contingent individual.

IV

Kierkegaard interprets the emergence of romantic irony as a re-emergence of subjectivity that Socrates had first sent into the world, but this time the strength of subjectivity is greater. Irony reappears as "subjectivity raised to the second power."[60] Hence, Kierkegaard follows Hegel in seeing a parallel between the movement of thought in the age of Socrates and that of the age of German idealism and romanticism. The key figures of this movement now concern Kierkegaard: Kant, Fichte, Schlegel, Tieck, Solger, and Hegel. But Kierkegaard's discussion does not focus, as does Hegel's, on the similarities and dissimilarities in the respective configurations of *Moralität* and *Sittlichkeit*, but on the disintegrative aspects of *Moralität* itself. Unlike Hegel, Kierkegaard has no belief that such an age of positivity can produce a new form of substantial ethic *(Sittlichkeit)*. There is no secular utopia; for when Kierkegaard is not playing at a nordic Socrates, he seeks his comfort in the lonely relation of the individual to God. To focus on the disintegrative aspects of *Moralität* is to focus on romantic irony. Kierkegaard approaches this new form of irony by making a distinction that antiquity did not make: between, as previously mentioned, executive or dramatic irony and theoretical or contemplative irony. Executive irony consists of the kind of dissembling that occurs in dialogue, whereas theoretical irony ends in an attitude that turns against the whole of existence. Modernity, therefore, not only splits apart what antiquity held together, but also radicalizes one term of the opposition. It is clear that we are in a totally different phase of world history with this latter concept. Whereas executive irony is dialogical in nature, theoretical irony finally comes close to religious devotion in its assertion that existence has no reality. The ironic subject has now become alienated from the whole of existence.

The three main romantic figures that Kierkegaard discusses are Friedrich Schlegel, Ludwig Tieck, and K. W. F. Solger. Both Schlegel and Tieck develop their aesthetic practice on the basis of their interpretation of the philosophy of J. G. Fichte, whereas Solger develops, according to Kierkegaard, a more independent aesthetic theory with which Hegel also enters into dialogue in an extended book review of Solgers's *Nachgelassene Schriften*. The post-Kantian philosophical debate revolves around that remainder impervious to thought in the object that Kant refers to as the *Ding an sich*. The Fichtian solution to the problem is to bring it also within thought and, thus, render the ego infinite. Thereby, Kierkegaard argues, "the producing ego is the same as the produced ego; I=I is the abstract identity. With this he emancipated infinite thought. But this infinity of thought [is] . . . a negative infinity, an infinity without finitude, an infinity void of all content."[61] The ego is like a king who has lost his realm and despite never being able to recover it is condemned to long and to strive for it. Schlegel and Tieck took this metaphysical position and turned it into a concrete life attitude that achieves its unity in the principle of boredom. They do this by a twofold operation. First, they substitute the everyday ego for the eternal ego, and second, they replace metaphysical actuality with historical reality. In other words, they bring a speculative construction down to earth by making earthly things a speculative construct: "all historical actuality was negated to make room for a self-created actuality. . . . [What emerged] . . . was an eccentric subjectivity, a subjectivity raised to the second power."[62] Irony turns nihilistic, and the ironic subject plays out its exhausting game of cat and mouse with reality, letting reality continue to endure in the sure knowledge that at any moment it can annihilate its artificial construct. Reality loses its capacity to surprise, to frustrate the ironic subject and, hence, loses its interest. Phenomena lose their ideal content, and ideas lose their ability to relate to reality. The world becomes stale and vacuous, and the individual only feigns a show of interest. The production by the poetic individual both of himself and of his reality leads these two self-created actualities to lose all substance; they become playthings of the ironist who thereby aestheticizes both himself and his reality.[63]

The ironic subject's production of reality leads to the ahistorical idealization of certain past epochs of human history, notably, classical Greece and the Middle Ages. The afterglow of the movement can be seen in the early works of German sociology, in particular in Tönnies distinction between *Naturwille* and *Kürwille* found in his *Gemeinschaft und Gesellschaft*. According to Kierkegaard, the romantics dispose of authentic history in order to seek refuge in the mythical. Irony demands unbridled control over the production of the historical material, and as a consequence, the historical moment loses its independent validity. The ironist soon becomes bored with his own creation. "At one moment," Kierkegaard argues, "it dwelt in Greece beneath the beautiful Hellenic sky. . . . But when it grew tired of this arbitrarily posited actuality it thrust it away so far that it wholly disappeared. . . . At the next moment it concealed itself in the virgin forests of the Middle Ages."[64] The ironic subject not only poeticizes reality, but it also tries to live poetically. This results in aesthetic gesturing devoid of substance, of which perhaps Lord Byron is the most famous European example. Kierkegaard argues that the romantic subject has no *an sich* to posit over and against the world, but this does not mean that the former is determined by the world; rather, the romantic subject stands over it in the guise of its creator. In sum, the ironist shifts so quickly from one guise to the next—from Roman patrician to Turkish pasha, to use Kierkegaard's example—that the only continuity that remains is boredom. What is equally important for the whole of the future aesthetical production of Kierkegaard is the triumph of the aesthetic and the displacement of ethics and morals. "Still," he argues,

> it cannot properly be said that the ironist sets himself above ethics and morals, for he lives much too abstractly, much too metaphysically and aesthetically ever to arrive at the concretion formed by ethics and morals. Life is for him a drama, and what engrosses him is the ingenious unfolding of this drama. He is himself a spectator even when performing some act.[65]

One could think of no better description of the life-attitude of the seducer in the "Diary of the Seducer," which is the last part of the first volume of *Either/Or*. It has as its consequence the fact that guilt, remorse, and all the other moral sentiments become aesthetically determined: "He feels remorse, but aesthetically not morally. At the moment of remorse he is aesthetically above his remorse examining whether it be poetically correct, whether it might be a suitable reply in the mouth of some poetic character."[66] One might say, with the analytical philosophers, that the ironic subject of romanticism lives within an enduring category mistake.

Kierkegaard endeavours to substantiate his theses on romanticism through an analysis of Schlegel's *Lucinde* and some of Tieck's satirical dramas and lyrical poetry; however, I shall return to his analysis of Solger's aesthetics in order to bring into the sharpest possible contrast Socratic and romantic irony. According to Hegel, ethical and aesthetic categories are intertwined in the ancient concept of the individual. This does not lead to the same aestheticization of existence as it does in the romantic concept because here the two categories are split apart; what, in effect, occurs is the hypertrophic growth of the aesthetic. Added to this is Kierkegaard's point that romantic irony negates all of existence and not just prevailing customs, as in the Greek case. Irony loses its Socratic lightness as jest, a hovering over Attic reality. It acquires in its place a more fundamental and more pathological relation both to reality and to the self. Romantic irony is morbid; it lacks the dialogical merriment of Socratic irony. Solger brings out some of these considerations particularly clearly. Kierkegaard refers to Solger as the "metaphysical knight of the negative"; he is the embodiment of contemplative irony.[67] His doctrine is summarizable under three points: man as finite must be made into nothing (the *Nichtige* or annulled/abrogated); that which is the *Nichtige* must be destroyed; "yet the *Nichtige* in us is the divine."[68] From God the creator of heaven and earth, we have arrived at God the creator of nothingness. God's creation of nothingness makes his whole existence ironical, for "God posits himself constantly over into nothingness, takes himself back again, then posits himself over once more, etc., a divine pastime which, like all irony, posits the most fearful oppositions."[69] This accentuation of the power of negative thinking has implications for Solger's aesthetic theory. "What exalts us" in tragedy, Solger argues, "is the destruction of the best itself, and this not merely because we take refuge in an infinite hope. Moreover, what pleases us in comedy is this same nothingness of human affairs, since this appears as the lot we have been assigned once and for all. . . . That mood wherein contradictions annihilate themselves and by this comprise our essentiality we call irony, or, in the comic sphere, caprice and humour."[70] Socratic ignorance is not Solgerian nothingness. Socratic negativity is dialogical and not metaphysical; it results in bafflement and not annihilation. Socrates destroys finite thoughts but does not turn nothingness into infinity. The

Socratic comportment is interested; it is never bored. The romantic is bored because everything that exists is rendered null. The ironist's self-created world of gesture and myth contains nothing *an sich*, no remainder, which resists the ironist's weary gaze.

Against the hypertrophic growth that irony undergoes in the hands of the romantics, Kierkegaard reasserts the validity of irony as a part or moment of a wider oeuvre or a wider existence. The exemplar of such a poetic existence is Goethe, whose antipathy to the German romantics is well known. Irony as a mastered moment "now limits, renders finite, defines, and thereby yields truth, actuality, and content; it chastens and punishes and thereby imparts stability, character, and consistency."[71] Irony, however, is not allowed to have the final word; for Kierkegaard points toward his doctrine of humor, which is essentially bound up with his notion of paradox. What remains is the fact that irony is the highest possibility for man as man existing outside the God relationship. As such, the Socratic employment of irony stands closer to an authentic life-attitude than its romantic employment. This is a point that can be indirectly read into Kierkegaard's subsequent aesthetical pseudonymous production, such as *Either/Or* and *Stages on Life's Way*.

V

The next important work in the Kierkegaardian interpretation of Socrates is the *Philosophical Fragments* of 1844, issued under the name of that admirable dialectician Johannes Climacus. Whereas in *The Concept of Irony* the contrast between the Socratic and the Christian teaching takes place in the margin of the text, in this work it stands at the center. In the book's moral, Kierkegaard characterizes the work as an attempt "to make an advance upon Socrates," an advance that he is presenting before the "master of irony" himself.[72] Kierkegaard is sure that such an attempt is un-Socratic; whether the Christian teaching is more true than the Socratic is something he cannot say. Nevertheless, he must make the attempt to settle accounts with his "erstwhile philosophic (Socratic and not Hegelian) consciousness." He presents himself in the preface as an idler, as useless, non-systematic, and willing to accept the charge of *apragmosynē* or indifferentism, which is, of course, the charge the Greek state levies against Socrates. In sum, Kierkegaard's project is to submit the Christian teaching to Socratic dialectic. Indeed, even the pseudonym chosen, John the Climber, indicates his desire to make a dialectical ascent. He asks the question "How far does the Truth admit of being learned?" There are two possible answers: the immanent approach, which is Socrates', and the transcendent approach of Christianity. Both presuppose fundamentally different relationships between the teacher and the disciple. The argumentation follows this form: if we do not presuppose this, then we lapse back into the Socratic standpoint.

"How far does the Truth admit of being learned?" can be approached through another question: "Who is in possession of Truth?" Here the Socratic and the Christian begin, according to Kierkegaard, with fundamentally different starting points. The Socratic doctrine of recollection puts truth fundamentally in the possession of man; Socrates' maieutic activity has the task of bringing out what man already possesses. Truth or the forms are what we are born with; the task between teacher and disciple is to come to a remembrance of them. From the Christian standpoint, everyone is not in the possession of truth but in a state of error by reason of his own guilt. Hence, the reality and the consciousness of sin are absolutely paramount. From the Socratic standpoint, sin is neither linked to guilt and the will (the sphere of the ethical) nor to any notion of hereditary sin (a concept belonging to the religious sphere). It is merely ignorance. Greek intellectualism, as Kierkegaard puts it in *Sickness Unto Death*, lacks all understanding of the will:

> What determinant is it then that Socrates lacks in determining what sin is? It is will, defiant will. The Greek intellectualism was too happy, too naive, too aesthetic, too ironical, too witty . . . too sinful to get into its head that a person knowingly could fail to do the good, or

knowingly, with knowledge of what was right, do what was wrong. The Greek spirit proposes an intellectual categorial imperative.[73]

This division between Greek intellectualism and Christian activism, between thinking and willing, is one that runs throughout Kierkegaard's work. I have already pointed out the distinction Judge William makes between "knowing oneself" and "choosing oneself." Yet the problem for Kierkegaard is that he is too fascinated by the figure of Socrates ever to subscribe to the following imperious judgement that Hannah Arendt attributes to the will: "In short, the will always wills to *do* something and thus implicitly holds in contempt sheer thinking, whose whole activity depends on 'doing nothing.'"[74] Hence, Kierkegaard's dismissal of Socratic intellectualism hides a more profound admiration for the proponent of sheer thinking. Kierkegaard is, in his fascination for Socrates, thinking against his own Christian heritage.[75]

If the disciple is in error, then the teacher must remind him that he is in a state of error. The truth comes from God; the teacher is God himself as our savior and redeemer. In the relationship to truth, therefore, there is a far greater and more radical gap between the teacher and the disciple in Christianity than in Socratic teaching. This may, in part, explain the fundamentally differing social institutions in which Christianity and Socratic irony are embedded: a hierarchical Church and a *polis* characterized by *isonomia*. For Socrates, any and every occasion offers the possibility of discourse; the occasion is characterized by accidentality. For the Christian, the moment has decisive significance. It is the moment in which the eternal enters and the individual is raised to the eternal through conversion. From a state of error the individual is reborn as a new creature. It is a moment, of course, that is beyond reason; it is the leap. In the Socratic framework the individual is central; the task is to bring him to self-knowledge, and such self-knowledge involves knowledge of the eternal, whereas in Christianity it is the eternal or rather the God in time that is central. He brings truth to the individual. The relationship between God and the disciple is a nonreciprocal one—God needs no disciple to understand himself—whereas that between Socrates and his disciples is reciprocal. Kierkegaard argues that in that relationship "between man and man no higher relationship is possible; the disciple gives occasion for the teacher to understand himself, and the teacher gives occasion for the disciple to understand himself."[76] The question, therefore, becomes one that asks how learning is possible between God and his disciples when such an abyss separates them. The answer is, according to Kierkegaard, that out of love God elevates the disciple by coming before him in the form of a servant: God becomes man. The learner still owes the teacher everything, whereas Socrates only owes Asclepius.

According to Kierkegaard, "all thought is the attempt to discover something that thought cannot think."[77] He refers to this idea as the paradoxical passion of thought and argues that it is a property of Greek and Christian philosophy alike. So long as Socrates remains at the level of wanting to know what man is, however, reason must come to a standstill; what thought cannot think must lie outside of man and his recollection. Kierkegaard calls this "the God," an unknown against which reason passionately collides. The task of proving that this unknown exists must include in its proofs something that goes beyond them; the remainder that cannot be covered by reason is crossed in a leap. Reason can go no further because it has come up against a limit: "the Unknown as a limit" is both "a torment for passion" and "an incitement."[78] The will conquers where reason fails; and where reason fails to acknowledge that it needs this eternal supplement, it suffers offense. It cannot understand the paradox that the eternal can and has appeared in time, and as a result it will not make room for what lies beyond its ken. The paradox and reason cannot "come together in a mutual understanding of their unlikeness."[79] The paradox is the stumbling block *(skandalon)* of reason. Reason views the paradox as absurd, but it is reason that must yield. Hence, we come to faith, for "no knowledge can have for its object the absurdity that the Eternal is the historical."[80] In *Sickness Unto Death* Kierkegaard characterizes the knight of faith both as he who cannot become himself and as he who renounces the universal in order to become the individual:

The paradox of faith is this, that the individual is higher than the universal, that the individual . . . determines his relation to the universal by his relation to the absolute, not his relationship to the absolute by his relation to the universal. The paradox can also be expressed by saying that there is an absolute duty toward God; for in this relationship of duty the individual as an individual stands related absolutely to the absolute.[81]

The universal is that which is determined rationally by the ethical. In the story of Abraham it would ethically prohibit Abraham from taking the life of his son; however, Abraham as an individual is to be determined in his actions by his relation to God or the absolute and not by his relation to the universal. Hence, he must undergo the trial God has set for him and make the movement of resignation and prepare to sacrifice his son. According to Kierkegaard, however, Abraham makes a second movement: that of faith. He believes, in short, that God will not ask him to sacrifice his son or, if he does, then God will provide him with a new Isaac. Kierkegaard argues that the ritual of faith must be carried out in silence, whereas for an "intellectual tragic hero," as he now refers to Socrates, death cannot be met with silence. It must be met with that ironical jesting that overturns everything. Socrates relates to the universal and not to the absolute, and he relates to it as a limit and not as something of which he claims to be in full possession. Hence, Socratic irony is foreign to faith. In the *Euthyphro* Socrates challenges the authority of the gods with this question: "Is that which is good loved by the gods because it is good, or is it good because it is loved by the gods?." For a style of thought that relates only to the universal, however ironically, and not to the absolute, the answer is clear.

The remaining problem that Kierkegaard discusses in the *Philosophical Fragments* with relevance to the Socrates problem concerns once again the question of discipleship. To say that we moderns continue to learn from Socrates is a truism, but to say that we do so from a position of discipleship makes no sense. The same, however, is not true of Christianity.

Kierkegaard wants to claim that there exists no difference between the contemporary disciple, who experiences Christ's teaching directly, and the disciple at second hand, who comes centuries later. The one who can see the teacher is in no better position than the one who comes centuries later because the paradoxical nature of the appearance of the eternal in time determines faith as a passion independent of immediacy or contemporaneity. According to Kierkegaard, everything that comes into existence suffers; as the necessary cannot suffer, everything that comes into existence does so freely. If we cannot, like Hegel, impose necessity onto the past, the disciple is faced only with the 'thusness' of God's coming into existence. In the face of this thusness, it is up to the disciple to choose faith, which Kierkegaard defines in this context as "a sense for coming into existence."[82] Only if God's being is determined historically, and not eternally, does it make sense to say that the contemporary disciple has an advantage, for then the question of faith is suspended. Needless to say, Socrates' appearance is not that of the eternal in time, and hence, the problematic of faith is irrelevant. The disciple at second hand cannot have the same relationship to him as the contemporary disciple. Because the learner is the one who possesses the truth, the Socratic activity, as has already been suggested by Kierkegaard, is a purely maieutic one. The disciple does not owe the teacher anything because, not being in possession of any truth, the teacher is unable to beget anything that deserves payment. The object of faith, if this is an appropriate expression, is in the teaching and not in the teacher, as it is in Christianity.[83] Therefore, the form and content of Socratic teaching is obviously available to future generations; however, we cannot stand in the same maieutic relationship to Socrates as the contemporary disciple does. But we can replicate the maieutic relationship of Socrates to his contemporaries with our own; and in the behavior of Kierkegaard within Copenhagen literary circles, we can see the pathetico-comic nature of such an attempt.

The *Philosophical Fragments* is probably the work in which Kierkegaard draws the sharpest possible dividing line between the essentials of his own Christian doctrine and the Socratic doctrine. First, the *Fragments* are, as he puts it in the moral, presented for inspection before "that master of irony"; furthermore, Kierkegaard cannot say whether his doctrine is any more true than the Socratic. In any case, what he claims to have put forward is a new organ—that of faith—whereas the Socratic organ *par excellence* is reason or, more accurately, *logos.* Second, he puts forward a new presupposition—that of sin— whereas the Socratic presupposition is the intellectual one of ignorance. Third, he presents a new decision—that of the moment—whereas for Socrates the moment in which truth can be delivered is totally accidental. Fourth, he presents a new teacher—the God in time—whereas Socrates as a teacher is a peripatetic ironist and *accoucheur.* The motto of the *Fragments* is "Better well hung than ill wed," which Niels Thulstrup interprets as "Better crucified with Christ than . . ."; however, such an interpretation lacks any feeling for Kierkegaardian irony.[84] It would be preferable to interpret it as "Better well hung between the Socratic and Christian standpoints than entered into any uneasy reconciliation of the human and the eternal, as in Hegel."

VI

Whereas the *Philosophical Fragments* counterpoises the Socratic and the Christian doctrines, the *Concluding Unscientific Postscript* contains such a fundamental and radical attack on what Kierkegaard calls variously Hegelianism, the system, or speculative thinking that there occurs a greater rapprochement between the Socratic and the Christian. This occurs, paradoxically enough, because there is a shift in his assessment of Socrates away from the unilateral assertion of the Socratic standpoint as irony to a seemingly more Hegelian standpoint that emphasizes the Socratic standpoint as subjectivity, inwardness, and individual existence. Hegel's Socrates interpretation is one thing, however, and his system another. Hence, this rapprochement is only apparently contradictory; in the same way that Hegel takes the side of the state against Socrates, these principles of *Innerlichkeit* and *Moralität* are but moments in the edifice of Hegel's thought rather than its core. In the *Postscript* Kierkegaard wants to turn Hegel on his feet by emphasizing what the 'primacy of the whole' in Hegel liquidates: not subjective reflection on the particular, as in Adorno's *Minima Moralia*, but reflection on the subjective or the subjective thinker as such.[85] This does not mean that Kierkegaard's relationship to Christianity weakens, but rather that his interpretation of Socrates changes in such a way that the Socratic standpoint comes to approach that of faith. As we shall see, Kierkegaard achieves this in part by a historical deformation of the Socratic standpoint but also in part through a greater recognition of the role that the concept of concern for the self or *heautou epimelia* plays in antiquity. In further focusing his attention on the relation of the individual to the Christian doctrine rather than the doctrine itself, Kierkegaard deepens and modifies the problematic opened up in the *Philosophical Fragments* instead of providing its historical complement. He acknowledges this fact in the introduction.

With regard to objective thinking, the truth of Christianity can be viewed either from the standpoint of historical or philosophical truth. The former involves a critique of our knowledge of the historical sources of Christianity, an enterprise that Spinoza launches in his *Theologico-Political Treatise*, in order to ascertain the exact nature of Christian teaching. The latter involves the decipherment of the eternal truth in the historical phenomenon. Both kinds of enterprise are subjected to the same critique because they both ignore the fact that, according to Kierkegaard, Christianity is, first and foremost, only thinkable in terms of subjectivity and inwardness. The individual's relationship to Christianity and the passion it generates within is central; the individual's passion for eternal happiness is predicated on a concern for the self that has its roots in antiquity. "The Socratic secret," Kierkegaard argues,

> which must be preserved in Christianity unless the latter is to be an infinite backward step, and which in Christianity receives an intensification, by means of a more powerful inwardness which makes it infinite, is

that the movement of the spirit is inward, that the truth is the subject's transformation in himself.[86]

While Kierkegaard is keen to draw parallels here, even he is at pains to draw dividing lines elsewhere in his work. I have already mentioned *Either/Or* in this context, but *The Concept of Anxiety* is also relevant. There Kierkegaard clearly recognizes the aesthetic impurity of Greek ethics:

> What is said of the law is also true of ethics: it is a disciplinarian, and by its demands only judges but does not bring forth life. Only Greek ethics make an exception, and that was because it was not ethics in the proper sense but retained an aesthetic factor.[87]

He also recognizes its ironical, and nonreligious, suspension of the erotic:

> In Christianity, the religious has suspended the erotic, not merely as sinful, through an *ethical* misunderstanding, but as indifferent, because in spirit there is no difference between man and woman. Here the erotic is not neutralized by irony, but it is suspended because the tendency of Christianity is to bring the spirit forward.[88]

Kierkegaard can cite the doctrine of *kalokagathia* and the Aristotelian definition of virtue, which is substantive and not merely formal, in defense of his first argument and the famous Socratic ugliness and Socrates' injunction to love the ugly in defense of the second. It is no accident that these quotations appear in *The Concept of Anxiety*, for there Kierkegaard is concerned with the Christian doctrine of hereditary sin and, hence, is at his most psychological and most un-Socratic. While, therefore, we cannot identify the Socratic and Christian standpoint, Kierkegaard is right to point to "the Socratic secret" because the ideal of "infinite abstention" did lead to a "style of existence" that both deepened considerably the subject's relationship to himself and led to the formation of a moral subject.[89] Hence, Kierkegaard is right to claim the backing of Socrates in his defense of Christianity as a form of subjective, as opposed to objective, thinking. The moral subject, which is born out of this intensified care of the self *(heautou epimelia)*, returns to haunt a modern world in love with the positive, the objective, the system, the world-historical, etc. Kierkegaard's intellectual concern with Socrates is also motivated by his contempt for the present age.

In the *Postscript*, however, Kierkegaard chooses a more contemporary figure, the German dramatist Lessing, to analyze the contours of the subjective thinker; but before he even begins this discussion Kierkegaard lays down some general distinctions between the objective and the subjective existing thinker, which necessitate a recourse to the figure of Socrates. Whereas the objective thinker is not interested in the subject that does the thinking but in what is to be thought, the subjective thinker thinks in what Kierkegaard calls a "doubly reflected" manner due to the fact that inwardness is, for him, the key determinant. "The reflection of inwardness," he argues, "gives to the subjective thinker a double reflection. In thinking, he thinks the universal, but as existing in this thought and as assimilating it in his inwardness, he becomes more and more subjectively isolated."[90] This difference in types of thinking corresponds to a difference in the style of communication appropriate to each: direct communication in the case of objective thinking and indirect communication in the case of subjective thinking. Direct communication is characterized by the fact that as it contains no relationship to inwardness, it does not and cannot transmit ideas pertaining to subjectivity that are essentially private and secret. For the transmission of such ideas only a form of communication that possesses artistry will suffice. The indirect communication of the subjectively existing thinker constitutes a work of art. The whole of Kierkegaard's authorial strategy, which he reveals to the public in the "First and Last Declaration" and which is included at the end of the *Postscript*, embodies the doubly reflected nature of indirect communication, whose "very first form is precisely the subtle principle that the personalities must be held devoutly apart from one another, and not permitted to fuse or coagulate into objectivity."[91] This holding apart dictates the pseudonymous or, as he calls it, polynonymous character of his aesthetic production, which permits Kierkegaard to both reveal and conceal the essential character of his own subjectivity, of his own inwardness. It permits him to be "personal in the second person."[92]

Socrates as ironist and as hearer of voices is also, according to Kierkegaard, a master of indirect communication. In *The Concept of Irony* Kierkegaard follows Schleiermacher in distinguishing the dialogical from the constructive dialogues of Plato; of course, the difference between the two is determined by the presence or absence of irony. Irony as an indirect form of communication possesses both an artistry and a revelation/concealment of Socratic inwardness that the later dialogues, where Socrates is reduced to a cipher, cannot possess. The irony analyzed in *The Concept of Irony*, however, is also a power to suck the intellectual content out of a question and leave the questioner in a state of intellectual disorientation. This aspect of irony now takes a back seat to its relationship to inwardness. From Socrates as the very public intellectual *trouble-fête* we have apparently moved to a more private Socrates. "When Socrates isolated himself from every external relationship by making an appeal to his *daemon*, and assumed," as Kierkegaard supposes, "that everyone must do the same, such a view of life is essentially a secret, or constitutes an essential secret, because it cannot be communicated directly."[93] Irony as seen earlier by Kierkegaard is an indirect communication of truth because it presupposes nothing and adds nothing. It merely draws out through questioning what is there. The emphasis on the secrecy of the Socratic *daimonion* gives irony a more irrational character by emphasizing the sheer arbitrariness of conscience as the subjective foundation of modern ethics—that is, morality or *Gewissensethik*. Hence, the emphasis on the subjective isolation of Socrates leads Kierkegaard to emphasize the connection of inwardness with madness. "In the merely subjective determination of truth," he argues, "madness and truth become in the last analysis indistinguishable."[94] Irony, with its use of inversion to bring out the truth of the matter, albeit indirectly, appears in this context as a form of madness; through its negativity it brings forth the infinite. The power of madness is both the power to plumb inwardness and the power to make opposites cohere. Hence, Socrates as a "subjectively existing thinker is as bifrontal as existence itself."[95] Existence is bifrontal because while infinite striving may contain the highest pathos, such striving in the context of infinity takes on the appearance of the comic. The subjectively existing thinker must encompass these opposites: the positive and the negative, the comic and the pathetic. This is precisely what Socratic irony does with its comic inversions that belie a greater seriousness. The greater seriousness stems from the inner infinity of Socrates himself, which characterizes his existence as one of striving, of becoming. "The Socratic principle," Kierkegaard argues, "is naturally not to be understood in a finite sense, about a continued and incessant striving toward a goal without reaching it. No, but however much the subject has the infinite within himself, through being an existing individual, he is in the process of becoming."[96]

Kierkegaard's attempt to read the concept of inwardness into an interpretation of Socrates is very strange indeed given the clearly Protestant, and more particularly Lutheran, character of the concept of *Innerlichkeit*. Weber has most incisively explored the theological core, which is found in Lutheranism and Calvinism, of this concept. In *The Protestant Ethic and the Spirit of Capitalism* Weber argues that the replacement of the Catholic doctrine of good works with the typically Protestant emphasis on faith alone *(sola fide)* leaves the individual alone and isolated in relation to a remote, unknown, and unknowable God. In its Lutheran form this inwardness takes on a mystical form that is foreign to the activism of its Calvinist form. In Lutheranism man realizes himself not in his works but in his inner attitude and feeling. The political and economic spheres, as the spheres of action in the world, are devalued in comparison to the value of inner freedom. The typically German split between *Zivilisation* and *Kultur* results from this theological complex of ideas. Although Kierkegaard does not systematically separate out the effects of Lutheranism and Calvinism, he is profoundly aware of the decline of Lutheranism into a purely secular ethic. The argument of Judge William in the second book of *Either/Or* presents the ethic of the calling *(Berufsethik)* in a nontheological context. Here the concern is merely to refute the romantic or aesthetic doctrine that work is self-expression by arguing that unless man submits himself to a calling, the development of his potential will rely purely on the accident of talent.[97] Judge William as the representative of the ethical stage is the embodiment of a Protestantism in decline. Elsewhere Kierkegaard asks, "When Protestantism degenerates, what form of corruption will appear? The answer is easy: spiritless secularism."[98] In response to such secularism, Kierkegaard tries both to radicalize the Protestant doctrine of inwardness and also to reconstruct the Catholic doctrine concerning the imitation of Christ. As a wider consideration of Kierkegaard's theology is out of place here, I would merely like to emphasize the Lutheran origins of Kierkegaard's radical *plaidoyer* for a faith that is beyond reason and that is borne by the individual in the solitariness of the God-relationship. The Socratic side of Kierkegaard rests on his unwillingness to give up arguing about what lies beyond argument. Kierkegaard himself is caught up within the polarity of faith and despair. It is this inner conflict, this inner torment that propels his thinking forward. Hence, inwardness may be a category applicable to Kierkegaard, but it is difficult for him to read it into the philosophy of Socrates. Furthermore, Kierkegaard's retreat into inwardness is obviously accompanied by a profound estrangement from the world that he characterizes as an age of positivity and that he chooses to allow him to be its pathetico-comic martyr when he needlessly provokes the journal *Corsair*. If Socratic thinking can at all be described as an inwardness, or at least as an analogue to inwardness, then it must be said that it involves no such devaluation of public life that is inherent in the Lutheran-derived concept of *Innerlichkeit*, which largely underlies Kierkegaard's thinking.

Kierkegaard claims the authority of Lessing to argue, as he did in the *Fragments*, that as historical and eternal truths are clearly separate, the only way to effect the transition is via the leap. The leap of faith, as he refers to it in *Fear and Trembling*, is the ethical decision that suspends the logical impossibility of deriving a belief in God from the fact of his historical existence. In other words, an inner leap is required to overcome the indifference of historical criticism to the fact that it is dealing with the eternal. Kierkegaard also claims the authority of Lessing in arguing that the striving for truth is preferable to its possession, for although the system or Hegelianism claims finality, existence knows no such thing. In becoming objective through its service to the world-historical, the system can conveniently forget what the subjectively existing thinker cannot, anymore than Greek philosophy could: the ethical. Yet due to the overwhelming importance of inwardness and the God-relationship, Kierkegaard scarcely rises to the level of the ethical; when he does, or when rather Judge William does, it is a very Kantian ethic that does not escape the polarity of inner freedom and external conformity to social institutions such as marriage and vocation. It certainly has nothing to do with Greek ethics. Yet it is always Socrates who provides him with the additional argument in favor of becoming subjective. ("Did Socrates go about talking of what the age demands . . . ? No, Socrates was concerned only with himself."[99]) Socrates also provides the argument in favor of the idea that truth is subjectivity or inwardness. In this latter context Kierkegaard refers to the Socratic doctrine of immortality. Here he contrasts those who give merely theoretical proofs for immortality with the attitude of Socrates in the face of death who stakes all on the question "if there is an immortality."[100] Socratic ignorance becomes, therefore, not simply a form of courage in the face of death but "an expression of the principle that the eternal truth is related to an existing individual, and that this truth must be a paradox for him as long as he exists."[101] With Socrates, of course, the truth is only negatively related to the existing individual because Socratic irony produces no knowledge; it merely destroys all pretentions to knowledge. Hence, he leaves his companions at the end of the *Apology* with the thought that only the gods know if their continued life or his immanent death is the happier prospect.

The Kierkegaardian equation of subjectivity with the truth identifies, or perhaps reduces, truth to faith. He gives the following definition of truth, a definition that has nothing to do with objective knowledge: "*An objective uncertainty held fast in an appropriation-process of the most passionate inwardness is the truth,* the highest truth attainable for an *existing* individual."[102] From a Habermasian standpoint such a position could be accused of reducing the validity claim of truth *(Wahrheit)*, which belongs to the domain of statements or propositional contents, to that of the validity claim of truthfulness or sincerity *(Wahrhaftigkeit)* of the participating subject of the discourse. This is the old conflict of knowledge versus faith. Habermas argues that the undisturbed unfolding of communication can only take place when *inter alia* the "truthfulness of the participating subject cannot be put in doubt."[103] From the Kierkegaardian standpoint, the other three presuppositions of understandability *(Verständlichkeit)*, truth *(Wahrheit)*, and rightness or appropriateness *(Richtigkeit)* are nothing compared to the importance of the disclosure of the "speaker's subjectivity," which occurs when the "expressive attitude" is adopted.[104] If we take the validity claims one by one, we can see that Kierkegaard puts them all at risk except that of truthfulness. The Kierkegaardian doctrine of indirect communication is designed to repel easy understandability; and as Kierkegaard's love of Socratic irony shows, he was always tempted to risk misunderstanding, as Socrates did, through a type of thinking that constantly disorients. The Kierkegaardian doctrine of truth is based on the rejection of objective reflection; that is, it refuses to isolate propositional content and even reduces the latter to that of truthfulness. He can also claim the authority of Socrates for this; although Socrates knows nothing as true, he lives and dies as a subjectively existing thinker in the pursuit of what he can only negatively approach. For Kierkegaard the claim of correctness is not something that governs the interpersonal relationship between two subjects but concerns rather the individual's relationship to God. This is the old conflict between ethics and theology. Although Kierkegaard claims the Socratic relationship to his *daimonion* as a parallel, his concept of the God relationship is different in its grounding in Christian theology. The concern with the correctness of the relationship between subjects does arise in the context of the famous Socratic ugliness and the effect that this has on the teacher-disciple relationship, for the repellent effect of his appearance has the same effect as irony; namely, it keeps the learner at a distance from the teacher in order to bring him closer to the truth, even if it can only be grasped negatively. Within Christianity, however, the master-disciple relationship is only a virtual one if the contemporary disciple has no advantage over those who come later, the disciples at second hand. The Socratic ugliness is also a sign of inwardness. Because inwardness or subjectivity is truth, it is the truthfulness of one's subjective existence that is of overriding importance for Kierkegaard. As he puts it, *"The objective accent falls on WHAT is said, the subjective accent on HOW it is said".*[105]

What Kierkegaard credits Socrates with discovering is not the objectivity of knowledge but the fact that "the knower is an existing individual."[106] This fact makes Socrates an existing thinker rather than a speculative philosopher; that is, he is one who speaks not with the authority of world history but with the authority of a mortal. It also brings the Socratic principle closer to that of faith; if inwardness becomes the truth, then the truth becomes paradoxical as it loses its purely eternal character. Like Christianity's God—the eternal in time—the eternal becomes mixed up with existence. Kierkegaard can conclude, therefore, that "the Socratic inwardness in existing is an analogue to faith."[107] Being an analogue, of course, does not make it identical to faith, yet the analogy drawn is a strong one. The difference lies, as mentioned previously, in the incompatibility of the Socratic principle of ignorance with the Christian one of hereditary sin. Yet for both positions the task of existing becomes central. The emphasis on existence is what distances Kierkegaard from speculative philosophy, but for him existence is not something one-sidedly absurd and irrational. The critique of an overblown concept of reason should not be mistaken for a critique of reason *tout court*. "Because abstract thought is *sub specie aeterni* it ignores the concrete and the temporal, the existential process, the predicament of the existing individual arising from his being a synthesis of the temporal and the eternal situated in existence."[108] Whether it be a case of nineteenth-century idealism, which later mutated into historicism, or nineteenth-century materialism, the supposition that thought should be related to the knowing individual situated in existence, and not either reduced to an expression of historical development or to some logical or pseudosubstantive principle, is a radical and untimely one. It smacks of ancient modes of thought and not of modern ones, as Kierkegaard correctly realizes. It is on this point that Kierkegaard is most legitimately able to claim Socrates and the inheritance of antiquity. He argues that he knows "that in Greece, at least, a thinker was not a stunted crippled creature who produced works of art, but was himself a work of art in his existence."[109] Here we are close again to Foucault's analysis of ancient ethics as centering on giving a style to one's existence; as we shall see, a similar problematic emerges in Nietzsche's thought when he attacks the loss of significance of history for life. The Kierkegaardian antidote to this indifference of thought and life is the subjective thinker's passion, a passion in and for existence. With Nietzsche the solution is slightly different and summarizable in the phrase: will to power. In both cases, however, and notwithstanding Kierkegaard's religiosity, which is foreign to Nietzsche except as parody, the turn toward existence is determined by the category of the aesthetic in its ancient employment. Kierkegaard argues that "the subjective thinker is not a man of science, but an artist. Existing is an art. The subjective thinker is aesthetic enough to give his life aesthetic content, ethical enough to regulate it, and dialectical enough to inter-penetrate it with thought."[110] For Kierkegaard, even Christianity is a question of existence: an existence-communication.[111]

Toward the end of the *Postscript*, Kierkegaard reiterates his theory of existence-spheres and places irony on the boundary between the aesthetic and the ethical, and humour on the boundary between the ethical and the religious. The ironist brings forth the contradiction between the finite and the infinite ethical requirement, according to Kierkegaard, and for this reason irony functions as the incognito of the ethicist. "Socrates," Kierkegaard notes, "was in this sense an ethicist, but it is well to note that he was an ethicist who tended well up toward the limit of the religious."[112] Here Kierkegaard presents a self-criticism, for he argues that Magister Kierkegaard, and one must not forget that he is writing here in the name of Johannes Climacus, one-sidedly presents Socrates as an ironist. The ethicist can use irony in order to travel incognito because "irony is a synthesis of ethical passion which infinitely accentuates inwardly the person of the individual in relation to the ethical requirement—and of culture, which infinitely abstracts externally from the personal ego, as one finitude among all other finitudes and particularities. This abstraction causes the emphasis in the first attitude to pass unnoticed."[113] Here we arrive back at the notion of litotes or underemphasis; the ironist underemphasises his own inwardness by interposing the comical between him and those who have no relation to the universal, thereby deluding them into believing that the ironist also shares their superficiality. For Kierkegaard, Socrates is obviously one who has so assiduously cultivated his inwardness that he comes as close as a pagan possibly can to being what the religious individual undoubtedly is: "a knight of the secret inwardness."[114] In his analysis of Religiousness A and B, however, which we have already discussed, Kierkegaard stresses that although the Socratic position is analogous to the kind of faith required in Religiousness B, there are essentially "no analogies to the paradox-religiousness of faith."[115]

VII

In a literary review Kierkegaard contrasts the "age of revolution," which he describes as passionate, with his own age, which he describes as "a sensible, reflecting age, devoid of passion."[116] Given the importance of passionate inwardness that is at the heart of his dictum that subjectivity is truth, this is the harshest possible criticism that Kierkegaard could have laid against his present age. Furthermore, he argues that "in an era of negativity the authentic ironist is the hidden enthusiast."[117] The example he gives of such an ironist is, of course, Socrates; and it is not hard to come to the conclusion that this is precisely what Kierkegaard sees himself as—a Socrates of the present age, a Socrates for this mass-dominated, passionless nineteenth century. Kierkegaard wants to see himself in the way he characterizes Socrates: namely, as a single individual who is prepared for self-sacrifice, a person who lives his life as an existence-communication, a person whose intellectual convictions are not merely set forth in a system but constitute a style of existence that is aesthetically shaped as a protest against an age of positivity where even the Christian church has lost any idea of what Christianity is about. His self-sacrifice duly comes about through the intermediary of Regine Olsen, the journal *Corsair*, and the Danish church. There is as much of the comic as of the tragic in these self-sacrifices, but even in this he is in line with his own interpretation of Socrates' fate as pathetico-comic. The difficulty with such an interpretation is where to place Kierkegaard's Christianity, his attempt to be a religious individual, a "knight of the hidden inwardness." It is possible to see him as never reaching these high peaks of Christian illumination but remaining like Socrates, forever shuffling between the aesthetic, the ethical, and the religious without ever stopping at any, as an authentic ironist could never do. Hence, we can arrive at the result that Kierkegaard lives his life in conformity to, and to some extent as a parody of, his own interpretation of Socrates. As a single individual, he toys with immediacy both in life and through the personnage of A; he is the ironist who goes through intellectual positions dialogically sucking out their content; he is the ethicist, either of the negative, Socratic kind or of the more Kantian law-oriented kind, as is Judge William; and he is the religious individual, either of the edifying or paradoxical kind. Yet he remains apart from all the spheres—extraterritorial, atopic, like Socrates; and this means that the concept of irony is crucial, for irony performs the work of intellectual asphyxiation, which sucks the life out of all one-sided forms of existence. Kierkegaard, in a revealing passage that compares his life with Socrates', goes on to argue that "outside of Christianity Socrates is the only man of whom it may be said: he explodes existence, which is seen quite simply in his elimination of the separation between poetry and actuality."[118] A prosaic age such as the nineteenth century knows nothing of poetry, of the eternal, of truth, of inwardness, of subjectivity. It only knows the positive, the passionless, the world-historical, the objective. Kierkegaard's fragmented subjectivity, emitted in various forms of existence-communication, exists in the tension between romantic inwardness and enlightenment positivity.

Chapter Three

Nietzsche: Socrates As Theoretical Man

If modernity stands under the principle of subjectivity, then the last great representative of this principle is Hegel. Hegel, as I have already argued, attempts to reconcile "reason as self-conscious spirit and reason as existing reality" by raising subjectivity out of particularity and acidentality, and by securing what is substantial from reality. Hence, reason can be described quite rightly for Hegel as "the rose in the cross of the present" because it is the reconciling power par excellence.[1] It reconciles subjectivity and objectivity, the real and the rational. The metaphysical nature of such a solution, however, does not escape criticism as the nineteenth century progresses. Its breakdown provokes that intellectual crisis called "nihilism." This crisis calls into question not only the modern principle of the freedom of subjectivity, but also the entire tradition of Judaeo-Christian ethics that underlie it. In the thought of Nietzsche, the rose of reason does not wither; rather, it is crushed. The total critique of reason he inaugurates has far-reaching consequences that lead to the invocation of the archaic and the tragic in the midst of modernity as a way out of the impasses that afflict thinking, willing, and valuing. Nihilism is, for Nietzsche, both something we must get over and something we must go through. If we do not go through it, we live in the naive belief that the highest values have not already devalued themselves. We live an easy life and not the dangerous life of the experimenter and seeker of new values. In this, Nietzsche is ironically at one with the rationalist impulse to eschew forever the merely given, whether it be a question of customary or logical principles. He describes himself "as a spirit of daring and experiment that has already lost its way once in every labyrinth of the future."[2] On the other hand, if we do not get over nihilism, if we do not find a way out of the labyrinth, then nihilism leads to a decline and not to an increase in the power of the spirit. Nietzsche's preference for an active, as opposed to a passive or reactive, nihilism is one made in full consciousness of the ambiguity of the phenomenon.[3] An active nihilism, as opposed to the weary nihilism that finds its expression in Buddhism, makes possible the countermovement (*Gegenbewegung*) that Nietzsche sees embodied in the formula of *The Will to Power: Attempt at a Revaluation of All Values*[4]—an attempt that also implies the creation of new values.

The recognition that we have no right to posit any principle as the principle, that all our past forms of moral valuation, including the one that establishes subjectivity as the principle of modernity, are incapable of being grounded, leads to the insight that the world in which we live is one and only one. "Radical nihilism," Nietzsche argues, "is the conviction of an absolute untenability of existence when it comes to the highest values one recognizes; plus the realization that we lack the least right to posit a beyond or an in itself of things that might be 'divine' or morality incarnate."[5] The absence of any metaphysical foundation for our values means that the phenomenal world is the only world. Hence, the attempt to seek meaning in a world without a goal is meaningless; the attempt to posit totality in a world without unity is senseless; and the attempt to impute truth in a world without a true world is fruitless. This feeling of valuelessness (*Gefühl der Wertlosigkeit*) is the highest form of nihilism. The absence of any metaphysical foundation for our values also means that with the disappearance of the noumenal world, reason is devalued. "The faith in the categories of reason," Nietzsche argues, "is the cause of nihilism. We have measured the value of the world according to categories that refer to a purely fictitious world."[6] Not only is there an absence of value, but there is also an inability to measure value. The nihilistic mode of thinking takes on that destructive and negative aspect that both Hegel and Kierkegaard ascribe to irony. This idea does not escape Nietzsche as well, for he describes nihilism as "partly destructive, partly ironic."[7] Ironic freedom is, however, not interpreted as an intensification of subjectivity and inwardness, as in Kierkegaard, but as "an expression of an increase in power."[8] This replacement of the principle of subjectivity with the notion of an economy of forces or power is just one of the consequences that flows from Nietzsche's radical assault on foundationalism. The consequence that I would like to emphasize here is the fact that it is only from the very edge of nihilism that Nietzsche can make the Dionysian leap of world affirmation. He argues that nihilism emerges when "one interpretation has collapsed; but because it was considered *the* interpretation it now seems as if there were no meaning at all in existence, as if everything were in vain."[9] The joyful acceptance of this "in vain" is opposed to the pessimistic feeling of valuelessness. The idea that everything is necessarily in vain, that existence is without meaning, unity, or goal is embodied in his doctrine of the eternal recurrence, which he further describes as "the most extreme form of nihilism: the nothing (the 'meaningless'), eternally!"[10] This is European Buddhism, not merely the Asiatic variety.

Nietzsche's distinction between passive and active nihilism results in both an increasingly one-sided and virulent attack on Socrates. In Nietzsche's early work, Socrates is read as a passive nihilist in as much as he attacks the higher values then in existence; insofar as those higher values are seen as a product of the archaic in Greek society, Socrates' nihilism is viewed as a purely destructive force. Hence, the playfulness that Kierkegaard attributes to Socratic irony is not possible for Nietzsche because Socratic nihilism is seen not so much as a product of irony as of theoreticism. The nihilistic force of irony obtains its validity for Nietzsche only when it is turned on the highest values of Judaeo-Christian civilization. When Nietzsche attempts this project, he is at his most receptive to a certain kind of Socratic irony. As I shall try to show in this chapter, Nietzsche's early reading of Socrates as a type of theoretical man sees the emergence of the principle of reason in Greek society both as an obstacle to the creativity embedded in nature and as an obstacle to the radicalization of the nihilistic impulse. In Nietzsche's later reading of Socrates, however, the emergence of the peculiarly Greek idea of reason is read simply as a stage in the emergence of the Judeo-Christian world view with its dualistic image of the cosmos that still dominates Kantian philosophy. Hence, Socratic irony becomes a kind of plebeian nihilism against aristocratic custom, and the Socratic employment of reason is read as the revenge of the suprasensible world on the sensible one. Nietzsche's later reading of Socrates is, therefore, a Platonizing one insofar as the constructive, rather than corrosive, side of reason is both emphasized and impugned. It is a reading of Socrates as the archetype of intellectual resentment that finds its modern embodiment in Kant. The Socratic becomes, therefore, the chief obstacle to the counter-movement against nihilism because its ascetic Platonism, as institutionalized in modern science, becomes the hallmark of modernity's intellectualization of culture. Nietzsche's attempt at a radical counter-movement in modernity brings with it, therefore, a complete reevaluation of the figure of Socrates. From the status of a philosophical hero, as he was for Hegel, Socrates emerges as a far more negative figure in modernity. Before we turn more specifically to Nietzsche's interpretation of Socrates, however, we must examine his theory of culture.

I

The attack on foundations, the insistence on one world, the insistence that reason presupposes a belief in a higher world, and the affirmation of this one world are four of the main constituents of Nietzsche's countermovement. The scaffolding that helped to erect subjectivity to the principle of modernity is dismantled by Nietzsche. The principle itself is disarmed when its foundational role is viewed as "the *hyperbolic naiveté* of man: positing himself as the meaning and measure of the value of things."[11] Rather than being considered a unifying principle, the subject must be thought of as a multiplicity *(Das Subjekt als Vielheit)*.[12] The fact that there is thinking does not imply a subject that thinks; the subject is not given but is itself an interpretation. An interpretation that implies a unity in existence, although fictitious, cannot be criticized as fiction but only as a weakening in our economy of drives. "The assumption of one single subject is perhaps unnecessary," Nietzsche argues. "Perhaps it is just as permissible to assume a multiplicity of subjects, whose interaction and struggle is the basis of our thought and our consciousness in general. A kind of aristocracy of 'cells' in which dominion resides. To be sure, an aristocracy of equals, used to ruling jointly and understanding how to command?"[13] Such a conception effectively undermines any notion of subjectivity that relies on the attendant principles of individualism, rationality, and autonomy.[14] The subject becomes transindividual; it moves beyond reason and is driven by scarcely conscious forces. If subjectivity is the principial origin of the modern world, then in the thinking of Nietzsche there is indeed a break in the "epochal economy," as Reiner Schürmann points out.[15] Schürmann characterizes this epochal economy as humanistic, for it elevates subjectivity as individuality, reflectivity, transcendentality, and morality into a unity.[16] Except for transcendentality, Hegel would have had very little difficulty in agreeing with this definition of modernity; his difference would be with the valuation that accompanies it. The cause of antihumanism, which Schürmann quite rightly sees Nietzsche as furthering, is also countermodern. Rather than the pathologies of modernity being put into question, as in Hegel, the whole of modernity itself is being sounded.

Together with the critique of foundationalism and the rejection of subjectivity, there is a far-reaching naturalization of man in the work of Nietzsche. Whenever Nietzsche speaks of man, he usually refers to him as an animal. Nietzsche radicalizes the affront paid to the dignity of man by late nineteenth-century science in his attempt to place man back into a nature resembling that of those hardheaded realists of the seventeenth century, whom Nietzsche admires, rather than the sentimental view of nature taken by an eighteenth-century figure like Rousseau. Nature is for Nietzsche not only cruel, however, but also valueless and purposeless. God has no place in the garden of nature other than what that "sick animal (*das kranke Tier*)" creates for him. As Nietzsche points out, man is the sickest animal because he is also the most gifted, dynamic, and experimental.[17] Hence, the idea that man is simply another animal in a cruel and purposeless creation is counterbalanced by a recognition that man is the most dynamically creative cultural force in nature. As Nietzsche puts it earlier in *On the Genealogy of Morals*, man is "the 'valuating animal as such *(das abschätzende Tier an sich)*."[18] If this aspect of his naturalization of man is not understood, then his critique of the concept of usefulness as the principle behind the mechanism of natural selection can also not be understood. Man as the value-creating animal is, indeed, capable of producing values that are not only useless but also positively dangerous: for example, values such as the ascetic ideal that is the subject of Nietzsche's critique in the *Genealogy*. What cannot be denied, however, is that behind this de-deification of nature and naturalization of man there lies a thorough-going naturalization of the measurement of value: the increase or decrease in the feeling of power or of force becomes the criterion of moral evaluation. The principle of universalizability as the moral regulative principle is cast aside in favor of a moral substantive principle parading as a quasi-scientific datum: life. This idea of Nietzsche's is particularly prominent in the unpublished writings of the 1880s, although it features in his works since *Zarathustra*. It finds its lapidary formulation in the following: "The criterion of truth resides in the enhancement of the feeling of power."[19]

The idea that man has become overrefined and overspiritualized by the moral contagion and, therefore, has become sickly, weak, and degenerate not only leads to a reevaluation of the natural, but also to the rehabilitation of the archaic. The three key events that give rise to the creation of the modern world are, for Hegel, the Reformation, the Enlightenment, and the French Revolution. All these events, with the exception of the Voltairian strand of the Enlightenment, are detested by Nietzsche. The scientific gaze of the nineteenth century and the realism of the seventeenth century are valued more highly. Beyond these epochs, however, the Renaissance and, above all, pre-Socratic Greek society and culture are awarded the palm. In this context Löwith is right to speak of an "anti-Christian repetition of antiquity."[20] The choice of pre-Socratic Greece as a horizon for the interpretation of modernity turns Socrates into the first spreader of the moral contagion and constructs the history of the world since Socrates as a process of decline, degeneration, and decadence with, of course, the partial exception of the above-mentioned epochs. The return of the archaic in the midst of modernity is not looked upon with the sober sense of alarm that Freud had when he looked upon the return of the repressed in the midst of war-torn Europe, but with the joyously affirmative gesture of the convalescent who has only just recovered his strength, his sovereignty. The value-creating power of the archaic is something that Nietzsche recognizes in the very earliest of his works, and its final consecration in the God Dionysos of the last writings is testimony to the power of the idea in Nietzsche's thinking. It is not the free and rational subject of modernity that is the truly value-creative power; it is rather the disordered and intoxicated subjects under the sway of both archaic and natural, unconscious and supraindividual forces that are the truly creative power. Nietzsche is surely justified in calling the god of wine and of intoxication his own. Burkert argues that Dionysian intoxication refers to the irruption of the divine and that, as a consequence, "the experience of Dionysos goes far beyond that of alcohol and may be entirely independent of it; madness becomes an end in itself. *Mania*, the Greek word, denotes frenzy, not as the ravings of delusion, but, as its etymological connection with *menos* would suggest, as an experience of intensified mental power."[21] Not incidentally, of course, Dionysian revelries were accompanied by great cruelty and ritual sacrifice. In *The Bacchae* of Euripides, a herdsman describes to Pentheus, the king of Thebes, how a group of Bacchae, led by Agauë who is the mother of Pentheus, fed animals with their own milk and made streams flow with wine. Overshadowing the Bacchic oneness of with nature is the violent frenzy of Bacchic sacrifice. The herdsman describes the frenzied dismemberment of his herd of cattle and the plundering of two villages. In listening to this story Pentheus is, in fact, receiving a warning that he fails to heed, for he is the rationalist and the moralist who refuses to recognize this god, son of Zeus, whose credo is joy and intoxication. His mother, filled with the strength of the god, tears her son apart. The central conflict in the play is not, however, over whether or not religious intoxication should be given its due. But in this respect, Pentheus is definitely *anaisthetos* or insensible—that is, one who pays too little attention to bodily pleasures.[22] What concerns Euripides is, rather, the question as to whether Pentheus is right to use his power as king to repress the cult, whether, in effect, self-mastery *(enkrateia)* or force is to prevail. Teiresias, the blind seer, gives Pentheus the proper advice:

> Petheus, pay head to my words. You rely
> On force; but it is not force that governs human affairs
> Do not mistake for wisdom that opinion which
> May rise from a sick mind. Welcome this God to Thebes
> Offer libations to him, celebrate his rites
> Put on his garland. Dionysos will not compel
> Women to be chaste, since in all matters self-control
> Resides in our own natures.[23]

The play opens up a whole series of problems that are treated in Nietzsche's thought under the rubrics of morality, decadence, and the overman.

The critique of morality is at the heart of the Nietzschean enterprise, an enterprise that replaces the philosophical grounding of a rational morality with a natural history of morality. This natural history sees in moral and religious valuations either an increase or decrease in the feeling of power. They are, in sum, interpretations that either strengthen or weaken life. The metaphysical *proton pseudos* that makes them possible is the division of the world into two: the true and the apparent world *("die 'wahre' und die 'scheinbare' Welt")*. The genealogy of the emergence of this distinction can be found in a preliminary form in the *Nachlaß* of 1888 and in a more polished form in the *Twilight of the Idols* of the same year. In the *Nachlaß* we are presented with three sources from which the idea of another world has emerged *("die Entstehungsherde der Vorstellung 'andre Welt'")*. They are the philosopher, whose inventions of a rational world results in the emergence of the "true world"; the religious man, whose invention of a divine world results in the emergence of a "denaturalized and antinatural world"; and finally, the moral man, whose fabrication (*fingieren* rather than *erfinden*) of a free world results in the emergence of the "good, perfect, just, and holy world."[24] The first thing to note is that philosophy, religion, and morality are inventions and as such are exemplars of human value-creation that have, however, gone wrong at birth. They emerge out of an instinct of negation, out of a tiredness with life. In short, they are the product of reactive forces or, more simply, of resentment. The critique of morality is, therefore, a part of a wider critique of morality, religion, and philosophy that gains its metaphysical warrant from the reconstruction of what is called in the *Twilight of the Idols* "the history of an error."[25] The idea of the abolition of both the true and the apparent world that is presented there leaves us in a world of forces and powers—an idea that is also used to reconstruct the emergence of moralities, not in terms of the emergence of metaphysical principles, God-given laws, or rationally grounded moral principles but as the outcomes of the struggles between life-enhancing and life-denying forces. This is only possible in the nineteenth century due to the emergence of the positivistic outlook that eschews any and all notion of a hidden and more true world than that before one's eyes. The three previous forms of this error are, in chronological order, the Platonic or philosophical idea that the real world is attainable by the wise; the Christian or religious idea of a real world promised to the wise; and the Kantian or moral idea of the real world as both unattainable and yet also an imperative. Against these three errors or prejudices—the philosophical, the religious, and the moral—stands the value-creating force of the aesthetic, of the natural, of the archaic, of the transindividual, all of which find their emblem in the god Dionysos.

Later, I will trace the exact path that leads from the aesthetic to the Dionysian; for the moment, I would like to fasten on more intensively to Nietzsche's critique of morality. In the preface to the *Genealogy* he claims that the hierarchy of moral values has been taken for granted but that now they must be called into question. He proposes a genealogy of moral phenomena that would not only investigate "morality as consequence, as symptom, as masks, as tartufferie, as illness, as misunderstanding; but also morality as cause (Ursache), as remedy, as stimulant, as restraint, as poison."[26] Although this twofold character of moral phenomena is never forgotten by Nietzsche, the more archaic forms of moral subjectivation are looked upon more favorably than the more modern ones, which are more likely to be read unilaterally as symptoms of decadence. I would like to look first at his treatment of archaic forms of valuation and subjectivation because his material is usually Greek and therefore of utmost relevance to an assessment of his interpretation of Socrates. I will begin with his chapter on moral sensations in Human, All Too Human, where, as Nietzsche notes, he first begins his sounding of morals. The title of this work implies, of course, his program of undercutting man's lofty assessment of himself; it belongs to the works of his most nihilistic period. This first fruit of the period of the 'free spirit' contains in embryo many of the ideas of the later Genealogy, particularly those concerning the emergence of the distinction between the good and the bad. Nietzsche argues that the word 'good' originated among those with the power to requite like with like—that is, among the rulers, the nobles, or the aristocracy. 'Bad', on the other hand, arises as an epithet for those without such power to requite. Hence, it is not the enemy who can do us harm who is bad, rather he who is beneath contempt. According to Nietzsche, "good and bad is for a long time the same thing as noble and base, master and slave."[27] In the Genealogy he claims to be able to trace the Latin bonus back to the word meaning 'warrior' and the German gut back to its root meaning 'godlike'; Greek words for 'low', 'bad', and 'pitiable' have similar connotations, as do 'happy' and 'well-born', 'noble and upright'.[28] The idea of justice arises, therefore, among those who have a roughly equal capacity to requite like with like and can see, as a consequence, the advantage of negotiating demands. Exchange as the characteristic of justice means that it has its origins in egoism, in enlightened self-preservation. Only we moderns believe the just act to be the unegoistic one.

In the Genealogy Nietzsche also traces the emergence of the valuation of the unegoistic back to the reversal effected by Christianity and its Mitleidsethik (ethic of pity). He argues that punishment has its origin in the relationship between two parties of fundamentally unequal power: the creditor and debtor. He argues that guilt has its material foundation in debt, which in German can be illustrated by the etymological connection between *Schuld* (guilt) and *Schulden* (debts).[29] Punishment is an exchange in which the culprit pays in pain the injury done to his victim, just as the debtor must compensate his creditor. Punishment is not dependent on the imputation of will to the guilty party and is not designed to act as a means of arousing conscience, but takes place with the simplicity of barter exchange. With the Christian reversal, guilt and duty are now both pushed back into the debtor (culprit) as bad conscience, and the force that would have been directed outward is now internalized *(Verinnerlichung)*. It is also turned back onto the creditor (victim); for example, Christianity renders life itself worthless in the doctrine of original sin. Bad conscience and the devaluation of earthly existence go hand in hand. Christianity, however, not only inaugurates this nightmare, but it also provides its own form of consolation, which involves an inversion of the creditor-debtor relationship: "God himself sacrifices himself for the guilt of mankind, God himself makes payment of himself . . . ; the creditor sacrifices himself for his debtor, out of love (can one credit that?), out of love for his debtor!"[30] The Christian God and his ethic of pity makes man a self-lacerating animal, the sick animal, whereas the Greek gods inhabited a world in which the animal in man was preserved and not merely annulled. The coming god is, for Nietzsche, Dionysos.

Behind this latecomer—the ethic of pity and the valuation of the unegoistic—lies custom. Nietzsche's project is not simply a critique of Christianity; he also wants to perform a genealogy of that animal who has "the right to make promises *(Ein Thier heranzüchten das versprechen darf)*."[31] Here, neither Christian nor Kantian morality *(Moralität)* is the key, but the "morality of mores *(die Sittlichkeit der Sitte)*" performs the "prehistoric labour *(vorhistorische Arbeit)*," which "notwithstanding severity, tyranny and idiocy involved in it" finds its justification in the fact that "with the aid of the morality of mores and the social straitjacket, man was actually *made* calculable *(berechenbar)*."[32] From the standpoint of the morality of mores or custom, good and evil simply means either acting in conformity or nonconformity with custom and tradition; and the purpose of the latter is quite simply the preservation of the community.[33] According to Nietzsche, we moderns live in such an "*unsittlichen Zeit*" (misleadingly translated as "immoral age") that we cannot see that "the origin of morality *(Enstehung der Moral)*" is in custom.[34] Nietzsche broaches here the opposition between tradition and morality in a way that radicalizes the opposition between *Sittlichkeit* and *Moralität* that Hegel employs. Hegel would mostly agree with Nietzsche's opposition between a tradition that commands us to obey whether or not we find it useful, and morality as a form of self-direction. But the degree of cruelty Nietzsche associates with custom and the depth of sickness he argues that morality brings to man go beyond the Hegelian diagnosis of the pathologies of modernity. Yet despite this fact, at the beginning of *Daybreak* we find an interpretation of Socrates that places him firmly within the context of the rise of individualism out of custom's demand that the individual should unreservedly sacrifice himself to its demands. From the standpoint of the morality of custom, which is not Nietzsche's own standpoint, moralists like Socrates are evil. "Those moralists," he argues, "who, following in the footsteps of Socrates, offer the individual a morality of self-control (*Selbstbeherrschung* or *enkrateia*) and temperance (*Enthaltsamkeit* or *sophrosyne*) as a means to his own *advantage*, as his personal key to happiness, *are the exceptions* . . . they cut themselves off from the community, as immoral men, and are in the profoundest sense evil."[35] The Greek enables us to see the affinities of the Socratic standpoint with the Euripidean one mentioned earlier; the idea of self-mastery provides the individual with his distance from custom. Even though Nietzsche's standpoint is not one of simple reversion to the morality of mores, his genealogy of morals does operate with the idea that our modern morality with its individualism is a reactive force compared to the active, value-creating, and world-affirming force of custom. Morality is the misbegotten child of custom.

Instead of the Hegelian project of the creation of a kind

of reflective custom in the midst of modernity as a solution to both the philosophical problem of the empty formalism of Kantian ethics and the real social conflicts engendered in civil society, Nietzsche's project involves a more radical repudiation of modernity as hostile to life and, as a consequence, a more favorable depiction of the archaic as a sphere that lacks our modern differentiations of science, art, and morality and in which an undifferentiated will toward creation predominates. Nietzsche's most direct and earliest ruminations on this theme are found in his famous essay on 'The Uses and Disadvantages of History'. The essay proper begins with an analysis of the happiness of animals who live entirely for the moment and possess no sense of the past; they live only in the blissfulness of the present. He compares animals to children; and in his later thinking concerning the eternal return, it is once more the child who is seen as the embodiment of a joyful, creative force. We adults, however, are overburdened by the past. We have learned the meaning of the phrase "it was," and our capacity to remember has destroyed our capacity to act. The historical sense has become particularly hostile to life in modernity as our plastic power is weaker. By plastic power, Nietzsche means "the capacity to develop out of oneself in one's own way, to transform and incorporate into oneself what is past and foreign, to heal wounds, to replace what has been lost, to recreate broken moulds."[36] The historical counterpoint to modernity is, for Nietzsche, the Greeks, whose unhistorical sense was accompanied by great plastic powers. He argues that "we moderns have nothing whatever of our own," that we have become "walking encyclopedias" whose value lies within and not outside.[37] Modern culture is "subjective culture for outward barbarians."[38] This dualism of subjective and objective culture, which had its reverberations in the history of German sociology, is a reaction against the flat and superficial type of inwardness typical of the *Bildungsbürgertum*. Kierkegaard's reaction leads, as we have seen, to a religiously deepened form of subjectivity, whereas Nietzsche's reaction leads to an overthrowal of the autonomy of the subject. Nietzsche pursues the genealogy of the triumph of subjective over objective culture not simply back into early

modernity but also into antiquity through the figure of
Socrates as the turning point in Greek culture (the theme of
Nietzsche's earlier writings) and in Western culture as a whole
insofar as Socrates prefigures the Christian development (the
theme of Nietzsche's later writings). In this context the pre-
Socratic philosophical unity between natural and ethical speculation is praised as a more productive employment of the
plastic powers of human intelligence. At the end of his essay,
Nietzsche argues that the two antidotes to the historical are
the unhistorical, which he defines as the "art and power of
forgetting and of enclosing oneself within a bounded horizon,"
and the suprahistorical as that which "bestows upon existence
the character of the eternal and the stable, towards *art* and
religion."[39] For Nietzsche, science is viewed as the antithesis
of these suprahistorical forces, which in pre-Socratic Greece
formed a scarcely differentiated unity as seen by the religious
context of dramaturgical performances. In the essay itself, historical science is directly attacked (and in attacking it, Nietzsche was attacking German culture's proudest monument),
for it sees things as historical and not as eternal. It is science as
a whole, including philosophy, however, that is implicated.
Nietzsche sees science as living "in a profound antagonism
towards the eternalizing powers of art and religion, for it
hates forgetting, which is the death of knowledge, and seeks
to abolish all limitations of horizon and launch mankind upon
an infinite and unbounded sea of light whose light is knowledge of all becoming."[40] Beyond the generalized critique of
enlightenment that can be read in this statement lies the theoretical framework of Nietzsche's earliest thoughts on Socrates:
the depiction of Socrates as the theoretical man who destroys
the archaic unity of art and religion found in pre-Euripedean
tragedy. From Socrates to the splintering of culture in modernity may take two and a half more millenia, but the intellectual decision in favor of science that leads to this end is
already made with Socrates. Nietzsche ends the essay with
the hope of a renewal of the Greek concept of culture "as a
new and improved physis, without inner and outer, without
dissimulation and convention, culture as a unanimity of life,
thought, appearance and will."[41] To achieve such a culture the

first thing that needs to be forgotten is Socrates, for his thought is only possible as a self-reflection upon the distinction between *physis* and *nomos* inaugurated by the sophists.

II

The periodization of Nietzsche's writings usually divides up his oeuvre into an early, middle, and late stage. According to Löwith, the first period comprises the early writings such as *The Birth of Tragedy* and *Untimely Meditations*. The second includes works such as *Human, All Too Human; Daybreak;* and the first four books of *The Gay Science*. The third begins with *Zarathustra* and ends with *Ecce Homo*. The periodization attains its authority from the fact that it corresponds to Nietzsche's own understanding of his development.[42] In a note from the *Nachlaß*, Nietzsche argues that there are three paths to wisdom. The first path is that of collecting all values worthy of admiration and setting them against one another; Nietzsche refers to it as a "time of community." The second path is that of shattering those worthy values, of reevaluating them; it is the time spent in the wilderness. The third path is that of world affirmation, of the overthrowal of all idols, and of the triumph of the creative instinct over all reactive forces.[43] The interesting thing about this conception is that the paths are construed not simply as stages in his own development but paths that indicate stages in the overcoming of morality, which are applicable to all philosophical positions in general. Another note from the *Nachlaß* mostly confirms Löwith's linkage of these paths to Nietzsche's published works. The possible exception is *The Birth of Tragedy*, which Nietzsche describes as an artist's metaphysics.[44] This seems to make the work more a foretaste of his post-*Zarathustra* affirmation of creativity than a confrontation between esteemed values, which really only describes *Untimely Meditations*. From the standpoint of the Socrates problem, this distinction also makes sense because the Nietzschean preoccupation with Socrates, although it can be discerned throughout his oeuvre, is particularly intense during the period of *The Birth of Tragedy* and in the post-*Zarathustra* period.

This view is confirmed when one looks at the *Nachlaβ* for signs of interest in the Socrates problem. From the autumn of 1869 to the winter of 1872-1873 and from spring 1884 to autumn 1888 are Nietzsche's two most intense periods of intellectual preoccupation with the figure of Socrates. Nietzsche's time spent in the desert is not a time spent reevaluating Socrates. Yet it is a time, as Dannhauser rightly remarks, when Nietzsche speaks most favorably of Socrates.[45] The reason for this is that the free spirit recognizes in the master of irony the same skepticism that constantly tests values. An aphorism from the *Nachlaβ*, which dates from the same year as *The Wanderer and His Shadow*, reads as follows: "Socrates' skepticism with regard to all knowledge concerning morality is still the greatest event—yet we have forgotten all about it."[46] In *The Wanderer and His Shadow* itself, a similar thought is expressed: "this putting of the god to the test is one of the subtlest compromises between piety and freedom of spirit that has ever been devised."[47] Irony is here identified with that critical, jesting spirit that sounds idols, gods, and values. It is an attitude that Nietzsche most identifies with during this middle period, although the attempt at revaluation, the attempt to sound out all idols is something that remains throughout his work. Nietzsche adds at this point that we no longer need such compromises. The nihilistic mood of the 'free spirit' is beyond all piety. Not even Nietzsche, however, could sustain this negativity, and the shift to his philosophy of the eternal return results in a reevaluation of both negativity and Socrates. The middle period is also the time when Nietzsche counterpoises favorably the figure of Socrates to that of Christ. He looks forward to the day when the *Socratic Memorabilia* of Xenophon will have replaced the Bible, as he argues that Socrates' diverse temperaments were all directed to "joy in living and in one's own self."[48] Hence, Socrates "excels the founder of Christianity in being able to be serious cheerfully and in possessing that wisdom full of roguishness that constitutes the finest state of the human soul. And he also possessed the finer intellect."[49] This is probably the mildest and kindest portrait of Socrates that Nietzsche draws, and it is the least interesting because of that fact. The hostility of the early and late Nietzsche toward Socrates contains truth only because of its exaggerations.

In what follows, I shall try to focus exclusively on Nietzsche's treatment of Socrates in the early and late periods, drawing upon works outside these periods only insofar as they further illuminate the respective problematics. In the early period, Nietzsche begins as a good philologist attempting to disclose the historical sources of Greek tragedy and the reasons for its subsequent decline. The philological enterprise is deepened, however, through the reflection that what the Greeks most prided themselves on—their reason—might have been the destructive principle that undermined both Greek tragedy and ultimately the Greek polity itself. Nietzsche extends the theme of the dangers of reason for social life, with its customs and mores, into the homeland of Western reason. Given that the ancient employment of reason had not degenerated into that hubris toward nature that Nietzsche sees as a product of our excessive curiosity, to attack reason there is to attack it at its strongest point—namely, where its discursive employment constructs a form of sociality centered on leisured conversation.[50] Reason had not yet become disembodied, located in processes that function independently of the conscious control of humans. It was still located concretely in time and space in the person of the philosopher himself, in his discourse, and in his actions. Something had changed in the emergence of what was then called philosophy, however, which had irrevocably set apart the employment of reason from the world in which it was embedded. Nietzsche is, in effect, the first to write what Blumenberg later calls "*eine Urgeschichte der Theorie.*"[51] Blumenberg sees in the story of the Thracian maid, who laughs at the philosopher who is so preoccupied with the heavens that he falls into a well, the paradigmatic emergence of the gap between a theoretical world view and the world view of ordinary people. Nietzsche sees in the emergence of this gap the downfall of Greek tragedy, its murderer being that type of theoretical man who emerges with Socrates and his artistic pupil Euripides.

In the later period, Nietzsche's emergence from his nihilistic period into a Dionysian philosophy of world affirmation, of which the doctrine of the eternal return is the main component, leads to the reemergence and radicalization of his earlier split between pre-Socratic and Socratic philosophy. Socrates and Plato, and their ancient and modern successors who crowd together under the name of philosophy, are assimilated into Western Christianity's world-denying morality—a morality that, because of its inversion of the higher values, functions as a means of social leveling. The triumph of the idea, which Socrates brings about albeit in the negative form of irony, is the *proton pseudos* of philosophy. It is also that which undermines the very possibility of a strong and creative culture. Philosophy's downfall and social decline begin with Socrates. It is clear that what is being attacked here is what Heidegger later calls the onto-theological tradition. The Platonic mode of philosophizing, with its realm of forms, is for Nietzsche closer to theology than to the healthy, realistic cosmological speculation of the earlier Greek philosophers. Nietzsche would like to reverse the Socratic error and turn philosophy out of the city where it only corrupts the citizens. Apart from the extension of his attack from tragedy to thinking itself, Nietzsche's later work on Socrates is remarkable for its return to his most original insights. For example, the idea of an artistic Socrates, which emerges in the early period, represents the triumph of the aesthetic over reason, which in the later works is reworked at the level of cosmology: the world as ceaselessly creative and, hence, something to be affirmed. This further underlines the relative unimportance of Nietzsche's work on Socrates between his two most fruitful periods and illustrates the need to pay attention to these parallels even as I proceed to a separate discussion of Nietzsche's early and late work on Socrates.

III

The passion for Socrates is due to the recognition that with him something fundamental changes in the history of the Occident. This view is common to Hegel, Kierkegaard, and Nietzsche. With Nietzsche, however, the valuation of that change alters. Either as finite subjectivity, as with Hegel, or ironic subjectivity, as with Kierkegaard, the essence of the Socratic turn has been identified with the emergence of free subjectivity.

This new principle is seen as the only possible principle compatible with the new republican constitution *(politeia)*, but it is viewed with ambivalence by both Hegel and Kierkegaard because it involves the destruction of custom *(Sittlichkeit)*. This ambivalence in the case of Hegel is lessened by his historiosophical presupposition that the Socratic moment is a necessary one in world history, and in the case of Kierkegaard by his somewhat anachronistic attempt at a Christianized interpretation of Socratic subjectivity. In the case of Nietzsche, the ambivalence remains unmuted. As the nineteeth century progresses, its untimely ones grow more and more disenchanted with the nature of modernity, particularly its relativization of values that they reasonably associate with democracy. Hegel attempts to rescue a new form of *Sittlichkeit* from the snares of an anarchic individualism that is at the heart of civil society. Kierkegaard turns away from the established Church and the public sphere, as symbolized by the self-chosen martyrdom at the hands of the *Corsair*. With both thinkers, however, Socrates is never completely identified with what is wrong with modern society, and hence, their valuation of Socrates is predominantly positive. On the other hand, the attempt to trace back to the beginnings of Occidental thought the malaise that lies at the heart of the most modern of its forms radicalizes Nietzsche's critique of reason and consequent image of Socrates. The passage of thinking from self-determining thought to subjectivity, as Hegel reconstructs it, becomes for Nietzsche the *via dolorosa* of instincts and creativity. If modern society's domination by the principle of subjectivity is at the heart of modern decadence, then its ancient representative—Socrates—becomes the negative turning point in world history. This thesis can be confirmed by a comparison of Nietzsche's reconstruction of Greek philosophy in *Philosophy in the Tragic Age of the Greeks* with the Hegelian account in the first volume of his *History of Philosophy*, both posthumously published volumes. Although the tragic age for Nietzsche signifies first and foremost the pre-Socratic period, he appears to include Socrates among that "republic of geniuses," for Socrates also embodies the unity of thinking and character that appeals to Nietzsche. Yet the work ends with Anaxagoras and does not even begin to discuss the sophists, let alone Socrates. The preference for cosmological speculation over ethical reflection that this decision implies is made explicit throughout the work. In fact, Nietzsche states that philosophy's entry into the city already means turning against the city. The philosopher should be a "major star in the solar system of culture," as he was in the fourth and fifth centuries, and not an "accidental lonely wanderer in a hostile environment."[52] In this transformation it is Plato, rather than Socrates, who is the culprit. In comparison with the pure philosophical types that precede him, Plato's philosophy has a mixed character and, what is worse, does not "protect and defend" its homeland. "Since Plato," Nietzsche argues, the philosopher "is in exile and conspires against his fatherland."[53] This antiphilosophical motif once again stems from a preference for premodern forms of sociocultural life as the more creative. For Nietzsche, the creative as such finds its elaboration in the cosmological speculation of the pre-Socratics. Thinking requires the abandonment of reason.

The interest of his work on the pre-Socratics lies, therefore, not only in its intrinsic worth, but also as a prefiguration of his Zarathustran elevation of the principle of creativity to a cosmological idea in the philosophy of the eternal return. The pre-Socratics have an importance for modern philosophy through Nietzsche's recuperation of their aesthetico-cosmological character. The amoral character of their universe particularly appeals to Nietzsche. The quarrel between the aesthetic and the moral of *Either/Or* is both decided in advance and shifted to another plane. Within the pre-Socratics themselves, Nietzsche notes a fundamental division between the Anaximanderian and the Parmenidean halves, which revolves in essence around the admission and treatment of becoming in the two stands. The Anaximanderian principle of unboundedness *(apeiron)*, the Hericlitean principles of flux and strife *(panta rei and polemon)*, and the Anaxagorean principles of chaos and mind *(Xaos* and *nous)* exemplify better a cosmology of perpetual creation or becoming than the Parmenidean half. The amoral and playfully creative character of such a vision of the universe is continually pointed out. One quotation dealing with Anaxagoras suffices here:

The Anaxagorean mind *(Geist)* is an artist, and truly the most powerful genius of mechanics and architecture who creates with the simplest means the greatest forms and lines and, as it were, a mobile architecture, but at any rate from that natural and arbitrary will *(irrationalen Willkür)* which lies in the depth of the artist. It is as if Anaxagoras pointed at Phidias and in the face of that prodigious work of the artist, the cosmos, cried to us just as he would do before the Parthenon: becoming is no moral phenomen, but only an artistic phenomenon *(ein künstlerisches Phänomen)*.[54]

Hence, instead of a history of the pre-Socratics as the steady progression towards the discovery of the self-determining mind, as in the Hegelian account, we have the counterpoising of two traditions of which only one fully grasps the nature and significance of becoming as the main philosophical problem. Furthermore, creativity is something that exists beyond the artist and is not simply an attribute of subjectivity. Subjectivity as such, which Hegel sees as coming into existence already with the *nous* of Anaxagoras and even more so with Socrates, is here of no concern to Nietzsche.[55]

It is true, of course, that Hegel does not view the Greeks as having reached the stage of pure infinite subjectivity, as it is a world still imbued with a relationship to beauty, which is not the case for modern times. Hegel's historiosophical relativization of the aesthetic stage of mankind, however, is not followed by Nietzsche. Instead of progression toward truth, truth itself is reduced to an aesthetic effect: that is, it becomes an event within language, an act of interpretation. Nowhere is this more apparent than in the small essay "Truth and Lies in an Extra-moral Sense," which was written in 1873, the same year as the work on the pre-Socratics. Truth is here depicted as coins that have lost their faces and are now merely perceived as metal and not as coins, which is, of course, a metaphorical way of stating a relativistic theory of truth. Truth is "a moving source of metaphors, metonyms, anthropomorphisms," which is to say that truths are illusions of which we have forgotten the made and created nature.[56] It has been erased like the faces of coins. The culprit here goes by many names: it is the intellect with its art of disguise *(Verstellungskunst)*; it is the concept that renders identical the nonidentical *(Gleichsetzen des Nicht-Gleichen)*; it is self-consciousness; it is science; it is the rational man; or, finally, it is Socrates. The identification of the conscious mind with the censor—that which erases, bars, and disguises from view the arbitrary and created nature of truth—is clear. Under the weight of this censor, man forgets the metaphorical nature of truth and mistakes metaphors for reality and, in the process forgets himself as subject—that is, "as artistically creative subject."[57] There is, therefore, no necessary relationship between subject and object but only a kind of infinite translatability between these differing languages made possible by the ceaselessly inventive character of language. In opposition to the rational man, Nietzsche talks of the intuitive man, whom he claims reigned supreme in the time of the ancient Greeks and founded "the domination of art over life."[58]

How this domination was created and how it was destroyed is, of course, the subject of Nietzsche's first published book, *The Birth of Tragedy*, which appeared in 1872. The structure of this work is compellingly simple, as it rests on two fundamental oppositions. The first is that between the Apollinian and the Dionysian, and the second is that between the Dionysian and the Socratic. The first opposition explains the nature, if not the origin, of Attic tragedy as a fusion of two of nature's artistic drives: that toward individuation and intoxication respectively. The second opposition reveals the impasse of culture after the demise of tragedy, where the only possible fusion of intoxication and reason that can arise is the fantasy image of a music-playing Socrates. Instead of fusion, however, Nietzsche sees tragedy as having died at the hands of the theoretical man, who looks at reality not as an aesthetic phenomenon but as an object of knowledge, of reason, of theory, and of a discourse that gives an account of things as they are *(logon didonai)*. Although Nietzsche's explicit aim in the work is a theory of the rise and the decline of tragedy, it is also, as I have remarked, an *Urgeschichte der Theorie* because it is modernity's obsession with science and the nihilistic consequences of that obsession that form the hermeneutical horizon of his philological interrogation. Nowhere is this concern more apparent than in the final section of the work, which he himself later criticizes both for its stylistic inelegance and for its praise of Wagner. In a sense, the inelegance arises out of the fact of making overly manifest the questions animating the work so that they are no longer merely present as an underthought *(hyponoia)*. Nietzsche argues that there are three types of illusion with which we have tried to heal, what he rather beautifully calls, "the eternal wound of existence *(ewige Wunde des Daseins)"*: knowledge, art, and metaphysical consolation. According to Nietzsche, all culture is made up of these stimulants; and according to whichever is dominant, culture is either Socratic, artistic, or tragic. The historical manifestations of such cultures are the Alexandrian, Hellenic, and Buddhistic periods respectively. The identification of the Socratic with the Alexandrian is, of course, outrageous from a historical viewpoint, as Socratic knowing is not disembodied scholarship but a form of existence characterized by a concern for the self *(heautou epimelia)*. From the standpoint of Nietzsche's *Urgeschichte*, however, knowing itself, the will to know, is the fatal step that leads from Socrates to modernity. Nietzsche argues that "our whole modern culture is entangled in the net of Alexandrian culture. It proposes as its ideal the theoretical man equipped with the greatest forces of knowledge, and labouring in the service of science, whose archetype and progenitor is Socrates."[59] Instead of knowledge, Nietzsche opts for wisdom; instead of an optimistic culture, a tragic one.

The concept of a fusion of horizons implies that both the present and the past enter into dialogue; hence, Nietzsche is not simply reading back into Greek antiquity his own critique of modern science, but using Greek antiquity as an estrangement effect in order to facilitate the understanding of modernity. This thought is summed up in a fragment from the summer of 1875. "Greek antiquity," Nietzsche argues, is "a classical collection of examples for the explanation of our whole culture and its development. It is a means *to understand ourselves*, to judge our times and through that to overcome them. The pessimistic foundation of our culture."[60] It is not only Greek antiquity, but the figure of Socrates in particular, that is an excellent means to understand ourselves in *The Birth of Tragedy*. Let me turn first, however, to the opposition between the Appollinian and the Dionysian with which the book begins. This opposition is, for Nietzsche, a nonantagonistic one, unlike the one between the Dionysian and the Socratic. He identifies the Apollinian with sculpture or the imagistic in general. Apollo as the "god of all plastic powers" and "at the same time the soothsaying God" also rules over "the beautiful illusion of the inner phantasy world."[61] The reference to *Schein* (illusion or appearance) illustrates the continuity between Nietzsche's conception of the Apollinian and the idealistic tradition of German aesthetics.[62] *Die schöne Schein*, however, is not conceived of by Nietzsche as a mediating or reconciling power, as it is in Schiller, but as one of the two artistic states of nature *(unmittelbaren Kunstzuständen)*.

Nietzsche's parallel between the Apollinian and dreams and the important identification of the Apollinian with the *principium individuationis* makes, in effect, the subject who bears the Apollinian within him the artist. The bearer of the Dionysian, even though it is one of the two art deities *(Kunstgottheiten)*, is not so much an artist as an artwork. The Dionysian is beyond illusion; it is the collapse of the *principium individuationis* and the forgetting of the self in the collective ekstasis of a reconciliation not simply of man with his fellow man but, more importantly, of man with nature. Although it is not associated either with the dream or illusion, but with intoxication and the displacement of illusion, the Dionysian is still a part of the aesthetic and, indeed, the fundamental experience that lies behind the possiblity of beautiful illusion in the Apollinian sense. The bearer of the Dionysian, Nietzsche argues, "is no longer an artist, he has become a work of art: in these paroxysms of intoxication the artistic power of all nature reveals itself to the highest gratification of the primordial unity."[63]

Nietzsche now turns from the manifestation of the Dionysian and the Apollinian as drives of nature to their manifestation, via the mediation of man, in the culture of antiquity. What interests him first is the break effected by the Greeks in the natural history of these two principles and the inauguration of their cultural history. For Nietzsche, the Dionysian barbarian, as distinct from the Dionysian Greek, could not have become a culture-creating force as it merely represents desublimated cruelty and sensuality. Only with the emergence of the Dionysian spirit within Greek culture and its reconciliation with what stood opposed to the Dionysian barbarian, namely the Apollinian spirit of Doric art and culture, does the break occur, which Nietzsche describes as an uneasy peace treaty. This uneasy truce between the two principles results in Dionysian orgies attaining "the significance of days of world redemption and days of transfiguration *(Welterlösungsfesten und Verklärungstagen)*."[64] The destruction of the *principium individuationis* is described, therefore, not as a regress of culture to a lower level of development but as an "artistic phenomenon *(künstlerisches Phänomen)*". The notion of an artistic phenomenon as a redemptive principle is the key to Nietzsche's text because it stands opposed to the philosophical view of the world as an object of *theoria*, which Nietzsche identifies with Socrates. *Theoria* versus the Dionysian are the two redemptive principles at odds in the later part of the text. If the Dionysian in Greek culture is even now identified with what is beyond good and evil, Nietzsche is at this stage of his intellectual development still not radical enough to eschew the form-giving power of the Apollinian in Greek culture as the bearer of the principle of beauty. The Apollinian as beautiful illusion is retained even though it is clear that what primarily fascinates Nietzsche is the Dionysian as *pharmakon*—that is, the idea that art emerges from cruelty just as much as from an impulse of beauty, that art is, indeed, both a remedy and a poison.

The Dionysian is mere appearance and the Apollinian the mere appearance of appearance *(Schein des Schein)*. Both are needed:

> For the more clearly I perceive in nature those omnipotent art impulses, and in them an ardent longing for illusion, for redemption through illusion *(Sehnsucht zum Schein, zum Erlöstwerden durch den Schein)*, the more I feel myself impelled to the metaphysical assumption

that the truly existent primal unity *(das Wahrhaft-Seiende und Ur-Eine)*, eternally suffering and contradictory, also needs the rapturous vision, the pleasurable illusion, for its continous redemption *(den lustvollen Schein, zu seiner steten Erlösung braucht)*.[65]

The fusion of the Dionysian and Apollinian is the redemptive principle in the early Nietzsche, whereas in the later Nietzsche there is an incorporation, and subordination, of the Apollinian to the Dionysian—to the power of intoxication. The emphasis on the redemptive power of beauty makes his aesthetics more idealistic and less idol-demolishing than his later position, for one idol—beauty—still remains. The fact that beauty requires cruelty as its necessary complement does not alter the idealist nature of his concept of appearance, although it clearly represents a romantic inflection within this tradition because the beautiful is no longer seen as a visible symbol of the morally good, as in Kant, but as in league with cruelty, suffering, terror, and torture. The beautiful is not merely morally neutral, as perhaps in Kierkegaard, but hostile to all morality. This is a position that is now possible, if not yet taken in *The Birth of Tragedy*. The necessary interdependence of the Dionysian and the Apollinian is rather strikingly conveyed by Nietzsche in a reference to the *Transfiguration* of Raphael, which I quote in full:

> In his *Transfiguration*, the lower half of the picture, with the possessed boy, the despairing bearers, the bewildered terrified disciples, shows us the reflection of suffering, primal and eternal, the sole ground of the world: the "mere appearence" here is the reflection of eternal contradiction, the father of things. From this mere appearence arises, like ambrosial vapour, a new visionary world of mere appearance, invisible to those wrapped in the first appearence—a radiant floating in purest bliss, a serene contemplation beaming from wide-open eyes. Here we have presented, in the most sublime artistic symbolism, that Apollinian world of beauty and its substratum, the terrible wisdom of Silenus; and intuitively we comprehend their necessary interdependence.[66]

The necessary interdependence of suffering and beauty, of excess and measure, of loss of self and self-knowledge, of intoxication and illusion is shown to its fullest, for Nietzsche, in Greek tragedy. The irony of this reference to Raphael's painting, however, which simultaneously depicts Christ's transfiguration and the prelude to the performance of a miracle, is that it is more a passionate expression of Raphael's belief in faith than an attempt to represent the coexistence of suffering and beauty. The two halves of the picture represent respectively a world with and a world without faith: the world of Christ, Moses, and Elijah and that of the disciples with little faith. Greek religion's basis in cult, as opposed to faith, is bound to prove a more favorable ground for the establishment of Nietzsche's aesthetic ideas, as the presubjective nature of its religion is more in harmony with his postsubjective aesthetic.

Nietzsche argues, in line with tradition, that Homer and Archilochus are the two paths that lead to ancient tragedy. Homer as "the type of the Apollinian naive artist" is unproblematic for Nietzsche; however, with Archilochus Nietzsche runs into a problem. This is the problem of severing the Dionysian from the subjectivity of the lyric poet. He solves this problem by separating out from the nongenial "I" the willing and desiring man called Archilochus, the genial "I" that is a pure medium for the expression of the transsubjective force of the Dionysian. Archilochus is here "a world genius expressing his primordial pain symbolically in the symbol *(Gleichnisse)* of the man Archilochus."[67] The artist falls thereby from his position of creator to become a mere medium. "Insofar as the subject is the artist, however, he has already been released from his individual will, and has become, as it were, the medium through which the one truly existent subject celebrates his release [*Erlösung* is better rendered as 'redemption'] in appearance."[68] Nietzsche's splitting of the empirical "I" from the "I" that is capable of being the identical subject-object of the aesthetic redemption and justification of existence is absolutely crucial for his artist's metaphysics. "Only insofar as the genius in the act of creation coalesces with this primordial artist of the world," Nietzsche argues, "does he know anything of the eternal essence of art . . . he is at once subject and object, at once poet, actor, and spectator."[69] As an empirical "I" the artist is not capable of such insight; he is merely a puppet for this primordial artist (Urkünstler) who is a product of Dionysian intoxications. Indeed, the empirical "I's" are nothing but the artworks of this primordial artist whose task is the aesthetic redemption of existence, "for it is only as an *aesthetic phenomenon* that existence and the world are eternally *justifed.*"[70] The interpretation of this passage in terms of the subject-object relationship is not unproblematic, for the Heideggerian interpretation of Nietzsche's theory of art as essentially ontological challenges such an interpretation. As this interpretation is based essentially on Nietzsche's late notes, we can adjourn any consideration of its implications.

The undercutting of the subject-centeredness of artistic creativity is further demonstrated for Nietzsche when he notes that it was Archilochus who introduced folksong into literature. Furthermore, due to its melodic character, language imitates music in folk music rather than the world of image and phenomenon. Despite its closeness to the Dionysian, folksong as well as lyric poetry remain distant from it insofar as they are dependent on the medium of language and have no immediate contact with the medium of the Dionysian par excellence music. The same problem arises in the attempt to uncover the origins of Greek tragedy—namely, to loosen tragedy from its rationalistic bondage, which derives from the lucidity of its dialogue. If Greek tragedy arises, therefore, from the tragic chorus, what precisely is the nature of this chorus? Nietzsche rejects Schlegel's idea that the chorus is the ideal spectator as well as Schiller's idea, although he has more sympathy with it than with Schlegel's, of the chorus as an ideal domain. According to Nietzsche, the Greek chorus is a satyr chorus born and nourished by myth and ritual. This religious nature of the satyr chorus has the effect of suspending the world of culture by leading man back to the sphere of the natural. The "metaphysical comfort" that tragedy is said to provide presages Nietzsche's later metaphysics, which goes under the name of the "eternal return of the same." "The metaphysical comfort," Nietzsche argues, "that life is at the bottom of things, despite all the changes of appearances, indestructibly powerful and pleasurable—this comfort appears in the chorus of satyrs, a chorus of natural beings who live ineradicably, as it were, behind all civilization and remain eternally the same."[71] The gap that the satyr chorus opens up between Dionysian reality and everyday reality, or between the sacred and the profane, is the gap through which the redemptive power of art enters to produce a type of knowledge into extramundane existence, which renders all action in our mundane existences absolutely pointless. The Greek chorus is a product of an artist's religion.

The satyr chorus, with its dithyrambic odes, leads to the dissolution of the boundary between the chorist and the reveler. The Dionysian reveler's will to transform himself into the bodies of others during intoxication is what Nietzsche calls the protophenomenon of drama. It is only on this basis that the Apollinian elements of tragedy, primarily the dialogue, emerge. Hence, Nietzsche understands "Greek tragedy as the Dionysian chorus which ever anew discharges itself in an Apollinian world of images."[72] The dialogue is, for Nietzsche, what has given the Greeks their undeserved reputation for "sweetness and light," whereas for Nietzsche such an interpretation is infantile. The emphasis on the chorus as preindividuation, as it is the Apollinian character of the dialogue that first introduces this principle into tragedy, leads to a reading of the manifest content of the tragedies themselves as circling around the theme of individuation and nonindividuation. The tragedies thematize the duality of their own structure in the stories of Oedipus and Prometheus. Sophocles' *Oedipus* teaches us, according to Nietzsche, that wisdom and the violation of the natural order go hand in hand. Aeschylus's *Prometheus* further teaches us, according to Nietzsche, that boldness and sacrilege also go hand in hand. In both plays, the curse of individuation is demonstrated even as it is praised. The dynamic element of the two is, of course, the Dionysian. Hence, Nietzsche goes so far as to argue that all the tragic heroes of ancient Greek tragedy are so many masks of the god Dionysos, and that the rebirth of Dionysos—"this coming third Dionysos"—would spell the end of individuation.[73] "The mystery doctrine of tragedy," Nietzsche argues, is "the fundamental knowledge of the oneness of everything existent, the conception of individuation as the primal cause of evil, and of art as the joyous hope that the spell of individuation may be broken in augury of a restored oneness."[74] What comes, however, is not the third Dionysos, this coming god, but a mere mortal and master of individuation—Socrates.

Nietzsche's aesthetic critique of individualism is without doubt a part of the wider critique of the nihilistic consequences of liberalism in late nineteenth-century Europe. Perhaps what he seeks in fifth-century Athens is a mirror image of his own epoch. To what extent it is a true image we shall see, for it is by no means certain that the intense intellectual speculation of fifth-century Athens is either nihilistic in character or fundamentally at odds with the religious character of the *polis*. In any case, individuation begins long before Socrates and is a characteristic of Greek religious theory (theo-logy) from the beginning.[75] So also is intellectualism, as the word *logos* in theology intimates. Both are, however, condemned by Nietzsche as parties to the destruction of the most dynamic value-creating power behind Greek tragedy—the Dionysian. Even if for the Greeks the intellect, nature, and gods were not irreconcilable, they were so for Nietzsche. That they could be so for a nineteenth-century intellectual is not difficult to imagine, for what goes by the name of intellect or reason is a mere remnant of its ancient embodiment that now, in its practical employment, is responsible, as Nietzsche notes in the *Genealogy*, for the devastation of nature. The modern inividual, as the bearer of modern reason, has also become a mere calculating machine incapable of the value-creating *ekstasis* of Dionysian intoxication. The linkage between the modern individual and the death of Greek tragedy is the emergence of the theoretical man *(anthropos theoretikos)* and his simultaneous refinement of reason and the use of that reason in the practice of the care of the self. This is the Socratic revolution for Nietzsche: the emergence of theory and of individualism. Although it is through Euripides that tragedy directly commits suicide, for Nietzsche the real and only figure behind its destruction is Socrates. With him important questions are posed for Nietzsche—namely, the relation between the conscious and the unconscious in cultural creativity, and the relation between the individual and the transindividual.

Before we tackle these questions, let me mention another question more directly concerned with Nietzsche's critique of Euripides' dramaturgy: that is, the relation between the drama and the spectator. Nietzsche's main complaint against Euripides is that he brings the spectator onto the stage. Nietzsche's reference to Euripides as giving civic mediocrity its voice indicates his eschewal of any public role for drama; that is, its articulation within a public sphere that recognizes itself therein is constrasted unfavorably with the aesthetic practices of Aeschylus and Sophocles. It is obvious that Euripidean dramaturgy is more in keeping with the democratic nature of the *polis*, which in fifth-century Athens submitted all things political to public consideration. Nietzsche, however, never looks on democratizing trends favorably in whatever sociopolitical context, and his argument here concerning Greek tragedy has its pertinence. Of the spectators that Euripides brings onto the stage, Nietzsche singles out Euripides and Socrates. Nietzsche criticizes Euripides for the subordination of aesthetics to extra-aesthetic criteria, principally to reason. The Dionysian is excluded from tragedy and tragedy itself reconstructed on the basis of an "un-Dionysian art, morality, and worldview" that is essentially the Socratic.[76] Accordingly, the new opposition is the Dionysian and the Socratic. For Nietzsche, the Socratic is a form of enlightenment that represents the mania for intelligibility that cuts man off from the gods and the form of life, an intensely creative aesthetic state, that contact with the gods makes possible. Again one can argue that this is a misinterpretation insofar as it underestimates the underlying theological concerns of the Greek philosophers who saw no unbridgeable gap between science and theology, as can be seen from the Aristotelian conception of philosophy as a theoretical science that begins with wonder *(thaumazein)*. As the knowledge of first causes, philosophy inherits, even as it transforms, the mythological accounts. Nietzsche, in his early phase, seems to read the philosophical revolution of the fifth century all too narrowly as a type of secularization familiar from the eighteenth-century pattern. The later Nietzsche avoids this interpretation; science then becomes the latest form of the ascetic ideal. The fact that science and philosophy are not equivalent to religious emancipation can be seen in Socrates as well as in Aristotle.[77] Even as Socrates individualizes the religious principle (the notion of *daimonion*) he recommends obedience to the traditional religious ethos and the laws they sanction. The fact that he was prepared to die for them indicates that they were not considered a part of a kind of provisional morality, in the manner of Descartes and Spinoza, to which one submitted in lieu of a fully rational morality as a concession to the way of the world. It is the mania for intelligibility, which Nietzsche sees as being brought onto the stage in the person of Socrates, that destroys tragedy. The supreme law of aesthetic Socratism reads, according to Nietzsche, "'To be beautiful everything must be intelligible,' as the counterpart of the Socratic dictum, 'Knowledge is virtue.'"[78] The rationalist illusion that evil or ugliness is a simple product of ignorance or confusion is not one shared by Nietzsche. Yet despite the truth of his observation, he goes too far in assimilating Socrates' mania for submitting everything to account with a secularized mythology of reason.

For Nietzsche, reason and art come into conflict in the person of Socrates. The "naive rationalism" that he credits Socrates with introducing means that "everything must be conscious in order to be ethical."[79] The conflict is, therefore, between a theoretical optimism, which sees the transparency of things as a sign of the potency of human consciousness, and a pessimistic world view, which sees in the opacity of things the precondition for the redeeming power of aesthetic illusion (*Schein*). Hence, the central theme of Nietzsche's interpretation of Socrates is the struggle between science and art as it was played out in ancient Greece. Socrates emerges in this context as the ideal type of theoretical man. The theoretical man can only be understood in opposition to the artist. "Whenever the truth is uncovered," Nietzsche argues, "the artist will always cling with rapt gaze to what still remains covering even after such uncovering, but the theoretical man enjoys and finds satisfaction in the discarded covering and finds the highest object of his pleasure in the process of an ever happy uncovering that succeeds through his own efforts."[80] The idea that the search for truth is more important than the truth itself, which is an idea first formulated by Lessing, has its roots in the optimism of the Socratic dialectic. Nietzsche argues this dialectic has "an unshakable faith that thought using the thread of causality, can penetrate the deepest abysses of being, and that thought is capable not only of knowing being but even of *correcting* it. This sublime metaphysical illusion (*Wahn* not *Schein*) accompanies science as an instinct and leads science again and again to the limits at which it must turn into *art*—which is the real aim of this mechanism."[81] The illusion is, to put it in Heideggerian terms, the idea that the knowledge of entities (*Seiendes*) will lead to a knowledge of being *(Sein)*, which, for Nietzsche, is more fully disclosed in tragedy. The impossibility of reason, despite the very power *(Kraft)* of its uncovering *(Enthüllung)*, to be able to ever fathom being is an idea that is just as much Nietzsche's as Heidegger's. What is not Heideggerian in Nietzsche's conception is the idea of a dialectical reversal, the idea that knowledge surpasses its limits and turns into art. This idea finds its image in the figure of the dying Socrates in which myth becomes the eternal supplement of reason. "Hence the image of the *dying Socrates*, as the human being whom knowledge and reasons have liberated from the fear of death, is the emblem that, above the entrance gate of science, reminds all of its mission—namely, to make existence appear comprehensible and thus justified; and if reasons do not suffice, *myth* has come to their aid in the end—myth which I have just called the necessary consequence, indeed the purpose, of science."[82] Here, there is not any simple repudiation of the Enlightenment, for liberation from fear and incomprehensibility are still very much in evidence; however, this liberation no longer presupposes the obsolesence of religion, but its very retention! Myth provides us with an access to being that reason, which is thereby reduced to the status of superficiality, cannot provide. Greek tragedy prior to Euripides has a similar access; its poetry is not simply an echo of a system of conscious knowledge but an echo of the Dionysian dithyramb, which is at its origin.

The opposition of the Dionysian and the Socratic, as well as their possible reconciliation, is also found in the *Nachlaß* in the more pointed form of opposition between the theoretical and the religious genius. The theoretical genius that destroys what Nietzsche calls here "Greek Apollinian art" has as its tasks the elaboration of "ever greater complexes of thought *(Denkkomplexe)*."[83] What is distinctive about Nietzsche's position in this note, however, is that the redemption of illusion is accorded to the religious genius. Hence, there is a possibility of a reconciliation between the "world mission of the Greeks and of Socrates," which is identified with logical thought, and the religious genius, which is identified with mythical thought. "There is a possible reconciliation," Nietzsche argues, which involves "on the one hand the sharpest determination of the boundary of the logical, and on the other hand the knowledge that illusion *(Schein)* is necessary for our existence."[84] Nietzsche had in 1870 no difficulty in substituting for the term Dionysian the concept of the religious as such, which in 1888 would have been unthinkable. The difference is that later on post-Platonic religion is seen merely as metaphysics for the masses; Socrates is seen as a forerunner of this form of decadence. In the early work, however, the emphasis on Socrates as scientist, as the nonreligious theoretical man is absolutely central to Nietzsche's image of him. "The theoretical man is," Nietzsche observes, "inactive, causality, pleasure in logical thinking, new form of existence *(Neue Daseinsform)*, boundless *(Grenzenloser)* Apollinianism, boundless *(masslose)* search for knowledge, lack of fear in doubt."[85] The emphasis on boundlessness puts the theoretical man firmly in the camp of the Enlightenment to which Nietzsche is not as yet its most radical opponent. What Nietzsche holds against the power of reason is its optimism, its confidence that knowledge can exhaust being and that ignorance is the only evil. "Socrates is the prototype of the theoretical optimist who," Nietzsche argues, "with his faith that the nature of things can be fathomed, ascribes to knowledge and insight the power of a panacea *(Universalmedizin)*, while understanding error as the evil *par excellence*."[86] Being is, however, inexhaustible, and only art can provide any sort of insight into that which remains beyond the illumination of science's power. The concept does not exhaust being without remainder.

From the boundary points *(Grenzpunkte)* of the circle of science, tragic insight surveys the remainder. Its access to remaindered being is through the medium of art. Its fictitious practitioner is the music-playing Socrates *(musiktreibenden Sokrates)*.[87] An example of such a being is, perhaps, Nietzsche himself. His own example from the *Nachlaß* is Shakespeare, whom he also describes as the completion of Sophocles.[88] The example that *The Birth of Tragedy* gives is Wagner.

With regard to the question of the relation between the conscious and the unconscious in cultural creativity, we must first recall the central concepts with which Nietzsche is operating: namely, thought, illusion, being, and redemption. The opposition between thought, or the logical, and illusion with which he operates leads to artistic creativity's being firmly placed on the side of illusion. "The projection of illusion is the primary artistic process *(das Projicieren des Scheins ist der künstlerische Urprozeß)*."[89] This elevation of illusion renders reason secondary; it becomes an adaptive structure: "Logic is adapted to the world of appearance; in this sense it must cover itself with the essence of art."[90] Indeed, Nietzsche's aim is, precisely, the construction of an artist's metaphysics. The identification of the unconscious with music and the presentation of music as the art of illusion par excellence leads to the identification of creativity with the unconscious. Hence, Nietzsche's main complaint against Euripides' Socratic dramaturgy is that it introduces *nous* into artistic activity, and that "his aesthetic principle" that "to be beautiful everything must be conscious" is, as I have said, the parallel to the Socratic "to be good everything must be conscious."[91] For Nietzsche, it is the unconscious that is the productive, while the conscious is merely critical. The perversity of the Socratic *daimonion* for Nietzsche is that it is both unconscious and nonproductive. In this inversion he sees the ground as being laid for the Platonic exclusion of the artist. The important note from the *Nachlaß* in which this idea is developed dates from the autumn of 1869. It reads:

> Greek tragedy found its annihilation in Socrates.
> The unconscious is greater than Socratic ignorance.
> The daimonion is the unconscious, but it only hinders

the conscious here and there: it does not have a *productive* effect, only a *critical* one. A most oddly inverted world! Usually it is the unconscious which is always the productive, the conscious the critical. *Plato's* banishment of the *artist* and the poet is the consequence.[92]

The Nietzschean unconscious is, therefore, a product of an artist's metaphysics and does not, as a consequence, function in the same way as the Freudian unconscious with which it has obvious points in common. Although the Freudian unconscious is greater than Socratic ignorance, the thread of rationalism that unites Freud and Socrates distances them both from Nietzsche. In any case, as Kierkegaard rightly sees, the irony of Socratic dialectic makes it a unique fusion of artistic and critical effect. There is a one-sidedness in the Nietzschean interpretation of Socrates as scientist, as the theoretical man. The struggle for the "rights of the unconscious" that Nietzsche reads into his interpretation of Socrates is typically romantic in its insistence that conscious control is the death of artistic creativity. "The principle of science has penetrated into Socrates," Nietzsche argues, "and with it the struggle and annihilation of the unconscious."[93]

In *The Birth of Tragedy* the same thought is expressed with the minor difference that Nietzsche speaks of the instincts becoming critical and of consciousness as the creative principle. He refers to this as "a true monstrosity per defectum."[94] What Nietzsche holds against Socrates is his pitting of himself, his individuality and the power of his own reason, against the anonymous forces of habit, myth, and instinct that underpin Greek life and Greek tragedy. With the phrase "only by instinct," Nietzsche argues, "we touch upon the heart and core of the Socratic tendency. With it Socratism condemns existing art as well as existing ethics. Wherever Socratism turns its searching eyes it sees lack of insight and the power of illusion; and from this lack it infers the essential perversity and reprehensibility of what exists. Basing himself on this point, Socrates conceives it to be his duty to correct existence."[95] In this regard, Nietzsche is at one with Hegel in seeing the danger that free subjectivity poses to the customary ethical order; where they part company is in their characterization of Greek antiquity. Hegel sees it more as a place of sweetness and light, whereas Nietzsche views it as a world dominated by a tragic pessimism. Apollo, the sun god, is also the god of individualism. Socrates, "the Apollinian individual," is his representative against the god who suffers, Dionysos.[96] Dionysos suffers because existence is no longer an unbroken unity due to the emergence of individuation. The Socratic tendency to want to correct being, which Nietzsche sees as the *Ursprung* of modern science, is counterpoised with the Dionysian desire to restore being, which presupposes a fundamentally different metaphysics that he will later develop under the concept of "the eternal return of the same." At this point Nietzsche merely recalls the hope of the epic poets for "this coming third Dionysos." More concretely, this rebirth of the Dionysian would mean a reconciliation of the two principles briefly united in pre-Euripidean Greek tragedy. "How can something new emerge out of two opposing principles, in which each split apart drive could appear as a unity," Nietzsche asks himself. His reply is that perhaps the tragic work of art may be considered as a pledge or security *(Bürgschaft)* for the rebirth of the Dionysian.[97]

In the writings in and around *The Birth of Tragedy,* which occupy the years from 1870 to 1872, the emphasis of Nietzsche is on a critique of the theoretical man that Socrates represents as the type of theoretical optimist; for Nietzsche, dialectics is the optimistic form of thinking par excellence, which leads to the collapse of the tragic world view. With his more detailed investigations into pre-Socratic philosophy, which were sketched in the year 1873 under the title *Philosophy in the Tragic Age of the Greeks,* and more particularly in the notes that accompany it, there occurs a shift away from the presentation of Socrates as a theoretical man to an even more disparaging depiction of him as a moralist, a depiction that is more in tune with Nietzsche's later interpretation. There are two main sets of notes. One was written from summer 1872 to winter 1873 and another much more important set was written in summer 1875. The study of pre-Socratic philosophy seems to have awakened Nietzsche to the fact that the theoretical attitude does not begin with Socrates; it is more the case that a new type of theoretical attitude, both more skeptical and more moralistic, begins with him. Nietzsche sees two distinct drives in pre-Socratic philosophy: one toward art and the other toward science. In either case, philosophy moves away from the culture of the people. This has four side effects according to Nietzsche:

> the harnessing *(Bändigung)* of the Mythical.—
> strengthening of the sense of truth against the
>   freedom of poetry . . .
> the harnessing of the drive to knowledge—
> or the strengthening of the mythic-mystical,
>   of the artistic . . .
> dismantling *(Zertrümmerung)* of rigid dogmas;
> a) in religion b) custom *(Sitte)* c) science.

> Skeptical characteristic. Every power (Religion, myth, drive to knowledge) has to an excess, a barbaric, immoral *(unsittliche)* and stultifying effect, as rigid domination (Socrates). Dismantling of blind secular-ization *(Verweltlichung)* (Substitute for religion) (Anaxagoras Pericles). Mystical characteristic.[98]

It is clear from this that Nietzsche does not view the develop-ment of Greek philosophy in any kind of linear fashion as a transformation from *mythos* to *logos* and that its development has more of an alternating gait *(alterno paedo)*. The only com-mon thread is philosophy's severance from ordinary culture and its inability to create culture. Even Socrates' willingness to practice philosophy publically, rather than from within the confines of a sect, is dismissed by Nietzsche as a "democratic-demagogical tendency."[99] But the real culprit at this stage is Plato, with whom the real enmity against culture begins. Niet-zsche's project is to turn the philosopher from the poisoner *(Giftmischer)* of culture to its doctor *(Artz)*. This would involve:

1. the dismantling of secularization (lack of popular philosophy)
2. harnessing of the barbaric effects of the drive to

knowledge (with that the development of a rumina-
tive philosophy)
    against the "iconic" history
    against the "working" scholars.[100]

The last two remarks are tackled by Nietzsche in *The Uses and
Disadvantages of History*, whereas the two points in general go
to the heart of his objections to the culturally corrosive effects
of Socratic skepticism. At this point, Nietzsche's Socrates interpretation is at its most Hegelian. "Socratic scepticism," Nietzsche remarks, "is a weapon against the hitherto existing culture and science."[101] This results in the new Socratic culture,
which focuses upon the individual, and the new Socratic science, which focuses upon the nexus between discourse and
action and is, as Nietzsche rightly points out, an enemy of natural scientific enlightenment.[102]

In the notes of the summer of 1875, the contrast between
wisdom and science, the pre-Socratic and the Socratic becomes
even greater. Socratism is seen as a peculiar mixture of wisdom
and science which, due to its fixation on the individual, is a
danger both to science, as natural-scientific knowledge and
ethical life, as the *unbefangene Sitte* of Hegel. The demand that
the individual should submit himself to rational inspection,
that his actions should be submitted to the test of discourse to
see whether the principles that underlie them are capable of
universalization, is the core of Socratism for Nietzsche.
Socratism is:

Wisdom in the taking seriously of the soul.
Science as fear and hatred of illogical generalizations.
Something strange in the demand for conscious and
logically correct action.[103]

This sudden increase in the importance of the individual, as
Nietzsche calls it, is the essence of the Socratic revolution.
"With Socrates begins the virtuosos of life" and the soul of
philosophy turns towards dread *(Angst um sich selbst)*.[104] The
consequences of such individualism are clear for Nietzsche:
"he sought *to create himself* and to refuse all tradition."[105] Furthermore, "the hateful man of the people struck dead the

authority of the ruling myth in Greece."[106] Authority, tradition, and finally, customary life *(unbefangene Sitte)* form the center of Nietzsche's very Hegelian argument against Socrates: "the natural regard *(unbefangene Blick)* of human beings is lacking in all Socratics, who have grey abstractions in their head like 'the good, the just.' . . . The Greeks lose through Socrates their naturalness *(die Unbefangenheit)*. Their myths and tragedies were much wiser. . . ."[107] So also was the pre-Socratic philosophy that directly preceded Socrates, as it was more closely related to art, "not the negation of *other* life," "not so individual-eudaemonistic"; it possessed a higher wisdom than "the cold-clever virtue of Socratism."[108] Nietzsche's argument ends with a powerful indictment of Socrates' effect *(Wirkung)*:

1. he destroyed the naturalness of ethical judgement,
2. he destroyed science,
3. had no sense for art,
4. tore the individual out of his historical bonds,
5. promoted dialectical chattering and talkativeness.[109]

There is a shift in Nietzsche's interpretation of Socrates, therefore, from a reading of Socratic individualism as an intellectual phenomenon, which is constructed in opposition to Nietzsche's interpretation of Greek tragedy in particular and existence in general as a primarily aesthetic or Dionysian phenomenon, to a reading of Socratic individualism as a primarily moral phenomenon, which is constructed this time mainly in opposition to Nietzsche's reading of pre-Socratic philosophy as embodying aesthetico-religious world interpretations. This shift leads from Nietzsche's possibly more original critique of Socrates as the theoretical man to a critique of Socratic moral skepticism reminiscent of Hegel's interpretation. The problem with this shift is that in Nietzsche's second, more nihilistic period he himself practices the very same skepticism for which he criticizes Socrates in these notes from 1875. Thus, in notes that date from 1880, Nietzsche's rejection of Socratic universalism as a form of moral classicism comes through very clearly but so, too, does his continued adherence to Socratic skepticism.[110] Nietzsche firmly states, for example, that "Socratic skepticism with regard to all knowledge and morality is still the greatest event."[111] Throughout this second period when Nietzsche's main preoccupation is the undermining of the spiritual history of values, Socratic intellectual skepticism is a most valuable tool when used in a non-Socratic fashion. But when it is used Socratically, it leads to precisely those value-demolishing tendencies that Nietzsche deplores. He does not succeed in escaping from this *aporia* during his second period. The words that he had already written in the summer of 1875 still apply: "Socrates, in order only to confess it, stands so close to me, that I am almost always engaged in a struggle with him."[112]

IV

In the third period the artistic Socrates or the music-playing Socrates *(musiktreibenden Socrates)* of the first period cedes his place to the dying Socrates *(der sterbende Socrates)*. Already *The Gay Science* of 1882 announces the new motif, which will only find its full development in 1888. At first this famous section leads us to believe we are on familiar territory with its fulsome praise of Socratic skepticism. Nietzsche writes that "this mocking and enamored monster and pied piper *(Rattenfänger)* of Athens, who made the most overweening youths tremble and sob, was not only the wisest chatterer of all time: he was equally great in silence."[113] We are very far away here from the Hegelian reproach that Socratic skepticism leads to the destruction of customary life, which Nietzsche developed in 1875. The reproach that Nietzsche now levels against Socrates is that at the last moment Socrates was not silent enough:

> Whether it was death or the poison or piety or malice—something loosened his tongue at that moment and he said, "O Crito, I owe Asclepius a rooster." This ridiculous and terrible "last word" means for those who have ears: "O Crito, *life is a disease (Krankheit)*." Is it possible that a man like him, who had lived cheerfully and like a soldier in the sight of everyone, should have

been a pessimist? . . . Socrates, Socrates *suffered life*! . . .
Alas, my friends, we must overcome even the Greeks![114]

Immediately following these remarks is a section that adumbrates the theory of the eternal return, and after that the famous section that is later used at the beginning of *Thus Spake Zarathustra*. The opposition that Nietzsche is just beginning to develop here is that between reactive and active forces, world denunciation and world affirmation, or in the words of nineteenth-century *Lebensphilosophie*, sickness and health. Nietzsche is beginning to remove some of the traces of ambiguity in his interpretation of Socrates and to identify him all too one-sidedly as a precursor of a Christian ethos in which Nietzsche sees the greatest reactive force. The identification of existence as a form of sickness plays no part in Socratic philosophy. The fact that it is a misinterpretation of Socrates' last words that Nietzsche has committed himself to here in this passage can be shown through an analysis of a remarkable little essay by Dumézil on these famous last words. Dumézil also begins his essay, which is cast in the form of an imaginary dialogue, with the same incomprehension that Nietzsche expresses concerning the possibility that such a soldier-citizen as Socrates could really have looked upon existence as a Buddhist does. Instead of adopting Nietzsche's interpretation, which is also that of Lamartine, Dumézil engages in a piece of good philology that even his fellow philologist would have been quick to admire. The question raised by the last words: what sickness has Socrates been cured of in the period before his death if these words do not refer to existence as such? The answer, according to Dumézil, is *aphrôn* or sickness of the spirit.

The sickness that assails Socrates in prison is the same sickness that assails Crito even more virulently. It is the sickness of bad judgment, which leads Crito to suggest to Socrates that he should be untrue to his calling and flee Athens; the fact that Socrates feels tempted to do so means that the sickness is present in him as well. In a dream Socrates receives from the gods a confirmation of the nature of his cure, a confirmation because he has already come to the same position through the use of his own good judgment. The cure is to await his death. It is bet-

ter for him to suffer the injustice of such a false conviction than
to commit the greater injustice of violating the laws of a city
that he has accepted as his own. Hence, Socrates owes a cock to
Asclepius for being cured of the sickness *(aphrôn)* of bad judgment; his judgment, at the point of death, has been rendered
healthy, wise, or regulated *(phronimos)* again. It is important to
note that the cure he affects upon Crito and upon himself is not
due to any external agency but to his remaining true to his
vocation as philosopher: the dialogical elimination of falsity
in the pursuance of true judgment. Yet his good judgment
does, in effect, require the confirmation of an external agency.
Dumézil, in the fictional personage of Kossyphidios, argues
that:

> The sickness which destroys the body is the twin sister
> of the false opinion which corrupts the soul. Physical
> sickness cannot be treated by the ignorant multitude,
> but by the only specialist, the man Asclepius, the doc-
> tor; false opinion, which mostly stems from an unre-
> flective submission to the opinion of the multitude, can
> only be corrected by an enlightened philosophical
> judgement, founded on certain principles. It is truly a
> question of establishing the equilibrium of the spirit,
> of rendering it *phronimos*, which one could translate as
> healthy, wise, tempered: it is all one . . . *aphrôn* is the
> "sickness of the spirit." The task of philosophy, the
> mission that the Delphic oracle has confided to him
> and that his daimon has often recalled to Socrates, and
> which will not allow him to be quiet, is to transform the
> *aphrones* into *phronimoi*, in brief to cure them.[115]

With this interpretation of Socrates' last words we are a long
way from Nietzsche's premature Christianization of these
enigmatic words. Nietzsche's interpretation, however, is completely in conformity with his all-out assault on the last sociocultural form to raise a claim to universality. Through his critique of Christianity, Nietzsche comes to suspect all such
claims as being onto-theological.

Hence, if in the early period Nietzsche's interpretation of
Socrates is determined in relation to the problem of tragedy,

then in the late period it is determined in relation to that of Christianity. This shifts the field of interpretation from aesthetics to morality. Nietzsche already begins to move in such a direction in the notes of 1875, and now that move is completed. One of the famous themes of the *Genealogy* is the argument that all forms of universal morality, of which Christianity just happens to be the most significant, have their sociogenesis among the slaves or underclasses. Universal moralities are the spiritual aroma produced by their resentment. Already in 1883 Nietzsche hones in on the plebeian character of Socratic philosophy as a product of resentment.[116] "With Socrates begins the downfall of morality . . . it is the collapse of older ideals. With it comes the prevailing plebeian character, these are men without power, pushed to one side, depressed, etc.[117] The opposition that Nietzsche is constructing is the familiar one of the morality of the people *(Volks-Moralität)* and that of philosophers *(Moral-Philosophen).*[118] The complaint is also familiar from the notes of 1875: the individual-eudaemonistic character of moral philosophy—the search for happiness—is ridiculed from the standpoint of an artist's metaphysics, which praises the hardness of the creator. The project is the construction of a genealogy of modern morality that sees its origins as spreading far back beyond Christianity to Plato and even Socrates.[119] The dying Socrates was the first decadent. The reason for why such an argument can attain any plausibility is, as I have remarked before, because universality as a principle is now conceived of as the primary cause of modern decadence. "From Socrates on," Nietzsche argues, "*aretē* is incorrectly understood,—it had always first to be grounded and was not conceived of in relation to the individual, but tyrannically, 'good for all.'"[120] Here once again, unconscious practices are valued above consciously grounded principles, as are particularistic criteria over universal ones. Not for the last time in the history of philosophy is the universal identified with tyranny.

It is now not so much any *Volks-Moralität* that Nietzsche wishes to defend against the *Moral-Philosophen*, however, but his new *Philosophie des Dionysos*, which he develops continually from *Zarathustra* onward. It is not possible to document this new orientation here in all its complexity; however, Nietzsche's abandonment of the opposition between the Apollinian and the Dionysian is of importance with regard to his interpretation of Socrates. In aphorism 799 from *The Will to Power*, we read that "in the Dionysian intoxication there is sexuality and voluptuousness: they are not lacking in the Apollinian."[121] The relativization of the opposition that is implied here is confirmed in *Twilight of the Idols* where Nietzsche asks himself the question "What is the meaning of the antithetical concepts *Apollinian* and *Dionysian*, both conceived as forms of intoxication, which I introduced into aesthetics?"[122] Instead of being the opposition between dream and intoxication, both are now types of intoxication *(Arten des Rausches)*. At the end of the work itself, the opposition that now animates his philosophy is clearly articulated:

> All this is contained in the word Dionysus. . . . The profoundest instinct of life, the instinct for the future of life, for the eternity of life, in this word experienced religiously—the actual road to life, procreation, as the *sacred road.* . . . It was only Christianity, with resentment against life in its foundations, which made of sexuality something impure.[123]

Dionysos as the world-affirming form of sacred intoxication is contrasted to the world-denying form of the socially instituted form of the sacred. Instead of the criterion of universality, we are left with an "increase in the feeling of power" as the touchstone for our judgments. "The condition of pleasure called intoxication *(Rausch)*," Nietzsche argues, "is precisely an exalted feeling of power *(das Gefühl der Kraftsteigerung und Fülle)*."[124] There is a deliberate category mistake, to speak the language of analytical philosophy, in Nietzsche's collapsing of aesthetic (beautiful/ugly), moral (good/evil), and cognitive (truth/illusion) categories into that of an enhancement or diminution of the feeling of power. Hence, beauty is a sign of enhanced strength and ugliness of diminished strength. "Ugliness," Nietzsche argues, "signifies the decadence of a type, contradiction and co-ordination between the inner—signifies a decline in organizing strength, in will, to speak psychologically."[125] The celebrated Socratic ugliness, which is a historical fact, is not an irrelevant fact for Nietzsche. It is an aesthetic, a moral, and an epistemological judgment.

Throughout the notes of 1884 and 1885 the themes that surface in the chapter on the problem of Socrates are prepared. Socrates as *Pöbel, schlau* (sly), *plebjisch, häßlich* (ugly)—these epithets appear for the first time in Nietzsche's interpretation of Socrates. The opposition between the Socratic and the noble revolves around the attempt of the former through dialectics to provide reasons for actions, whereas for the latter virtue remains without a 'why'. "Socrates: the common man: sly: who became master of himself through clear intellectualism *(Verstand)* and forceful will: humour of the victorious: always noting in his conversation with the nobility that they could not say *why* (it belongs to nobility that virtues are without a why? They acted thus—)."[126] In this context science loses its purity and is unmasked as a form of hypocrisy by Nietzsche, who views it as a means of revenge *(Rache)* used by the plebeian Socrates against the nobility. Hence, "the dialectic is plebeian by origin *(ihrer Herkunft nach)*."[127] With the Socratic infiltration of "the sickness of moralising into science," real science, as practiced by Democritus, Hippocrates, and Thucydides, whom Nietzsche constantly praises for their realism, disappears.[128] The hostility toward Socrates reaches its climax in the accusation that his condemnation to death concealed his own will to death *(Willen zum Tode)*, and that he, therefore, unnecessarily brought a slander upon his country. "Even more egoist than patriot," claims Nietzsche.[129] The accusation of plebeian cunning directed against Socrates is also a blow delivered by Nietzsche against the celebrated Socratic irony, which now loses all its playfulness. "The cunning self-deprecation of Socrates, which served to render his opponent guileless, so that he said what he thought: a trick *(Kunstgriff)* of the man of the rabble! Logic was not at home in Athens."[130] "The wonder of Socrates," Nietzsche argues, "was that he had one soul and behind that still another and behind that still another."[131] "The masterpiece of his art of seduction" was "the conversion of Plato."[132] The conversion, in other words, changed the man of noble origin into a purveyor of the tricks of the man of the rabble. The dying Socrates was the cultic fetish object of Athenian youth.

Even if he could not be accused of corrupting the youth during his lifetime, through his death the accusation found its mark. Only one art *(Kunst)* is accorded to Socrates by Nietzsche— the art of moralizing deception.

During the period between 1884 and 1885, however, the accusation of decadence *(décadence* rather than *Verfall)* is not leveled against Socrates, even though Nietzsche now constantly asserts the superiority of the pre-Socratics. This is probably due to the fact that his assessment of Socrates is still marked by ambivalence. An example of this is his treatment of the problem of faith and reason in Socrates, which appears as the problem of instinct and reason. Although Nietzsche argues that "Socrates had placed himself naively on the side of reason," he further asserts "that he had still basically followed all moral instincts, only with a false motivation: as if the motive came from reason."[133] The paradoxical vision of a Socrates who judges rightly, but not through right reason, is what separates still Nietzsche's vision of Socrates from Plato, who consciously wants to unify reason and instinct, reason and action. Hence, Plato and Christianity are still placed to one side, the side of unfreedom, and Socrates to another.[134]

In the main published works of 1886 and 1887, *Beyond Good and Evil* and the *Genealogy*, as well as in the notes, the main tone is also one of ambivalence. What is at stake here is a critique of Christianity, which is conceived of as a critique of truth that is posited as being. This is a Platonic invention, and Christianity is, as Nietzsche puts it in the preface to *Beyond Good and Evil*, "a platonism for 'the people.'"[135] The argument is put most fully in the *Genealogy*, where Nietzsche quotes from his own fifth book of *The Gay Science*, published also in 1887:

> The truthful man, in the audacious and ultimate sense presupposed by the faith in science, thereby *affirms another world* than that of life, nature, and history: and insofar as he affirms this "other world," does this not mean that he has to deny its antithesis, this world, our world? . . . It is still a *metaphysical faith* that underlies our faith in science—and we men of knowledge of today, we godless men and anti-metaphysicians, we

too, still derive our flame from the fire ignited by a faith millennia old, the Christian faith, which was also Plato's, that god is truth, that truth is *divine (dass Gott die Warheit, dass die Wahrheit göttlich ist).*[136]

Rather than any unification of faith and reason under the dominance of reason, this argument underlines the split between faith and reason itself. Reason, like the Freudian ego, is no longer master *(Herr)* in its own house. As Nietzsche concludes:

> Because the ascetic ideal has hitherto *dominated* all philosophy *(über all Philosophie bisher Herr war)*, because truth was posited as being, as God, as the highest court of appeal *(oberste Instanz)*—because truth was not "permitted" to be a problem at all, is this "permitted" understood?—From the moment that faith in this ascetic ideal is denied, a *new problem arises*: that of the *value* of truth *(vom Werthe der Wahrheit).*[137]

If truth is no longer being—that is, if the question of truth can no longer be struck in a metaphysical register—then what is the status of the discourse in which the value *(Werthe)* of truth can be raised? Heidegger has argued that "value and the valuable have become the positivist substitute for the metaphysical."[138] We know, of course, that for Nietzsche what stands behind values is the will to power, the will to preserve, affirm, and enhance life. Thus, instead of retaining their status as an independent realm, values also seem to undergo a reduction to will that cannot escape the Heideggerian accusation of positivism. In this context, the Nietzschean view of the Socratic concept of truth, which does not equate truth with being as an independent realm but sees it as the dialectical result of a process of communication that is in principle interminable, is initially looked upon with favor. But the more Socrates is looked upon as making the Platonic position possible by elevating moral values into the highest form of values, the more he falls into Nietzsche's disfavor.

In *Beyond Good and Evil*, therefore, Nietzsche is remarkably positive toward Socrates. His ambivalence toward Socrates is present, but the hostility of the notes of 1884-1885 is not. In section 191 Nietzsche develops the opposition between reason and instinct or faith alluded to at the end of the penultimate paragraph. Socrates is looked upon here as the dialectician who outwits himself. As a dialectician, he takes the side of reason against instinct. In this he is at odds with the Athenian nobility who do not ask themselves, "Why?"; however, Socratic self-questioning is reflective enough to question the power of reasoning itself. Dialectics outwits itself in thinking past its own limits. Hence, the falsity of Socratic irony for Nietzsche is that it compels reason to aid the instincts with good arguments. Socrates is still not viewed as a symptom of decadence for Nietzsche, because the instincts are still given their due. When the instincts become faith and when faith and reason are seen as inexorably leading to the same goal, only then does the herd triumph in the form of Platonic-Christianity.[139] Socrates is not yet part of the herd; and Nietzsche argues that at a time when the Athenian nobility were themselves showing signs of decay, the plebeian gadfly had a prophylactic effect. Nietzsche argues that "in the age of Socrates, among men of nothing but wearied instinct, among conservative ancient Athenians who had let themselves go . . . *irony* was perhaps required for greatness of soul, that Socratic malicious certitude of the old physician and plebeian who cut remorselessly into his own flesh as he did into the flesh and heart of the 'noble,' with a look that said dinstinctly enough: 'do not dissemble before me! here—we are equal!'"[140] Nietzsche immediately adds that in an age of equality like our own, the attack upon the noble can have no such prophylactic effect of enlivening weakening instincts.

In the notes of 1886 to 1887, which were published in part in *The Will to Power*, the critique of morals, which was intensified in the *Genealogy*, is carried through and begins to alter Nietzsche's portrait of Socrates. The predominance of morality is increasingly interpreted as a form of domination that casts its shadow over the entire history of the West. The will to power as morality is seen as a symptom of decadence. Instead of viewing Socrates ambivalently by making Platonic-Christianity the real historical turning point, Nietzsche takes another approach; Socrates now becomes, as Nietzsche puts it in 1888, "a moment of deepest peversity in the history of mankind."[141] The equation of the good and the true as a moral movement prepares the way for the postulation of truth as being. "The common factor in the history of Europe since *Socrates*," Nietzsche now argues, "is the attempt to make moral values dominate overall other values."[142] The drive for improvement *(besser-werden)* is led by the regressive instincts of the herd, the suffering, the underprivileged, and the mediocre. In many ways this is, as I mentioned earlier, the radical completion of Nietzsche's earlier thought that only as aesthetic phenomena are existence and the world fully justified. The emergence of the ethical in the person of Socrates, which Nietzsche now constantly ties in with both the physical ugliness and common origins of Socrates, is seen as that which has historically stymied the development of the culturally creative force of intoxication. From Socrates to Kant, the essential history of the West has been a lie shaped in the crucible of morality. Hence, Nietzsche asks himself "whether all hitherto specifically moral movements were not symptoms of decadence?"[143]

The corollary of the amount of value (and given that value is a term that stems from political economy, one can speak of amount)[144] that Nietzsche accords to the aesthetic is the simultaneous disinvestment of value that is accorded to the moral. The inflation of the aesthetic causes a run on the moral. "There are no moral facts whatever," Nietzsche argues; "morality is only an interpretation *(Ausdeutung)* of certain phenomena, more precisely a *mis*interpretation *(Misdeutung)*."[145] The only value that the moral retains is a semiotic *(Semiotik)* one; it provides us with the raw material for a symptomatology *(Symptomatologie)* of cultures and forms of inwardness *(Innerlichkeit)*. The moral, having lost its value as currency, has immense value still for the numismatist who delights in deciphering debased coinage. Despite the many things that Nietzsche says concerning Socrates in 1888, both in the chapter on the problem of Socrates and in the notes, what stands out as both novel and central is Nietzsche's attack on the morality of improvement or self-mastery *(enkrateia)* that he now reads into the figure of Socrates. The key note that probably encapsulates best Nietzsche's late attitude toward Socrates was written in the spring of 1888. "The struggle against Socrates, Plato, and all the Socratic schools is rooted deep in the instinct," according to Nietzsche, "that one does not make mankind *better (besser)*, if one presents virtue to him as provable and as calling for reasons *(gründefordernd)*."[146] This drive to betterment through morality is anti-Greek for Nietzsche, whereas the sophists and the pre-Socratics represent authentic Greek philosophy. Nietzsche even flippantly suggests that perhaps Socrates and Plato were Jews. For Nietzsche, of course, the improving of mankind is in reality a form of training and taming that weakens the instincts; hence, all forms of philosophy and religion that further this process are decadent. The forms that elevate reason over instinct, spirit over the body all operate on the principle of withdrawing all value from that which is unconscious and investing it in the conscious. "The progress toward the *better (Besseren)* can only be a progress *in becoming conscious (im Bewußt werden)*."[147] Nietzsche now fully identifies Socrates with this principle, and the virulence of his criticism increases as a consequence.

But the distance even now between the two is not absolute. At the beginning of *Twilight of the Idols*, Nietzsche refers to himself as "an old psychologist and pied piper *(Rattenfänger)*."[148] He had earlier referred to Socrates as the "pied piper of Athens," so there remains a residual identification between the one who wants to sound out idols and the one who seduces youth. The skeptical suspension of Socratic dialectic still holds an attraction for Nietzsche; however, the main argument of "The Problem of Socrates" is that Socrates was one who denied life, and hence, he was a declining type *(Niedergangs-Typ)* and symptom of decay *(Verfalls-Symptom)*. After arguments that point back to *Gay Science* and *The Birth of Tragedy*, Nietzsche argues that the famous Socratic ugliness is both a sign of thwarted development produced by inter-breeding and also a sign of criminality and decadence. Unlike Hegel, however, Nietzsche does not interpret Socrates' criminality as an act in a struggle that leads to moral progress but as an unequivocal act of moral rebellion and moral regression. The argument that runs through the chapter is, therefore, that the foreclosure of the instincts that the philosophical

(and the religious) operation perform leads to the displacement of the instincts into one or another of the ideal forms
(idols), which embody that instinct in such a twisted,
thwarted, and ugly fashion that these forms themselves can
only be described as perverse or decadent. Hence, all that is
left to investigate are the symptoms (a Symptomatologie) of
declining life that the philosophical elevation of consciousness, reason, and morality into idols represents. Decadence
not only goes together with ugliness but also with the comic.
Here, as elsewhere, Nietzsche separates the tragic from the
comic conviction, because for Nietzsche the Socratic conviction has become a symptom of the comic par excellence.
"Everything is over-driven, eccentric, caricatural in Socrates, a
buffo (buffo), with the instinct of a Voltaire in love."[149]
"Socrates was the buffoon (Hanswurst) who got himself taken
seriously."[150] Or, to quote from the end of the book where the
argument is put in its fullness:

> But the philosophers are the decadents of Hellenism,
> the counter-movement against the old, the noble taste
> (—against the agonal instinct, against the polis, against
> the value of the race, against the authority of tradi-
> tion). The Socratic virtues were preached because the
> Greeks had lost them: excitable, timid, fickle, comedi-
> ans every one, they had more than enough reason to
> let morality be preached to them.[151]

Socrates is a comedian among his own kind, and hence, he
was taken seriously. If the old instincts of the Greeks had still
prevailed, then Socrates would have been laughed at. The
question, however, is what did he offer to his countrymen that
they now had need of? And why did they need it?

Nietzsche's answers to these questions rest on the plausible
assumption that the displacement of instincts that occurs in
declining types or in decadent cultural forms like philosophy is
no historical accident. The Socratic notions of self-mastery and
rationality, which are at the core of his teaching, were a
response to a state of emergency in which a civil war had broken out between the instincts. What Socrates had understood is
that:

all the world had need of him—his expedient, his cure, his personal art of self-preservation *(Selbst-Erhaltung)*. . . . Everywhere the instincts were in anarchy; everywhere people were but five steps from excess: the *monstrum in animo* was the universal danger. "The instincts want to play the tyrant: we must devise a *counter-tyrant* who is stronger. . . ." When that physiognomist had revealed to Socrates what he was, a cave of every evil lust, the great ironist uttered a phrase that is the key to him. "That is true," he said, "but I have become master of them all *(über alle Herr)*." How did Socrates become master of *himself (über sich Herr)?*[152]

This is a development of Nietzsche's earlier argument concerning the timeliness of Socratic irony: the decay of the nobility required such a cure. Here, however, the emphasis is more on the poisonous, rather than the curative, properties of such a *pharmakon*. Reason, as a countertyrant, has all the symptoms of a hysteric. The cure turns out to be another kind of sickness:

The moralism of the Greek philosophers from Plato downwards is pathologically conditioned: likewise their estimation of dialectics. Reason=virtue=happiness means merely: one must imitate Socrates and counter the dark desires by producing a permanent *daylight*—the daylight of reason. One must be prudent, clear, bright, at any cost: every yielding to the instincts, to the unconscious, leads *downwards*.[153]

The severing of instinct and happiness that the Socratic equation contains is a formula for decadence, according to Nietzsche, as reason cannot reproduce at another, and higher, level the primal unity of instinct=action=happiness, which is that of tragic culture. Rationalist culture feeds off the illusion that it can restore a kind of unity to human life through reason once the tragic equation has broken down. Reason, however, misunderstands itself when it sees itself as a cure for decadence, for Nietzsche it merely alters its expression. "Socrates was a misunderstanding," Nietzsche argues; "the entire morality of improvement *(die ganze Besserungs-Moral)*, the Christian included, has been a misunderstanding."[154] Socrates is now seen as the moral-monomaniac *(Moral-Monoman)*.[155]

With this criticism Nietzsche joins together his critique of Socrates' theoreticism, which worships the "daylight," the "clarity" of reason, even more firmly with his critique of morality, which sees in the moralism of philosophy the undermining of any naturalism of morals.[156] The works of 1888 pursue the idea that morality is antinature and that nature is amoral. Whatever increases or stengthens the feeling of power is deemed to be both natural and healthy, whereas whatever enervates the instincts produces decadence. The surest instinctual forces are the unconscious, and cultures that are strong need no theoretical enlightenment as to what is right and wrong. When a culture starts to ask itself the 'why?' of its customs and practices, then decadence has already begun to set in. This is why Socrates is both a symptom and a kind of solution. He arrives at a point when the 'why?' is already beginning to be asked and distributes the questioning throughout the city of Athens. With his new intellectual weapon called dialectics, the question is not only distributed but made more intense, more troubling for the people of Athens. Hence, for Nietzsche, dialectics is not just a form of revenge by the man of the rabble against the nobility, because dialectics itself is a product of that agonal instinct that belongs to the very essence of Athenian nobility with its taste for gymnastic.[157] Socrates is a sign, a symptom of a state of emergency.[158] What solution, therefore, does he offer for this parlous condition? We know from Plato, of course, the famous Socratic saying that the unexamined life is not worth living; and it is a kind of solution, which with the exception of his early period has some attraction for Nietzsche. Nietzsche seems to say that the "superfetation of logic and the clarity of reason" as a cure for "the wildness and anarchy of instincts" might not be very good, but what other solution did the Greeks have left?[159] The solution does not posit truth as being, which is what still distinguishes Socrates from Plato, but is a product of the form of agon called dialectics. The uniqueness of the Socratic solution and of Socratic moral-monomania is that discourse, as a form of life, is productive of happiness and that happiness is inseparable from a life centered on discourse. "Logic as will to power, to self-mastery *(Selbstherrschaft)*, to 'happiness'"[160] is the highest formula of rationalist culture. As such, it commands more respect from the proponent of tragic culture than does the Platonic-Christian culture of pity, which followed it. Even if Socrates denaturalized morality, he did not irrationalize it. Nietzsche is enough of a rationalist to understand this.[161] The tension that Nietzsche posits between reason and morality, on the one hand, and power and creativity, on the other hand, is one that haunts not only his interpretation of Socrates but also his interpretation of the problem of modernity.

Conclusion

Socrates between Modernity
and Postmodernity

There is no common image of Socrates in the three nineteenth-century interpretations of the figure of Socrates that I have analyzed. Neither Hegel, Kierkegaard, nor Nietzsche takes Socrates to be a moral exemplar, on a par with Christ, in the same way he was for Renaissance thought.[1] Neither Hegel, Kierkegaard, nor Nietzsche takes Socrates to be the victim of intolerance, primarily religious in origin, in the same way he was for Enlightenment thought.[2] This is not to say, however, that there are no differences among Renaissance and Enlightenment thinkers concerning their interpretations of Socrates, only that strong lines of convergence can be drawn. Rather than searching for a common image in these three interpretations, it is more profitable to look at the central tension in modernity and how that tension expresses itself in a conflict of interpretations concerning the image of Socrates. This tension concerns the status of reason in modernity and is expressed in the conflict between the 'discourse of modernity' and its counterdiscourse.[3] The discourse of modernity assures us that after the collapse of the emphatic concept of reason, the unity of reason can still be preserved. Even if modernity is characterized by the reemergence of those old warring gods and demons *(Glaubens-mächte)* from their graves, then this does not necessarily lead to the forfeiture by reason of any right to legislate between the warring powers.[4] The counterdiscourse of modernity argues that after the collapse of the emphatic concept of reason, whose last great representative is Hegel, the shriveling-up of reason into sphere-specific rationalities, of which the most socially important is instrumental rationality, leaves thought in the dilemma of thinking after reason—hence, the reevaluation of the religious in Kierkegaard and the emphasis on the aesthetic in Nietzsche.

The discourse of modernity is, therefore, a continuation of the project of the Enlightenment, whereas the counterdiscourse of modernity has its intellectual ancestry in the romantic revolt against the Enlightenment. In this context, however, neither the Enlightenment nor romanticism is taken as a historical category. The Enlightenment as such, as Georges Gusdorf has shown, already contains the programmatic thoughts of romantic thought.[5] The thought of Rousseau is, of course, the most striking example, although he is by no means alone. The Enlightenment, however, was primarily concerned with the popularization of the new scientific world view invented in the seventeenth century. It is this aspect of the historical Enlightenment that primarily informs the modern use of the term. This means that, in many ways, the century of enlightenment was an intellectually derivative one and that the central period of European intellectual history for the discourse of modernity was the seventeenth century. It is too large a task to go into any extended discussion of what precisely the new world view entailed, so I shall merely rely on Koyré's succinct formulation that it involved both the "destruction of the cosmos" and the "geometrization of space," a mathematization of space that resulted in the "infinitization of the universe." As Koyré puts it, the world was no longer viewed as "a finite, closed, and hierarchically ordered whole," but as "an indefinite and even infinite universe which is bound together by the identity of its fundamental components and laws and in which all of these components are placed on the same level of being."[6] The transition from a cosmocentric to the modern world view resulted, therefore, in what Koyré calls "the utter devalorization of being." Furthermore, the infinite universe created by this new world view inherited, as Koyré wryly points out at the end of his work, all the ontological attributes of divinity. "Yet only these," he adds; "all the others the departed God took with him."[7]

As I remarked before, the historical Enlightenment popularized this new world view. It did so by elaborating a social mission for science and by extending its methods into the investigation of society and not merely of nature. I shall take the latter point first. Just as the world of nature had been transformed into a homogeneous and infinite space, freed from outdated values that were imposed by a closed, ontological framework, so also was the social world freed from closed, hierarchical concepts—those characteristics of the departed God that the eighteenth-century saw as having been left in the custody of the Church. After the collapse of this closed social world there were two possible directions for social theory. One was taken by eighteenth-century French materialists such as Helvetius, for whom society became the environment of man, which as the determinate factor in man's behavior became susceptible to scientific intervention. The other was taken by German idealism, for whom man was capable of making free and public use of his reason to shape his social and political world. This later view was, to some extent, a theoretical conclusion drawn from the historical experience of the social mission of the Enlightenment. Enlightenment in this sense meant the overthrowal of all accepted customs, traditions, and superstitions that could not withstand the probing criticism of the free and public use of reason. In this form, the project of Enlightenment burst the boundaries of scientific culture, to which it was confined in the seventeenth century, and became the ideology of large segments of liberal Europe. Although the two directions that I have indicated were guided by two widely divergent images of man, a heteronomous versus autonomous image respectively, both were subjected to criticism within the context of romantic thought. Romantic thought, in other words, turned not merely against the Enlightenment, definable as the subjection of the natural and social world to the power of science, but also against its completion, definable in terms of a trans-spheric power of public reason that is said to be all that is left to us in a society without a center. The thought of Hegel, Kierkegaard, and Nietzsche is marked, to varying degrees, by this romantic critique of the Enlightenment, and their respective interpretations of Socrates are shaped by the tension between these two discourses.

I

As I have tried to show, the early Hegel is directly influenced by Romantic ideas, and these help to shape his initial interpretation of Socrates. The influence of these ideas occurs in the context of Hegel's rejection of Kant's drawing of the boundaries of reason's proper employment. The Hegelian 'subject as substance', or philosophy of *Geist*, creates the foundational warrant for its own activity in the very process of its accomplishment. Reason learns to swim by throwing itself into the waters, rather than by damming the waters up to fit the circumference of its predefined displacement. Kierkegaard is also influenced by romanticism, an influence that helps to shape his hostility to Hegel. This can be seen, first, in his treatment of the concept of irony. Even as he tries to go beyond German romanticism's metaphysical irony to a form of irony as a mastered moment, irony in its negative Socratic employment is vital in the turn toward existence because of the intellectual disorientation it produces. Insofar as it unhinges Hegelianism as a system by making it impossible for the individual to live in the theoretical house that the system creates, the accent is shifted back onto the individual and his or her existential choice. It can be seen, second, in the notion of the religious with which Kierkegaard operates because it has affinities with a notion of the aesthetic in its stress on externality as compared to the immanence of ethics. His notion of the religious departs from any notion of the aesthetic, however, because of its emphasis on the radical inwardness of existential choice, a notion that is essentially a late Protestant development. Nietzsche's artist's metaphysics, despite being partially clothed in the trappings of a positivism borrowed from the natural sciences, also remains caught in the expressive individualistic strand of romanticism. All three stand opposed to key elements of Enlightenment thought: the Hegelian critique of Kant's notion of *Verstand* leads to a rehabilitation of a strong, metaphysical concept of *Vernunft*; the Kierkegaardian critique of the positivity of his age and the pallid rationalism of its ethics is an attack upon any notion of a rational morality; and, finally, the Nietzschean critique of science as the last decadent form of the ascetic ideal is a fundamental questioning of the *bios theoretikos*. There are, therefore, central counter-Enlightenment motifs in all three.

Whether this leads to antimodernism or not is another question. Hauke Brunkhorst has argued that the "paradox of romantic modernism" is that "romanticism, which begins as a critique of the instrumentalistic destruction of traditionalistic meanings, itself becomes an expressionistic destruction of traditional meanings."[8] This means that romanticism is fundamentally modern. It furthers both the differentiation of art and the erotic from moral and religious and also from cognitive and scientific demands, as well as furthers their internal differentiation. Both the internal differentiation of art and the erotic and the separation of the religious from cognitive demands is particularly clear in Kierkegaard. What is unique to Kierkegaard, however, is that the expressivistic destruction of traditional meanings occurs through an expressivistically transformed concept of the religious, which finds its opaque formulation in the phrase from the *Concluding Unscientific Postscript*: religiousness B. It is not a religiousness founded on immanently ethical principles, but one based on the immediate apprehension of the paradox. The paradox itself relates the individual to something outside himself or herself. It is this willing subjection of oneself to the heteronomous, this freeing of oneself from the demand of autonomy, that defines both the aesthetic and the religious. Of course, the God relationship demands something different from the individual than does the relationship to one's senses—namely, the hidden inwardness of the knight of faith as opposed to the dizzying freedom of the ever-changing self who uses what Kierkegaard calls the rotation method. Nevertheless, this freeing of the religious from ethical demands, which are cognitive in nature, makes the choice of the religious an aesthetically conceived act of self-assertion.

With Nietzsche, the aesthetic critique of reason is carried out more directly. In "The Three Metamorphoses" from *Thus Spake Zarathustra*, the transformation of the camel into the lion sees the birth of the opposition between the freedom of the will, symbolized by the lion, and the inherited Christian values, symbolized by the dragon. The lion, however, cannot create new values, only the freedom for new creation: "To *create* new values *(Neue Werthe schaffen)*—even the lion is incapable of that: but to create itself freedom for new creation *(aber Freiheit sich schaffen zu neuem Schaffen)*—that the might of the lion can do."[9] Enlightenment can, in other words, clear the field of dragons, but it cannot create new values. The negativity of the Enlightenment, which is something Hegel complains of from the conservative standpoint of customary authority *(Sittlichkeit)*, is criticized here from an aesthetic standpoint: its inability to create. Hence, the three metamorphoses are necessary from the standpoint of a metaphysics in which the redemption of the world is seen primarily as an aesthetic phenomenon. Nietzsche argues that "the child is innocence *(Unschuld)* and forgetfulness, a new beginning, a sport *(Spiel)*, a self-propelling wheel, a first motion, a sacred yes.—Yes, a sacred yes is needed, my brothers, for the spirit of creation *(Zum Spiele des Schaffens).*"[10] The child is that naive master of the arts of remembering and forgetting, which when perfected in adulthood enables one to play, as Kierkegaard puts it, "battledore and shuttlecock with the whole existence."[11] From *The Birth of Tragedy* onward, Nietzsche has praised forgetfulness, as a property of the Dionysian over and against the theoretical men of science who forget nothing. The gods treasure their obscurity; their power exhausts itself when subjected to the illumination of knowledge. The aesthetic becomes the other of reason when the feeling of an increase of power becomes the criterion of truth.

Kierkegaard can be accused of an expressivistic transformation of traditional meanings because of his redefinition of the religious. Nietzsche can be accused quite directly of an expressivistic destruction of traditional meanings. Hegel's critique of the instrumentalistic destruction of traditional meanings, however, issues in the expressivistic conservation of traditional meanings in the early works and a more liberal-conservative conservation of traditional meanings in the later works. What unites the two phases of his thought is the fact the emphasis throughout, from the early Hegel's project of a *Volksreligion* to the later Hegel's *Philosophy of Right*, is not as individualistic as it is for both Kierkegaard and Nietzsche. Hegel's concern is the attempt to reconcile the divisions that exist in modern civil society through recourse to some higher integration, be it a *Volksreligion* or the state. It is this emphasis on the communal dimension of social life that separates him from the asocial expressivism of romantic individualism. Hence, in the early, more romantic Hegel the project of *Volksreligion* is founded on three principles: reason, the imagination, and publicness. Here there is no one-sided emphasis upon imagination as opposed to reason as there is in Nietzsche, nor any one-sided disparagement of publicness as there is in both Kierkegaard and Nietzsche. Expressivism only turns destructive of traditional meanings when it becomes radically individualistic. Hegel's later thought does not take this turning. Instead it takes on both a more realistic and conservative character in that it is not some new imaginary construction charged with the task of reconciliation, but the actually existing institutions of the family, civil society, and the state. What these institutions are charged with reconciling is not so much reason, imagination, and publicness as reason, custom, and the split between the private and the public. The liberal in Hegel now forgoes the ancient ideal of a public *Volksreligion* through the recognition of the necessary differentiation of the three spheres with their necessarily differing levels of privacy or publicness. But the conservative in Hegel recognizes the formalism and impotence of a state based solely on abstract morality and formal law and, hence, tries to reconcile the morality of reason *(Moralität)* and the morality of mores *(Sittlichkeit)*. Whether such a construction is any less imaginary than that of a *Volksreligion* is a moot point; however, what is clear is that it represents both a more coolly modernist recognition of social differentiation and a less romantic and more conservative attempt to reconcile the conflicts generated by modernization.

II

All three thinkers share in the concerns of romanticism, although the later Hegel also shares in the concerns of conser-

vatism. For the early Hegel, Kierkegaard, and Nietzsche, therefore, the conflict between the Enlightenment and romanticism
which defines the field of tension *(Spannungsfeld)* constitutive
of our modernity is played out through an interpretation of
the figure of Socrates. In the late Hegel this field of tension is
defined by the poles of the Enlightenment and conservatism.
This does not mean, of course, that Socrates is interpreted in
any one-sided way: for example, as a specifically romantic figure. It simply means that with the disenchantment of reason in
modernity, the conflict of interpretations over the figure of
Socrates circles around the question of the authority of reason
in an epoch in which a shriveled concept of reason is increasingly attacked as deficient from both romantic and conservative positions.

In the early Hegel, Socrates is almost an Enlightenment
figure; however, given that Hegel is himself influenced by
romantic currents, he is at pains to distinguish dogmatic
instruction from the respect for the autonomy of the individual
he attributes to Socrates' teaching. Furthermore, given that
Hegel is also influenced by the Attic state and its religion, he is
at pains to point out the superiority of publicness as against
either the secrecy of magic or the privacy of a purely moral
religion—hence, the superiority in Hegel's eyes of Socrates'
life over that of a Jew or a modern. In the end, however, Hegel
places Jesus above Socrates, but only after he recognizes in the
person of Jesus the reconciling power of love that places Jesus
above both the normal prophetic model Hegel attributes to
Judaism and also the cold and formal command of the moral
law for which Hegel criticizes the Kantian philosophy. The
Socratic philosophy was not based on cold moralizing, but neither did Socrates know of love as the supplementary fulfillment of the law. In the context of Hegel's romantic transformation of morality through love, Socrates stands as an ancient
representative of the nondogmatic employment of reason in
the service of moral enlightenment. Socrates' mode of instruction could be defined, therefore, as naive enlightenment.

In the late Hegel, Socrates is introduced as a world-historical person, as the one who brings infinite subjectivity and the
freedom of self-consciousness into the world. The fate of

Socrates, however, is determined by the fact that he enters a world that is, paradoxically, not quite ready for him. I say "paradoxically" because within the context of Hegel's philosophy the world spirit is always destined to arrive on time. In this late reading, however, Socrates almost becomes the modernist proponent of *Moralität*, a kind of premature Protestant or ancient Kant who unsettles the customary order *(Sittlichkeit)* of the Attic state. From the person who merely brings out the good lying within the other through a naive *(unbefangen)* mode of instruction that facilitates the dialogue of the individual with his soul, Socrates is now seen as the person who revolutionizes the Attic state by listening to his *daimonion* and by interfering, as the meddlesome third, between the parent and child. From a romantic philosophy of the "clear and healthful milk of pure feelings," Hegel has moved to a conservative philosophy that seeks to preserve the *"Muttermilch der Sittlichkeit."* Socrates, as the modernist proponent of *Moralität*, sours the mother's milk of *Sittlichkeit*. Hegel tries, however, to remain faithful to both the freedom of subjectivity and the customary order by declaring Socrates a world-historical person who creates a new world that will survive precisely because of his death. In neither the early or the late Hegel is Socrates seen as a romantic figure; however, in the early Hegel the Socratic mode of instruction is seen to be superior to more dogmatic modes and, hence, is valued more highly by the romantic Hegel who believes, furthermore, that such naive enlightenment is perfectly in keeping with the times. The late and more conservative Hegel sees Socrates more in terms of the conflict between *Moralität* and *Sittlichkeit*, which Hegel views as being constitutive of modernity; hence, Socrates tends to be interpreted *nolens volens* as a thinker of the freedom of infinite subjectivity. Hegel interprets such a principle and the freedom of thought that it legitimates, as by definition, destructive of the closed order of value constituted by *Sittlichkeit*. In reconstructing Socrates as a proponent of such a principle, Hegel is, in a sense, reconstructing the prehistory *(Urgeschichte)* of that peculiarly modern conflict between those disintegrative aspects of reason as they emerge in the Enlightenment, which Hegel now sees in Socrates, and those naive and unreflected beliefs and customs which Hegel now believes give substance and force to social life. From a romantically conceived portrait of Socrates as a proponent of naive enlightenment, Hegel now draws a conservatively conceived portrait of a Socrates as a proponent of a form of reason destructive of naive custom.

The thought of the early Kierkegaard is influenced by German romanticism and, in particular, by the romantic concept of irony. In the Socrates interpretation of the early Kierkegaard, Socrates' position is, in the final analysis, clearly separated from romantic irony through the distinction that Kierkegaard draws between Socratic irony and metaphysical irony, and through his attempt to think of irony as a mastered moment. Nevertheless, the Kierkegaardian portrayal of the disorienting effect of Socratic irony is quite romantic and is reflected in the portrait of A in the first part of *Either/Or*. Socrates appears in Kierkegaard's early work as a kind of reflective seducer of the youth of Athens who employs dialectic as a vacuum pump to asphyxiate his interlocutors, not as a kind of naive moral instructor as he is for the early Hegel. Socrates is the existential thinker who chooses his way of life, a life of constant engagement in intellectual experimentation. Socrates is, in effect, so close to Kierkegaard that he feels compelled to recoil in horror before such a mentor and to rail, as a consequence, at the negativity of irony. Hence, Kierkegaard counterpoises Socrates as the cannibalizer of concepts to the power of reconciliation contained in Christianity. As it does for Hegel, such a position leads to the commendation of Aristophanes' image of Socrates as one who dwells in the clouds of dangerous speculation. Unlike Hegel, however, Kierkegaard does not fall back onto a conservative defence of *Sittlichkeit* but remains true to his romantic critique of Hegelianism as a system by insisting on the ineliminable element of existential choice of one's life conduct in modernity. The subject chooses himself or herself in the absence of the voice of reason for a form of life that may even be hostile to reason. Such is one of the paradoxes of romantic modernism.

Kierkegaard's identification of Christian faith with the asystematic dialectician in the *Concluding Unscientific Postscript* is, at first sight, puzzling. Why has dialectics lost its destructive character? The answer lies, to a large extent, in Kierkegaard's reaction against the system and its exclusion, as he sees it, of the subject and ethics. Dialectic is not simply an intellectual method but a style of life in which thinking lives. Kierkegaard argues that "most systematizers in relation to their systems are like a man who builds an enormous castle and lives alongside it in a shed; they themselves do not live in the enormous systematic building. But in the realm of mind or spirit, this nonresidence is and remains a decisive objection. Dialectically understood, a man's thoughts must be in the building in which he lives—otherwise the whole thing is deranged."[12] The notion of an existential, as opposed to a speculative, thinker is definable in terms of a person who is at home with his or her thoughts. This is the task of thinking after philosophy—that is, after the collapse of the metaphysical concept of reason. Hence, even if what separates the knight of faith from Socrates is the fact that the teleological suspension of the ethical (that is, a relationship with something higher than that of the universal) is only possible for the former, then what draws them together is precisely the intimate relationship between thinking and being. After Hegel, truth is determined in relation to existence and not the system. Hence, Kierkegaard's Socrates, *qua* existential thinker, can ultimately be seen as an analogue to faith. Insofar as the accent of Kierkegaard's interpretation falls on either the notion of dialectical asphyxiation or existential thinking, it is a more romantic Socrates than is portrayed in the interpretation of Hegel. The antisystematic impulse in Kierkegaard when aligned with his very Protestant reading of Christianity, which places faith above that devil's whore that Luther calls reason, further supports such a conclusion.

With Nietzsche, the romantic motif of creativity is erected into a metaphysics that replaces any and all metaphysics that privilege reason. In opposition to the attempt to view the world as an aesthetic phenomenon stands the figure of Socrates, interpreted unambiguously as the theoretical man par excellence. The identification of the unconscious with the creative and the Socratic unconscious, *qua daimonion*, with the critical makes knowledge the enemy of the aesthetic. In the figure of Socrates Nietzsche reads the *Urgeschichte* of theory as an objectifying mechanism that underlies modern science and that stands counterpoised to the unity of individuation and intoxication, which he sees as embodied in Greek tragedy. Socrates becomes, therefore, the Enlightenment figure who in shaping the dramaturgy of Euripides destroys the ancient Greek tragedy. Despite this attack upon the theoretical, Nietzsche remains attracted to the skepticism embedded in the *bios theoretikos*, a skepticism that comes to the fore in the middle period but in fact is never far from him. In the late Nietzsche the confrontation with Christianity is central, and it shapes his interpretation of both ancient society and thought accordingly. Christianity's genealogy is pushed further and further back into the Greek world until Socrates himself is implicated in its moral-monomania. But the ambivalence that marks Nietzsche's interpretation of Socrates does not quite leave him, for even here Socrates is viewed as a brake, a necessary prophylactic, who halts the further slide of Greek culture in the period of its decadence. In the late Nietzsche, therefore, the image of Socrates shifts from being one of the theoretical enemy of the view of the world as an aesthetic phenomenon to being one of its moral enemies. What unites these two views of Socrates is Nietzsche's construction of Socrates as the proponent par excellence of truth as the higher value, a view that is anathema from the standpoint of Nietzsche's totalistic and romantic critique of reason.

What Nietzsche says of Socrates could apply to all three thinkers—namely, that he stands so near to them that they are always fighting with him. The reason for this, I have suggested, is that the central problem of reason in modernity, which centers upon the sundering of the integrity of reason into divergent spheric rationalities, puts into question key elements of the Western philosophical tradition as represented by Socrates. Socrates as the mythical embodiment of the *bios theoretikos* illustrates that unity of life-conduct and philosophical practice that made the life of reason more than simply a metaphor and that is now no longer possible in modernity. Of course, the decline in the charisma of reason that Enlightenment thinking furthers is not reversed by romantic thought in the course of the nineteenth century, although the thought of

Hegel comes close to it in his stress on the reconciling power of *Vernunft* as opposed to the divisive power of *Verstand*. This romantic motif in Hegel increasingly gives way to a conservative motif, however, which sees the decline in the authority of *Sitten* as the central problem of modernity. Socrates becomes, in this later context, the protagonist of that sphere-specific rationality that underlies morality. Trans-spheric power is now accorded to *Sitten* and not to *Vernunft*. In the more unambiguously romantic and modernist thought of Kierkegaard no trans-spheric power is accorded even to the religious. Instead, the attack upon the shriveling-up of the concept of reason takes the form of an insistence upon the existential character of thinking. This is what saves Kierkegaard's decision for the religious from the charge of irrationalism. It may not be rationally groundable, but the leap of faith is a product of thinking. This leap finds its analogue in the *bios theoretikos* of Socrates. In the context of Nietzsche's aestheticized metaphysics, the attempt to construe the aesthetic phenomenon, called simply intoxication in the late Nietzsche, as the redemptive power leads not merely to an assault upon the Enlightenment's shriveled-up concept of reason, but toward an *Urgeschichte* of the theoretical attitude itself as the embodiment of the *proton pseudos*. Socrates as the first proponent of the *bios theoretikos* becomes, therefore, the originator of this lie.

It is these tensions between the Enlightenment and romanticism, as well as between the Enlightenment and conservatism, that define the fields within which the interpretation of Socrates takes place. If no unitary interpretation of the figure of Socrates has emerged, then this is due to the fact that the tensions constitutive of modernity make possible only an irreducible and unresolvable conflict of interpretations. The fascination of modern thinkers with Socrates is, therefore, determined by this very irreducibility. The centrality of interpretation in modernity, which is due to its irremediably pluralistic character, turns Socrates into the hermeneutical figure par excellence. As a thinker whose thought exists only as interpretation, the task of interpretation is doubly reflected. As a thinker whose thought is governed by the concepts of dialectic and *daimonion*, the task of interpretation hinges on the question of the status of reason in human life. All three thinkers that I have discussed are, in various ways, engaged in a critique of universalistic ethics, either from the standpoint of *Sittlichkeit*, or from the standpoint of the ethical decision, or from the standpoint of an artist's metaphysics. Each standpoint corresponds to a differing assessment of the main pathology of modernity. For Hegel, it is the breakdown of customary authority. For Kierkegaard, it is the impossibility of faith. For Nietzsche, it is the generalized collapse of moral values. Their differing standpoints and diagnoses of modernity are also reflected in the differing concepts of truth with which they operate. For Hegel, truth is both absolute and a product of historical development. For Kierkegaard, subjectivity is truth. For Nietzsche, truth is reducible to the will to power or is, rather, an interpretation that corresponds to a particular configuration of power (*Herrschaftsgebilde*). This shift away from strongly universalistic positions in favor of antiuniversalistic ones, which may or may not be relativistic, is indicative of the polytheistic or hermeneutical character of modernity. The fact that this shift occurs through reflection and not naively is also indicative of the modernity of these thinkers. In all three thinkers, therefore, the difference between universalistic and antiuniversalistic positions is thought through to its completion.

III

The question of universalism versus particularism is one that is still very much alive, even though it takes vastly different forms in contemporary thought. The postmodern turn in contemporary thought can be thought of as a threefold critique of the notion of history as progress or liberation, of the notion of reason as uniform and universal, and the notion of modern society as involving the strict differentiation of cultural spheres. What concerns us here is, of course, the critique of the notion of reason. What is remarkable about modern debates concerning reason is that it is, once again, the emblematic figure of Socrates that emerges as an interpretative knot. Of course, no one any longer believes in the substantive notion of reason that was handed down to us in the metaphysical tradition. Hence, we tend to talk these days in terms of rationality and to construct typologies of rationality, such as that of Weber's between substantive versus formal rationality. The postmodernist turn in contemporary thought, however, would like to get rid of the notion of rationality as well, due to what it sees as the inevitably disputatious and contextually bound nature of any truth claim. The field of contemporary thinking about reason and rationality divides up into those who want to retain a weak, procedural unity for reason and those for whom the critique of identity thinking is employed as a kind of radical hermeneutics that demonstrates the arbitrary and contextual nature of all conceptual distinctions. What I would like to do now is to show how this field of tensions can be reconstructed through a comparative analysis of the interpretations of the figure of Socrates as they appear in the work of Apel and Derrida.[13] In this context, the work of Apel and Derrida is construed more broadly both as representative of wider schools or trends, such as discourse theory and deconstruction, and as examples of modernist and postmodernist theorizing respectively. Deconstruction is the inheritor, *inter alia*, of the Heideggerian destruction of the *logos*. Discourse theory seeks to reconstruct the presuppositions of rational argumentation as such. In sum, the former puts into question what the latter seeks to firmly ground—namely, the linkage between reason and speech. The former can be said to be postmodernist insofar as it only wants to listen to reason through the plurality of its voices, whereas the latter seeks to grant a weak procedural unity to the modern notion of rationality.

Derrida's philosophy is a philosophy of *différance*. "*Différance*," he argues, "is the non-full, non-simple, structured and differentiating origins of differences. Thus, the name 'origin' no longer suits it."[14] What Derrida is arguing against with this definition of *différance* is the metaphysics of presence, of the determination of being as presence *(Anwesenheit)*, as full, simple, and originary presence, in Occidental metaphysics. What Derrida is arguing for is a generative but nonunitary principle that gives rise to other differences or system of differences. As such, it is capable, as Derrida puts it, of "non-synonymous substitutions" such as "*archē-écriture*," or more importantly in this context, the *pharmakon*.[15] What I would like to point out here is one consequence of the erection of *différance* into, as Frank has rightly argued, a transcendental principle.[16] This is the fact that *différance* or *archē-écriture* as a transcendental principle generates the opposition between language and speech in which language, as a system of differences, has priority over a speaking subject that can no longer be thought of in terms of self-presence. Hence, speech is subordinated to language, and language is subordinated to what Derrida calls "a kind of writing before the letter."[17] What should be noted at this point is that this erection of *archē-écriture* into a transcendental principle feeds off the empirical concept of writing that it otherwise wants to cut itself off from as a writing before the letter. What also needs to be noted is that this interpretation of Derrida's philosophy as a species of transcendentalism has been subjected to criticism. In the work of Rorty, for example, the distinction between an early and late Derrida enables Rorty to both admit the cogency of this interpretation while at the same time arguing that Derrida has gone beyond his own earlier style of philosophizing.[18] According to Rorty, Derrida's ironist theorizing turns inevitably into fantasizing. The text that Rorty pins his interpretation on is *Envois*. There does not seem much doubt that this text does lead in the direction of what I would call a radical hermeneutics, wherein the context of the interpretative act becomes a fundamentally privatized space. Derrida's conceptual inventiveness, however, remains dependent upon the notion of a prior indetermination, which remains a constant theme in his *oeovre*. Thus, the notion of *démocratie* includes both the moment of *de fait* and *à venir*, and the notion of *jetty* that of *destabilization* and *stabilization*.[19] There is nothing particularly new and nothing that indicates a radical rejection of his earlier work in this kind of philosophizing. Furthermore, Rorty seems to miss what Derrida now considers to be of central importance to deconstruction—that is, its ability to question institutional structures. If there is a turn toward private fantasy in the late Derrida, then it is one that is complemented by a new type of political engagement.

Apel's philosophy is centered on the notion of discourse

ethics. In his *Diskurs und Verantwortung*, Apel argues that since his early work he has taken his ideas for a discourse ethics in basically two directions.[20] The first direction appears to be a continuation of his work and leads in the direction of a transcendental pragmatics. Its task is to establish the fundamental presuppositions that must underly any rational ethics. The second direction follows from Apel's self-criticism of what he now considers to be the main shortcoming of his earlier work. He formulates this shortcoming as one of assuming that the problem of the application of moral norms is one that can be simply solved by the application of discourse ethics to any historically concrete context. In other words, Apel argues that by making the *a priori* of the communication community something that is counterfactually anticipated, he spirits away the thorny problem of the nonidentity or "*Differenz*," as he puts it, "between real and ideal conditions of the application of the communication ethic."[21] This new distinction makes necessary the second direction that his work has taken: namely, the construction of an ethics of responsibility as an answer to the problem of the application of discourse ethics in a historical context. This involves, *inter alia*, a critical transformation of the work of Piaget and Kohlberg. The more purely post-Kantian approach of the early Apel that seeks to reconstruct the formal-pragmatic preconditions of an ethics of communication or discourse has now, therefore, been complemented by a quasi-Hegelian concern with the historical applicability of procedural norms. As Apel points out, the current situation of discourse ethics parallels that of the post-Socratic moment in the Greek Enlightenment and the post-Kantian moment in the German Enlightenment. Although Apel admits the force of the later Plato's rejection of the "critical *Logos-Principle* of Socrates," however, he does not accept as a potential alternative "the Platonic paradigm of the re-construction of 'substantive moral custom' in the form of a utopian state."[22] And although Habermas admits the force of the early Hegel's objections to the formalism, abstract universalism, impotence, and ahistoricism of Kantian ethics, he also rejects any substantivist solution that would alleviate the burden of moral responsibility that the politically active citizen must bear.[23]

Whereas formal pragmatics sets out to show how both truth claims and normative claims can be discursively redeemed, and that one can not deny the possibility of such a discursive redemption without falling into a performative contradiction, deconstruction construes this attempt to finally ground the rationality of knowledge and morality in a theory of communication as yet another species of logocentrism. Hence, as against the idea of the validation of claims through a form of argumentation that adheres to the fundamental norms of discourse, deconstruction underscores the impossibility of any final determination of a procedure for the production of truth. Furthermore, as against the touchstone of consensus as a way out of the dilemmas of the representational theory of truth, which discourse theory would agree remains tightly bound to the philosophy of consciousness, deconstruction underscores the improbability of consensus and multiplies the deconstruction of those framings through which truth is to be produced. Whereas discourse theory's response to the disenchantment of reason has been the development of a communications-theoretical analysis of types of rationality, deconstruction has responded by an endless repetition of the interment of the old bones. Deconstruction is bewitched by the magic of reason that it seeks to deconstruct insofar as it sees its task as one of multiplying the demonstrations of the impossibility of identity thinking by showing how all our inherited concepts can never fully exclude what is other than them. The critique of logocentrism leads to a radically contingent and indeterminant contextualization of interpretation. From Apel's point of view, Derrida's work is a continuation of the powerful nineteenth-century current of *Historismus-Relativismus* that includes both Nietzsche and Heidegger. Apel sees this current as resulting in a case of *Logos-Vergessenheit*. The *logos* that has been forgotten is not that of the *Gestell* or instrumental reason or what Derrida has recently called the "principle of reason," but the "logos of discursive understanding which is laid down in speech."[24] I do not want to proceed here any longer with this critical juxtaposition of the two paradigms. Let me simply indicate the fact that Apel reads Socrates as a representative of the logos of discursive understanding, whereas Derrida bases his interpretation of Socrates on the refutation of the Nietzschean remark that Socrates is "he who does not write."

IV

There are two main texts by Derrida in which he tackles the Socrates problem. The first is *Plato's Pharmacy*, which is found in *Dissemination*, and the other is *Envois* from *The Post Card*. In *Plato's Pharmacy* it is the concept of *pharmakon* or drug that functions as the nonsynonymous substitution for the concept of *différance*, whereas in *The Post Card* it is the concept of *poste*. In both cases Derrida exploits the semantic ambiguity of the concepts themselves to elaborate his philosophy of differing and deferral. In both cases Derrida is also engaged in a deconstruction of the metaphysics of presence, from its logocentric beginnings to the end of the era of postal rationalism. The specific target of *Plato's Pharmacy* is, of course, Plato's critique of writing. The work is lodged, therefore, in that peculiarly Nietzschean attempt at a reversal of Platonism. In particular, what Derrida wants to reverse is the Platonic dismissal of writing as poison for which speech is the cure, along with all the logocentric oppositions that are bound up with this initial distinction. He does so by showing the inescapably dual character of *pharmakon* as poison and remedy. What Derrida finally concludes is that the essence of the *pharmakon* is to have no essence—that it is, as he puts it, "aneidetic." Indeed, rather that being a thing at all, it is a medium or, to be more precise, a prior medium. "It is," as Derrida puts it, "the prior medium in which differentiation in general is produced, along with the opposition between the *eidos* and its other; this medium is *analogous* to the one that will, subsequent to and according to the decision of philosophy, be reserved for transcendental imagination."[25] The analogy drawn here between the notion of the *pharmakon* and the transcendental imagination links Derrida's philosophy of *différance*, of which the notion of the *pharmakon* is yet another nonsynonymous substitution, back to the Heideggerian interpretation of Kant. For Heidegger, Kant's notion of the transcendental imagination is a productive, and not a reproductive, notion of the imagination.[26] The formative or creative aspect of the imagination lies in both its horizon-constituting and in its image-furnishing capacity. The imagination constitutes both the temporality of the horizon itself and the images that both anticipate and constitute concepts as such. The notion of the imagination as a *facultas formandi* in Kant is one that is, according to Heidegger, originally constitutive both of time itself and of the very possibility of forming a concept. Derrida's work is a set of variations on the theme of the transcendental imagination. It is able to constitute itself as such by jettisoning the ontological implications of the notion of the transcendental imagination and by radically contextualizing the productive nature of the transcendental imagination—hence, the infinite number of variations that Derrida plays around the theme of *différance*, of which the *pharmakon* and the *poste* are but two.

The figure of Socrates is interpreted by Derrida through the notion of the *pharmakon* as yet another imaginary variation on the formative capacity of the transcendental imagination, which in the work of Derrida does not so much exist as a *facultas formandi* but as a series of formative contexts. What interests Derrida about the figure of Socrates and what he restages in *Plato's Pharmacy* is not the trial of Socrates, which haunts Hegel, but the trial of writing. Yet according to Derrida, Plato reconstructs the death of Socrates as an accusation against the indictment—the *graphē*—which was to cause his death. The sophists are the logographers or graphocrats who champion the written word over the spoken, whereas Socrates defends the spoken word against the *pharmakon* of writing. The Platonic text creates a whole series of oppositions dealing with the split between discourse and writing. For example, the city is associated with speech, whereas the countryside is associated with writing; that writing is appropriate for myth, but dialectics requires *logos*; that *logos* itself occupies the paternal position, whereas writing involves the absence of the father; that writing is associated with death or the breathless sign, whereas the *logos* is *pneuma* or the living voice; that the god of writing must also be the god of death whose authority must necessarily be secondary to the king who is the father of speech; and, most important, that writing and speech are related to each other as dead is to living *logos* or as rememorization is to living memory. The latter distinction determines writing as both external and dangerous, for it effects live memory while merely pretending to supplement it. As a *pharmakon*, writing becomes a dangerous supplement in the text of Plato.

The Socrates that appears in the text of Plato seems, therefore, to be a Socrates for whom the *logos* is identified with word and truth. Derrida, however, points to the existence of a wild *logos*, a *logos* that possesses all the indeterminacy of a *pharmakon*. This other *logos* can also be seen represented in the text of Plato by the figure of Socrates. Socrates is a *pharmakeus* or magician. He is the person who engages in sorcery, who bewitches other people, who is a piper, who is venomous, who numbs one like a sting ray, and who is, in sum, a wizard or *pharmakeus*. It is no longer a case of *logos* against *pharmakeus*, but of the Socratic *pharmakon* versus the sophistic *pharmakon*. What is in question here is, as in other romantic interpretations of Socrates, the status of irony. According to Derrida, "Socratic irony precipitates out one *pharmakon* by bringing it into contact with another *pharmakon*. Or rather, it reverses the *pharmakon*'s powers and turns *its* surface over . . . through the fact that the *pharmakon* properly consists in a certain . . . non-identity-with-itself always allowing it to be turned against itself."[27] The *pharmakon* as the identity of identity and non-identity generates what is non-identical to itself from within itself. Derrida argues that Socrates's taking of the hemlock, which is always referred to as a *pharmakon*, illustrates perfectly this capacity of the *pharmakon* to be turned against itself and made over into a remedy. "Although it is presented as a poison," Derrida argues that the *pharmakon* is "transformed through the effects of the Socratic logos and of the philosophical demonstration of the *Phaedo*, into a means of deliverance . . . it initiates one into the contemplation of the *eidos* and the immortality of the soul."[28] The *logos* is not, therefore, opposed to the *pharmakon* but is inscribed as remedy in what Derrida calls "*the general alogical economy of the pharmakon.*"[29] We are here once again back to the transcendental structure of the *pharmakon* as the identity of nonidentity (poison) and identity (remedy).

Derrida's answer to the question as to why the Athenians brought Socrates to trial is lodged, as I remarked earlier, in the question of the trial of writing. It is, therefore, lodged in the transcendental structure of the concept of *pharmakon*. It is, furthermore, implicated in the birth of philosophy. It involves the expulsion of the outside that is within, or of the nonidentical from the identical. This is an expulsion that does violence to *"the general alogical structure of the pharmakon."* It is an attempt to restore the purity of origins through the operation of the *logos*. What is happening here, according to Derrida, is the catching of the *pharmakon* by philosophy, by Platonism. The trial of Socrates is lodged, therefore, in this expulsion of the outside. There is another connotation of the word *pharmakon* besides wizard, magician, or prisoner, Derrida argues, and that is scapegoat. The ritual of the *pharmakos* involves the expulsion of evil from the city in order to purify it. It takes place in Athens on the sixth day of Thargelia—the day, as Derrida notes, that Socrates was born. The death of the one who does not write has a structure that is homologous to the death of writing as *archē-écriture*. Hence, as Derrida puts it, "Socrates ties up into a system all the counts of indictment against the *pharmakon* of writing"; his discourse upholds the "basileopatro-helio-theological dictum" by "transforming the *mythos* into *logos*."[30] The *logos* is the death of *archē-écriture* insofar as tries to expel its own otherness or moment of nonidentity. But this is not the end of the story. Although Platonism may want to do away with writing through the distinction between live memory and rememorization, or even through the distinction between good and bad writing, the graphics of supplementarity necessarily recurs. First, the fact that Platonism can never be done with writing is tied, in the first place, to Plato's own act of reparation to Socrates. Derrida argues that Plato "writes *out of his death*" as "reparations of and to the father made against the *graphē* that decided his death."[31] Second, and more importantly, it is due to the very "(non)logic of play and writing." It is this, ultimately, that explains why, according to Derrida, "Plato, while subordinating or condemning writing and play, should have written so much, presenting his writings, *from out of Socrates's death*, as games, *indicting* writing in writing, lodging against it that complaint *(graphē)* whose reverberations even today have not ceased to resound."[32] Third, the Platonic theory of the *khōra* from the *Timaeus* has the structure of a *trace*—that is, of *différance*. Fourth, and finally, Platonism as writing is tied to parricide. "The play of the other within being," Derrida argues, "must needs be designated 'writing' by Plato in a discourse which would like to think of itself as spoken in essence, in truth, and which nevertheless is written. And it is written *from out of the death of Socrates*."[33] The repetition of the formula "out of the death of Socrates" signifies the erasure of the proper name that the notion of writing as *archē-écriture* entails. It is, therefore, only the deconstruction of the paternal *logos* that establishes the interwoven system of difference that Derrida refers to as the *sumplokē*.

If in *Plato's Pharmacy* the deconstruction of the Socratic *logos* leads to the idea that writing as *archē-écriture* is analogous to the transcendental imagination, then the task of *Envois* is to show how the delegitimization of the paternal legacy leads to the idea that reception also has a differential structure. If in *Envois*, therefore, Derrida creates a Socrates who writes, then there is nothing to surprise us in that. Once again it is a question of thinking through the possibility of a nonunitary generative principle. Here it is the concept of the postal that functions as this principle. Derrida argues that "as soon as there is, there is *différance* . . . and there is postal maneuvring, relays, delay, anticipation, destination, telecommunicating network, the possibility, and therefore the fatal necessity of going astray, etc."[34] The principle of the postal is not, Derrida stresses, a technological determination of being; for as a generative principle it is thought "on the basis of the destinal of being; and as such it is the 'proper' possibility of every possible rhetoric."[35] Once again it is the question of the relationship between Socrates and Plato that concerns Derrida; however, what concerns him here is not simply the Platonic privileging of the paternal logos over writing that is necessarily an indictment of writing in writing, but the question of inheritance. The idea of the Socratic legacy in Plato is turned around when one conceives of Plato as the one who does write; that means, for Derrida, the one who translates/relays/leads-astray/interprets the legacy of the one who did not write. Yet is it really the case that Socrates is the one who did not write? With regard to this question, Derrida takes as his point of departure the frontispiece of a thirteenth-century fortune-telling book by Matthew Paris that shows a seated Socrates writing at a table with a standing Plato behind him and holding a finger to the middle of Socrates' back. This is an image that Derrida comes across on the back of a postcard that he discovers by *hasard objective* at the Bodleian Library at Oxford. Derrida's commentary on the Socrates problem through this image centers on the question of the relationship between the erasure of the proper name of the emitter and the necessary indeterminacy of interpretation or translation by the receiver. At this point, the reliance of Derrida's attack upon Western logocentrism reveals its Judaic provenance. Derrida argues that "YHWH simultaneously demands and forbids, in his deconstructive gesture, that one understands his proper name within language, he mandates and crosses out the translation, he dooms us to impossible and necessary translation."[36] The deconstructive gesture of Socrates is also one that simultaneously demands and forbids writing, interpretation, and translation. This deconstructive gesture hands over the legacy of the penman Socrates to the wanderings of his postman Plato. As Derrida puts it, "the writing of the proper name, that of the *penman* Shem, sees itself interminably given over to the detours and wanderings of Shaun the *postman*, his brother."[37] The Judaic legacy of Derrida surfaces in this text as a radicalization of hermeneutics insofar as it refers the fusion of horizons between the interpreter and his text, not to any stable understanding of a shared tradition; rather, it leaves it open to an unstable and open telecommunicating network.

In *Plato's Pharmacy* it is Thoth, the god of writing, over Thamus, the father of speech. In *Envois* it is the postman Shaun over the penman Shem. In *Plato's Pharmacy* what is central is the attempt to reverse the Platonic relegation of writing to the status of "that dangerous supplement." Hence, Plato is the one who writes out of the death of Socrates. In *Envois* what is central is the erasure of the proper name of Socrates; hence, the penman Plato becomes the postman Plato. The invention of the penman Socrates, however, who in a deconstructive gesture both demands and prohibits translation, is a kind of ventriloquism. In effect, the penmanship of Socrates is a kind of ventriloquism performed by the postman Plato who is, in every real sense, also holding the pen. The transformation of the Greek Socrates into the Jewish YHWH and the transformation of the Greek Plato into a Jewish rabbi are tied together by the notion of the *kolophon*. In Derrida's analysis, the legacy of Socrates is ultimately both graphic or textual and also, and more important, theologically inscribed in a peculiarly Judaic tradition. Hence, Derrida links the Platonic finger in the Socratic back to the Matthew Paris frontispiece to the *kolophon*, which the Jews use to point to the text of the Torah. In *Plato's Pharmacy* this term also appears in its Greek meaning of "inscription." What I want to suggest is that we employ a third *kolophon*, and that is the one that Lacan attributes to Descartes—namely, the *kolophon* of doubt, for the textual mark of the pointing finger points toward this theological reinscription of the problem of Socrates as the most problematic. Yet the usage that Derrida makes of the Judaic tradition at this point is one that determines the radically contingent turn that he makes within the hermeneutical tradition. If everything is in the post, for Derrida, then this does not mean everything is destined to arrive. With this idea Derrida deconstructs the notion of inheritance and reception that plays such a key role in the conventional interpretation of the relationship between Socrates and Plato. Yet the theological idea of Messianic hope and the impossibility of its fulfillment are what stand behind the idea of the contingent nature of reception. Derrida argues, therefore, that "the master-thinkers are also masters of the post. Knowing well how to play with the *poste-restante*. The post is always *en reste*, and always *restante*. It awaits the addressee who might always, by *chance*, not arrive."[38]

The context out of which the interpretation of Socrates emerges in discourse theory is not one shaped by hermeneutics but by transcendental pragmatics. The task of transcendental pragmatics is to establish the *a priori* or fundamental norm of argumentation as the basis for the final grounding of the rationality of both theoretical and moral-practical discourse. The interpretation of Socrates that emerges out of discourse theory is also one that is shaped by a certain reading of the history of philosophy that reconstructs it using a stage theory of development imported from the work of Piaget and Kohlberg in psychology. Although discourse theory is a complex philosophical research program, its guiding idea of the discursive redemption of validity claims and the implications of this idea for the foundation of ethics are quite clear. Apel's demand is that "the subjective, individual decisions of conscience [be] now mediated *a priori* with the demand for intersubjective validity; namely, by each individual acknowledging from the outset that public argument is the explication of all possible criteria of validity and . . . rational formation of the will."[39] There are, at least, three consequences that flow from such a demand. First, the turn away from conscience to intersubjective validity necessitates a turn also away from the philosophy of consciousness to one of intersubjectivity or communication. Second, the *a priori* of argumentation only gives us a rational means of testing our principles and gives us no indication of what these should actually be. Third, the communicative utopia envisaged by discourse ethics is one that was said to be counterfactually anticipated in every act of communication. This is the consequence that has since been rejected by discourse theory with its partial turn toward an ethic of responsibility. Yet the guiding idea of the discursive redemption of validity claims is one that remains. It is an idea that shifts the interpretation of Socrates in the history of philosophy away from the Hegelian emphasis on Socrates as the discoverer of morality and toward an interpretation of Socrates as the discoverer of the norm of rational argumentation and, hence, as a precursor of discourse ethics.

This interpretation begins to emerge in the introduction to Apel's *Transformation of Philosophy*. "At this moment," Apel argues, "it appears to me that the institutionalization of impotent philosophy as an island of communication this side of or beyond party political control, which has at least been reasonably successful since Socrates, is both necessary and, in a certain sense, comforting."[40] It only reaches its full development, however, in the *Funk-Kolleg* collection as well as in *Diskurs und Verantwortung*. In his contributions to the *Funk-Kolleg* Apel refers to this side of the Socratic revolution as the introduction of the meta-institution of discourse. The meta-institution of discourse involves, as Apel puts it, "the testing and justification of all traditional norms through rational argumentation."[41] The emergence of such a meta-institution presupposes the differentiation of discursive types. Therefore, philosophy can give up the Socratic and Platonic distinction between argumentative discourse and other forms of discourse, as well as the distinction between the discursive and the figural, only at the cost of considerable intellectual regression. Apel argues in *Diskurs und Verantwortung* that just such a regressive de-differentiation is now occurring due to what he calls the "hermeneutic-rhetoric-pragmatic turn" of philosophy with its cult of rhetoric and literature.[42] When, where, and how precisely does this possibility of progress or regress arise? Through the use of Kohlberg's stage theory of moral development, Apel tries to show that Socrates makes possible the transition from a conventional to a postconventional stage of moral development, which involves essentially both personal conscience and principles of reason. Apel argues that both Socrates and fifth-century B.C. Athens enjoyed a normal adolescence but that in the new wave of *Historismus-Relativismus* and Nietzschean *Machttheorie* the crisis of adolescence is sharpened. These theories remain trapped at the transitional level of "the putting into question of all moral obligations through the apparently regressive reversion to a pre-conventional moral consciousness."[43]

The problematic character of this ultrarationalist portrayal of Socrates becomes particularly clear when Apel admits in the *Funk-Kolleg* collection that Socrates not merely had a successful adolescence, but that he almost reached old age. Socrates and Athens reached maturity with the development of what Apel calls the *Logos-Grundsatz*, which he defines as the "claim only to recognize as true and good that which survives critical testing in dialogue."[44] Apel also argues, however, that Socrates developed elements of an ethic that presages the new stage of postconventional development that Apel and Habermas have dubbed stage seven. Apel argues that the Socratic maieutic involves both, on the one hand, the "logical rules of the conclusiveness of arguments and of the generalization of concepts" and, on the other hand, the "social rules of reciprocity in the sense of the freedom and equality of the right of discourse."[45] If this is the case, however, how can Apel convincingly maintain that the Greek Enlightenment was a transitional epoch, a kind of historico-philosophical adolescence? And if this is admitted, then does not the hyper-rationalism of this developmental logic come tumbling down? The consequences of such an admission would be, therefore, that even if Apel's criticisms of *Historismus-Relativismus* were allowed to stand, then this would have to be done in terms that avoid such evolutionary assumptions. Furthermore, if such assumptions are avoided, then so also must Apel's one-sided characterization of Plato and Aristotle as regressing to a *Polisethik*. Notwithstanding the fact that Apel is right to point out the fact that the moral norm of preferring to suffer evil than to commit it is not a universal principle in the Kantian sense and that, as a consequence, Socrates is not a totally modern figure, the turning of Socrates into a discourse theorist *avant la lettre* emphasizes both the rationality and modernity of Socrates' *Logos-Grundsatz* in a way that undermines the developmentalist logic of Apel's basic categories.

The two readings of Socrates could be described as different Socratic novels or even novellas.[46] Such a description, however, would prejudge the philosophical dispute that lies at the heart of these two narratives. The dispute revolves around the question of the linkage between speech and reason (*legein* and *logos*) and writing and protowriting (*écriture* and *archë-écriture*). This is essentially a dispute between those who argue for ascribing to reason a kind of unity, and those for whom the idea of dispersal or dissemination functions to dispel the totalizing magic of reason. The Kierkegaardian moment repeats itself. The existential critique of speculative reason returns as the deconstructive critique of procedural reason. Yet does it really repeat itself? Apel's reading of Socrates is a rationalist one; however, Apel's rationalism is one that is in line with that of the Enlightenment rather than Hegel's post-Enlightenment, speculative concept of reason. Hence, Hegel's romantic critique of the Socratic discovery of morality as the criminal force that breaks apart the customary order is alien to Apel. Apel's reading is more in line with Diderot's reading of Socrates as a hero in the struggle against intolerance. This struggle is tied up, for Apel, with the Socratic invention of the principles of rational argumentation. Socrates is a figure who tried to give rational grounds for whatever he said in a discourse that was free and open to all. Derrida's reading of Socrates relativizes the distinction between reason and nonreason by interpreting the distinction itself as a product of "the general alogical economy of the *pharmakon*." The *pharmakon* contains, as Derrida puts it, a certain "non-identity with itself"; it is this very indeterminacy that opens up the space for reversals, substitutions, elisions, and so on. In sum, it opens up a space for the nonidentical, which is definable as a space that includes the conceptual. Socrates as *pharmakeus* or magician employs the wild *logos* or irony, which is also governed by indeterminacy, to overturn the arguments of the sophists. It is a case of *pharmakon* against *pharmakon*, not knowledge *(epistemē)* against opinion *(doxa)*. This is a reading that clearly lies within a tradition of thought that commences with the romantic thematization of irony in the early nineteenth century. It belongs, therefore, to the type of reading of Socrates that both Kierkegaard and Nietzsche pursue. What we have here, then, are not only two narratives but also two different modes of philosophizing. One is based on the compulsion to determine, to ground, to give warrant; the other on the resistance to conceptual determination because of its insistence on the preconceptual matrix of all philosophical concepts. These two narratives constitute the philosophical outer boundaries of the field of interpretative tension between the currents of Enlightenment and romanticism that is constitutive of modernity. In the Socratic narratives of Apel and Derrida this tension between the Enlightenment and romanticism is only recoverable through a kind of parallel reading that presents to each the narrative of which they could not possibly have been the author.

V

The tension between the Enlightenment and romanticism has become even more acute in recent times with the debate over the question of the postmodern. Whether postmodernity is a condition or stage beyond modernity, as some claim, or a new attitude or consciousness that breaks with modern consciousness does not really matter. What either version of the argument represents is a new eruption of the romantic current in modern thought and a reformulated criticism of the nature of the Enlightenment project itself. This renewal of romanticism in contemporary thought, however, is both more reflective and less irrationalist than previous currents of romantic thought. As a post-totalitarian form of thought, the newer postmodernist current takes into account both the Enlightenment critique of myth and the romantic critique of progress. On the other hand, modernist currents of thought, as post-totalizing forms of thought, take into account both the romantic critique of speculative reason and the Enlightenment critique of secrecy. Hence, the more modernist currents of thought are also more reflective and less dogmatic than previous forms of Enlightenment thought. The quarrel between modernists and postmodernists is, as a consequence, both decidedly less contemporary and decidedly less polarized than their respective adherents tend to suggest.

The influence of Nietzsche on postmodern currents of thought is one that has been explicitly acknowledged. Hence, it is the more subterranean influence of Kierkegaard that is more difficult to reconstruct. But there is a more specific and uncanny parallel that can be drawn between the romantic and the postmodern moment: they are both responses to Hegelian modes of thought. In the case of the romantic moment, it is the influence of Hegel himself that is in question. In the case of the postmodern moment, it is Hegelian forms of Marxism that are in question. In the former, it is the speculative construction of reason in history that is placed in question, whereas for the latter, it is the transposition of this schema onto a redemptive concept of revolution that is the main concern. The critique of speculative thinking and the turn toward the existing thinker, which one finds in Kierkegaard, elevates sheer particularity over any kind of representative individuality. This idea undergoes further adumbration in the notion of irony as an expression of the romantic individual's negativity towards existence and in the notion of romantic subjectivity as a kind of playful set of variations through which the self alternates. In Derrida, the critique of speculative thinking is no less central even if his notion of thinking after reason is more influenced by Heidegegger's notion of *Denken* than Kierkegaard's notion of the existing thinker. Derrida does explicitly acknowledge, however, the parallel between Heidegger's notion of *Denken* and Kierkegaard's notion of the "instant," which he defines as a brief and paradoxical event that fractures time. This is in contrast to the Hegelian and Hegelian-Marxist idea of time as development, which renders the event a more rational and predictable outcome of previous forces. Furthermore, the Kierkergaardian experiment with plural authorship through his multiplication of authorial signatures in his pseudonymous writings both pluralizes subjectivity and ties it back into writing. Derrida's critique of intentionality in the context of his work on the signature, and the multiplication of the signature in the face of its legal-institutional foreclosure, are in the same vein as those of Kierkegaard. In the same way, therefore, that Kierkegaard's thought focuses on the marginality of the existing thinker in relation to the grandiose structure of the speculative system, Derrida's deconstructive philosophy sets to work on the closure of the system from the temporal location of the momentary *(Augenblick)* and of the liminal position of thinking *(Denken)*. Hence, the romantic anti-Hegelianism of the romantic moment of modern thought can be seen to repeat itself in the equally, but differently, anti-Hegelian (or anti-Hegelian-Marxist) current of the contemporary postmodern moment.

With respect to Nietzsche's influence on postmodernism, there have been two interpretative approaches that have been particularly influential. There is, first of all, that of Deleuze and Foucault, for whom Nietzsche is a thinker of power; and it is the Nietzschean theory of power that underlies the various genealogies of contemporary morals that have been undertaken. The task of genealogy is to undercut the notion that reason informs our contemporary discourses and that these discourses are best seen as emerging out of a naturelike process of conflict and struggle in which forces impinge on bodies. This denial of the discursive foundations of rationality is anti-Socratic in principle; however, Foucault's most sustained treatment of Socrates occurs after his partial and incomplete break with the paradigm of power/knowledge. In his later work, Socrates is viewed as a new "style of existence" that constitutes a philosophical solution to the problem of self-mastery peculiar to ancient Greek society.[47] The second influence that Nietzsche has had on postmodernism is through his critique of Western metaphysics, particularly as reinterpreted by Heidegger. This is the starting point of Derrida's attempt at a deconstruction of Western metaphysics, which is, as already mentioned, one that is also heavily influenced by Levinas and Judaic thought in general in its counterpoising of being as presence to the idea of absence or dissemination. Here, the idea of reason or, as we say now, of rationality is foregone in favor of that of the wandering of interpretation. The influence of Nietzsche on postmodern thought leads, therefore, either to the reduction of rationality to a calculus of forces or to its deconstruction by an interpretative strategy that reads it as another stage in the history of Greco-Occidental metaphysics.

As I mentioned earlier, the quarrel between modernists and postmodernists cannot only be reconstructed in terms of the notion of reason as universal or uniform, but also as a critique of the notion of history as progress or liberation and the notion of modern society as involving the strict differentiation of cultural spheres. What I would like to do by way of conclusion is both to look back at the nineteenth-century interpretations of Socrates and forward to contemporary interpretations in terms of this new quarrel between ancients and moderns.

The thought of Hegel represents the most powerful account of history as progress toward freedom. In the Oriental world only one was free, whereas in the Greek world the few were free. It is only within modern political forms, however, that all become free. Progress is, for Hegel, the progressive inclusion of the whole of the population within the political system or the universalization of citizenship. The ethical concomitant of this political transformation is a moral transformation. The modern world sees the universalization of moral conscience, which is at the heart of modern subjectivity for Hegel, and the emergence of the conflict between morality and custom. This conflict attains a political form in the tendency of modern political forms to disintegrate into moral terrorism, as was the case in the French Revolution. Indeed, the famous Hegelian analysis of the French Revolution in terms of the development of the notion of absolute freedom and the consequent emergence of a process of institutional de-differentiation is an analysis that already shows the self-reflexive nature of Enlightenment thought in its ability to analyze the immanent consequences of the Enlightenment project itself. The Hegelian dialectic is already one that is moving toward a recognition of both progress and loss, despite its basically progressivist characterization of history. The evolutionism of both Apel and Habermas also tries to explicitly take into account both what has been gained and what has been lost in the course of human history; however, their stage model of progress is, if anything, even more unilinear than Hegel's in its explicit use of ontogenetic models in the analysis of phylogenesis. Furthermore, even though their definition of reason is less substantialist than Hegel's, they both share a common tendency to read history as the unfolding of a concept of reason that was already there from the beginning. In both cases, a rationalist theory of history results in a rationalist reading of the figure of Socrates.

Hegel's reading of Socrates is a distinctly modernist one. The Socratic moment is the discovery of the rationality of morality. The Kantian moment is the realization of the rationality of morality. Hence, Hegel can draw a parallel between the Greek Enlightenment and the German Enlightenment. This moral progress is accompanied by political progress. The Socratic moment is only possible in a society where at least the few have become free. Yet the fact that it is not yet a society where all are free means that the Socratic moment must be repressed. The death of Socrates is a world-historical necessity because the Greek world is too small to accommodate the new principle. It must appear as the act of a criminal, even though Socrates himself has proved on numerous occasions his worth as a citizen. Hence, it is the act of a law-abiding criminal that sets world history in motion, that propels history forward. History is progress toward freedom only insofar as the exception, the criminal, emerges. The Socratic act of criminality—civil disobedience—does not have its full effect on his own society, but his struggle for the rights of the moral conscience to be recognized is ultimately realized in modernity. The progress that this principle's recognition brings is accompanied by both dangers (moral terrorism) and loss (of the customary order). The reading of Socrates by Apel is also a distinctively modernist one, but the rationalism of Apel is both necessarily more modest and unfortunately flatter. For Hegel, Socrates is both of his time and ahead of his time, whereas for Apel the Socratic moment is a stage in a unilinear sequence of stages. Yet the attempt to present the Socratic moment as a healthy adolescence in which the transition to a postconventional moral stage is successfully completed means that discourse ethics is already prefigured at the beginning of Western philosophy. What is also significant about the Apelian reading of the Socratic moment is its rationalist reading of Socratic irony as merely a demand for explicit argumentation. The complex and subversive character of Socratic discourse, which Hegel recognizes in his depiction of Socrates as a criminal, is thereby lost. Hence, the way dissent functions to make progress as increasing freedom possible is lost.

The notion of history as progress or liberation presupposes a unilinear concept of time that is foreign to Kierkegaard, Nietzsche, and Derrida. For Kierkegaard, the relationship of the individual to the absolute is one in which the privilege of being contemporary does not pertain. The privilege of being a contemporary of Socrates is, indeed, a privilege; however, the privilege of being a contemporary of Christ is not a privilege. The emergence of the absolute in time is an event that must be reappropriated anew by each new generation and by each individual in that generation. The absolute cannot, by definition, undergo change. The individual is that which must undergo internal change. With his emphasis on subjectivity as truth, Kierkegaard splits apart the historical dialectic of the universal and the particular as it appears in Hegel. Each moment of the life of the individual is potentially an absolute one. Truth is the leap of faith or the movement toward a religious stage, a stage that is not a historical stage but a permanent existential possibility. History loses its historical character. It becomes the scene of a contingent act, a decision for Christ. For Nietzsche, the modern concept of history as progress is one in which the notion of history loses all its relationship to life. Hence, Nietzsche variously counterpoises art, nature, life, power, and the drives as unhistorical or, perhaps, suprahistorical principles to the principle of history itself. The ultimate form that this rejection of the Western concept of time takes is constituted by the interrelated myths of the superman and that of the eternal recurrence. The myth of the superman is an elevation of the individual to the ahistorical decisional center that submits itself to no absolute, as does the Kierkegaardian self, but only to its own self-absolutized authority. The myth of eternal recurrence completes this self-legislated sovereignty by making time itself repeatable by subjective fiat. For Derrida, the Western notion of time is similarly rejected, and hence, the notion of history as progress cannot be posed. The time zone that Derrida operates in is messianic time. As with Benjamin, time is a door through which the Messiah may enter at any moment. Hence, the democracy that is to come is not merely in the post and as such destined to arrive. It is not futural; rather it is a promise that may or may not be fulfilled. Humans cannot create this future; they must await it. Derrida is still singing what Weber refers to as the beautiful song of the Edomite watchman.

The rejection of the Greco-Occidental notion of time leads to the devaluation of the historical as such. In the work of Kierkegaard, Nietzsche, and Derrida, there is no real attempt made to historically situate the Socratic moment. Indeed, what is important for all three thinkers is not so much a Socratic moment as the Socratic alternative. For Kierkegaard, the Socratic alternative is either one of the aesthetic attitude of irony or that of the ethical attitude guided by reason. For Nietzsche, the Socratic alternative is either that of the *bios theoretikos* or that of the *Moral-Monoman*. For Derrida, the Socratic alternative is what Apel describes as the *Logos-Grundsatz* or what he himself calls the privileging of the voice as pure presence. What both the Kierkegaardian and Nietzschean presentation of Socrates forgets is that the Greek invention of reason is not something that can be dispensed with either by a leap of faith or by a recourse to the unhistorical. What the Derridean presentation of Socrates ignores is that Greek culture is a literary as much as oral culture and that to import a notion of writing that is a peculiar transformation of Judaic theological motifs and Heideggerian philosophical motifs into the reading of the Socratic moment is, in effect, a reading in which the specificity of the Greek moment is lost. The supposed privilege that the voice has over writing in Greek culture is a privilege that does not exist if one is simply referring to the empirical notion of writing. The importance of writing in the development of the legal and political culture of Greece is both too obvious to be repeated here and also simply irrelevant. In the Judaic tradition, writing refers to the writing of God that is handed down to Moses, which then becomes the property of a specialized caste of interpreters.[48] The notion of writing as *archē-écriture* reframes this theological concept in terms of the Kantian notion of the transcendental imagination, reinterpreted by Heiddegger in his *Kant-Buch* as the matrix out of which all interpretation wanders or errs. The end product is a Socrates who writes—that is, who interprets. The ahistorical reading of Socrates is there simply to dramatize an overly theologically determined notion of writing.

The Hegelian notion of reason is modernist insofar as it affirms the unity of reason; however, it is also both curiously premodern and postmodern. It is premodern in its speculative attempt to overcome the Kantian bifurcation of reason into pure and practical reason; it is postmodern insofar as the unity of reason only occurs through a historical process that involves conflict and struggle. The Hegelian notion of reason already contains within it the romantic critique of the Enlightenment even as it tries to distinguish itself from romanticism proper. Hence, it also demonstrates the self-reflexive nature of the

Enlightenment and the theoretical tensions that are part and parcel of modernity itself. Apel's notion of reason is one that more fully accepts the fragmentation of reason in modernity even as it tries to reconstruct the linguistic foundations of reason itself. Such a project has the theoretical advantage of foregoing a speculative and totalizing concept of reason; hence, it is less ambivalently modernist. The project's theoretical disadvantage, however, lies in its resort to a kind of linguistified transcendentalism that makes our ability to understand the world dependent not so much on the categories of the understanding, but on the fundamental pragmatic properties of language. Hence, the notion of reason *qua* rationality is decontextualized in advance and immunized from any historical context. Therefore, Apel's Socrates must already have discovered what a stage theory of history must otherwise conclude that he could not discover—namely, the meta-institution of discourse. The emergence of the *Logos-Grundsatz* in Greek philosophy is, first of all, the discovery of a new usage of language. At the level of the discursive employment of language, Socrates is already a modern or post-conventional figure. The Hegelian reading of the figure of Socrates can more easily account for both the antiquity and modernity of the Socratic usage of reason because of its attention to the historical context. The criminal is the bearer of a new principle of rational morality that struggles for recognition in the marketplace of Athens. Even if Hegel ultimately reads this struggle between *Moralität* and *Sittlichkeit* in terms of a dialectic of world history in which the justly convicted criminal gains a posthumous victory, the reading of Socrates that Hegel develops is still one that is more sensitive to the historical vicissitudes of reason *qua* rational morality.

The critique of the idea of a uniform or universal notion of reason is executed more radically in the work of Kierkegaard, Nietzsche, and Derrida. In all three thinkers it is the status of theoretical reason that is in question. Although the immediate object of Kierkegaard's attack is the speculative construction of reason in Hegel, the real object of attack is the whole Greco-Occidental emphasis on the discursive and propositional properties of language. The Kierkegaardian elevation of indirect communication and his definition of truth as subjectivity are a response to the Greco-Occidental tradition that relies totally on the other fundamental source of the Western tradition—namely, the Judaeo-Christian emphasis on an ethic of redemption and the ensuing definition of truth in ethico-religious terms. The Nietzschean attack on reason is more radical still in that it is one that is directed to both strands of the Western tradition. His work is just as much a critique of the logic of identity and propositional truth, which get reduced to a mobile army of metaphors, as it is a critique of ascetic ideals and the ethic of resentment. The Derridean deconstruction of Western logocentrism represents, if anything, a partial retreat from the radicality of Nietzsche's philosophy. The reading of Western logocentrism as a phonocentrism that privileges the notion of the voice as presence implicates Christianity in the Greek tradition by reading Christianity as a species of Platonism. This enables Derrida to rehabilitate Judaic theological motives under the guise of a philosophy of writing and of the other. The reading of Derrida as a nihilist à la Nietzsche is a misreading one that he has quite rightly repudiated. The philosopheme of nonidentity and otherness that both Adorno and Derrida develop can ultimately be traced back to the Judaic reading of God as the absolute other that both forbids and demands mediation. The reading of Socrates that emerges out of this more radical critique of reason is a necessarily more negative one. For Kierkegaard, Socrates is at most the highest representative of the rationality that inheres in ethical life defined in terms of relationships among humans. For Nietzsche, Socrates is pilloried as both being anti-aristocratic in his worship of reason and the theoretical life and, finally, for being too Judaeo-Christian as well as anti-aristocratic in his emphasis on rational morality. If the first reading is a kind of Apelian reading à l'envers, then the second reading is a kind of Hegelian reading à l'envers. The Derridean reading of Socrates is one that turns him into a point of dissemination and, hence, into one who writes. This is not a critique of Socrates as anti-Greek and too Judaeo-Christian but a reading of Socrates that assimilates the figure of Socrates into the Jewish tradition due to its devaluation of discourse and its peculiar conception of writing.

The postmodernist critique of the notion that modern society requires a strict differentiation of cultural spheres is one that can be found already in the writings of Hegel. The Hegelian critique of the Kantian *Sollen* and the formalism of the modern state are all signs of a romantic suspicion of the increasingly indivualized concept of the self and the increasingly abstract and impersonal nature of social relations demanded by and within modern social institutions. But the early Hegel's attempt to see classical *polis* democracy as the germ of a new form of *Sittlichkeit* later gives way to a more sober assessment of modern society that accepts the fact of differentiation. In this context, Socrates is read as a premature advocate of a new concept of the moral self that is incompatible with the poorly differentiated character of ancient social institutions. The acceptance of the differentiated character of modern society is even more pronounced in the work of Apel, although one of the central presuppositions of transcendental pragmatics is that language constitutes a shared linguistic background. Language is itself differentiated out, however, and the capacity to use differentiated forms of speech constitutes the linguistic infrastructure of social differentiation itself. The Socratic moment becomes, within this framework, the moment in which language becomes conscious of its own discursive properties, of its ability to be used propositionally; the result is the establishment of communities of intellectual discourse guided by the meta-institution of discourse.

The opposition to the differentiated character of modern cultural spheres that is said to typify postmodern thought is quite clearly in evidence in the main nineteenth-century precursors of many nineteenth-century thinkers: namely, Kierkegaard and Nietzsche. Although the stage theory of Kierkegaard describes accurately the qualities and station of that denizen of the ethical life he calls Judge William, who both personally accepts and acts professionally within the differentiated institutions of sober bourgeois life, it is ultimately the rather strange figure of Socrates that becomes the embodiment of the virtues of the ethical life. With this choice, Kierkegaard seems even to be rejecting the type of modern bourgeois personality as an existential possibility with any degree of credibility. Needless to say, the other two types or existential possibilities (namely, the aesthetic and the religious) are ones that consciously refuse the sober conduct that differentiated social institutions demand by either a de-differentiating playfulness or a religious seriousness. For Nietzsche, the thematic of cultural decadence is, in effect, a critique of modern processes of social differentiation that misrecognizes itself as such. The critique of democratic forms as lacking cultural creativity and the celebration of aristocratic political forms as engendering cultural creativity identifies the differentiation of cultural spheres with cultural decadence. Hence, the later Nietzsche's diatribe against the lowly social origins of Socrates is a diatribe against the emergence of the cultural pluralism that political democracy brings about in ancient Athens. Socrates is the modernizing agent of cultural differentiation for Nietzsche who destroys the closed yet culturally productive customary society of pre-Socratic Athens. The de-differentiating motif in Derrida's thought is executed in and through a theory of ontological *différance* that thinks of being as *archē-écriture* or as the nonoriginating originary source of differences. This theory of ontological difference relativizes ontical differences to the differential and differentiating matrix that produces them. They become effects of the productivity of this transcendental imaginary. At the level of sociocultural institutions, Derrida is left with a one-sided critique of them as logocentric or onto-theologically determined or even phallogocentric because they fail to recognize the otherness or moment of nonidentity that invariably constitutes them as the products of the transcendental imagination. Within this framework the interpretation of Socrates is at one with the theory of ontological difference. The Socratic interpretation of writing as *pharmakon* or both poison and cure is such a nonoriginary originating substitution for the concept of *différance*. Socrates becomes a nonoriginating origin, both penman and postman in the terminology of *Envois*.

VI

The fact that the terms of the dispute in the quarrel between modernists and postmodernists can be read into nineteenth-century interpretations of Socrates as well as into contemporary interpretations demonstrates that the quarrel itself is still located within the field of tension between Enlightenment and romanticism that has characterized modernity from the late eighteenth century. Indeed, the extent to which postmodern quarrels are prefigured in the work of the three great nineteenth-century interpreters of Socrates is remarkable. The current controversy between the liberals and the neocommunitarians over the formalistic nature of modern notions of subjectivity, justice, and community is prefigured in the *différend* between Kant and Hegel. The other important current controversy between discourse theorists on the one hand and deconstructionists, historicists, and pragmatists on the other hand— over whether one can defend a weak notion of the unity of reason within the plurality of its voices—is also clearly prefigured in the *différend* between Kierkegaard and Hegel over the relationship between subjectivity and truth and in the *différend* between Nietzsche and the philosophical tradition over the relationship between being and time. Hence, Hegel's remetaphysicalization of the notion of the subject makes being itself a product of a rationalizing activity, which pre-endows existing institutions with a rationality that empirical citizens either as egoistic bourgeois or as bearers of formal rights can no longer provide, is quite clearly in line with the neocommunitarian emphasis on a non-rights-centered view of modern institutions. The postmodern polity is a postliberal one. Kierkegaard's de-metaphysicalization of the notion of the subject, which finds its expression in both the elevation of the existing individual and in the multiplication of his own authorial signature, is quite clearly in line with the postmodern stress on the problematic nature of the notion of a unitary subject. The postmodern subject is a master of the rotation method. Nietzsche's de-metaphysicalization of the notion of being, which results both in the elevation of creativity over order and the reduction of cultural creativity to an economy of drives and instincts, is also quite clearly in line with the postmodern stress on either the unconscious or on power. The postmodern world is one of immanence and difference.

In the same way, therefore, that the romantic assault on

the Enlightenment brings forth new interpretations of Socrates, so also does the postmodernist assault on modernism. Yet even if one can detect a clear sign of a postmodernist Socrates in the emphasis on a Socrates who writes (Derrida) or, even more recently, on a plurality of Socrate(s) (Kofman) or in an emphasis on the notion of *atopia* as the key to the understanding of Socrates *(Böhme)*, such interpretative possibilities simply constitute one pole of a field of tensions in which a Socrates, *qua* discourse theorist (Apel), currently occupies the other pole.[49] Contemporary interpretations of Socrates still exist within the distinctively modern field of tensions that was first developed around the turn of the nineteenth century. The disenchantment of reason in modernity calls forth a reaction that fastens on the strangeness of Socrates as a figure through which to interpret both the de-intoxicating and intoxicating power of thinking after reason.

Notes

Introduction

1. Although the nineteenth century prepared the way for the generalized culture of nihilism prevalent in the twentieth century, those who prepared this way were outside the mainstream traditions of nineteenth-century thought. On the general context of nineteenth-century German philosophy, see Hans Schnädelbach, *Philosophy in Germany, 1831-1933* (Cambridge: Cambridge University Press, Cambridge, 1984).

2. Max Weber, "Science as a Vocation," from *Max Weber*, trans. H. H. Gerth & C. Wright Mills (London: Routledge and Kegan Paul, 1970), p. 148. ("Wissenschaft als Beruf," *Gesammelte Aufsätze zur Wissenschaftslehre*, ed. J. Winckelman, [Tübingen: J. C. B. Mohr (Paul Siebeck), 1922], p. 604.)

3. Ibid., Eng., p. 148; Germ., p. 604-5.

4. Weber, "Religious Rejections of the World and Their Directions," from *Max Weber*, p. 342.

5. Ibid.

6. Johann P. Arnason, "The Imaginary Constitution of Modernity," *Revue européenne des sciences sociales* 10 (1989): p. 333.

7. See Georg Lukács, *The Destruction of Reason*, trans. P. Palmer (Atlantic Highlands: Humanities Press, 1981).

8. Michel Foucault, *L'usage des plaisirs*, vol. 2 of *Histoire de la sexualité* (Paris: Gallimard, 1984), p. 16.

9. Some of the terminology and ideas in this paragraph are developed from a reading of the work of Adorno and Castoriadis. See Theodor W. Adorno, "Die Aktualität der Philosophie," from *Philosophische Frühschriften, Gesammelte Schriften*, vol. 1 (Frankfurt am Main: Suhrkamp, 1973), pp. 345-66; and Cornelius Castoriadis, "Le social-historique," from *L'institution imaginaire de société* (paris: Seuil, 1975), pp. 233-96.

10. Hans Blumenberg, *Work on Myth* (Cambridge, Mass: MIT Press, 1985), p. 68.

11. Karl Löwith, *Meaning in History* (Chicago: University of Chicago Press, 1949), p. 1.

12. Karl Löwith, *From Hegel to Nietzsche: The Revolution in Nineteenth Century Thought* (London: Constable, 1964), p. 12.

13. Löwith, *Meaning in History*, p. 199.

14. Hans Blumenberg, *The Legitimacy of the Modern Age* (Cambridge, Mass: MIT Press, 1983), p. 137.

15. Jürgen Habermas, *Der philosophische Diskurs der Moderne* (Frankfurt am Main: Suhrkamp, 1985).

16. Blumenberg, *The Legitimacy of the Modern Age*, p. 138.

17. Ibid., pp. 177-78.

18. Johann P. Arnason, "Die Moderne als Projekt und Spannungsfeld," in *Kommunikatives Handeln, Beiträge zu Habermas' "Theorie des kommunikativen Handelns,"* ed. Axel Honneth and Hans Joas (Frankfurt am Main: Suhrkamp, 1986), p. 318.

19. Ibid., pp. 318, 320.

20. Ibid., p. 318.

21. Ibid., p. 319.

22. Ibid.

Chapter 1

1. Charles Taylor, *Hegel* (Cambridge: Cambridge University Press, 1975), p. 6.

2. G. W. F. Hegel, *Phenomenology of Spirit*, trans. A. V. Miller (Oxford: Oxford University Press, 1979), p. 11. (*Phänomenologie des Geistes*, in *Werke* [Frankfurt am Main: Suhrkamp, 1986], 3:24). References to the German edition of Hegel's works will follow this format: *Werke* volume:page.

3. Ibid., p. 10 (*Werke* 3:22-3).

4. Ibid., (*Werke* Ibid.).

5. Ibid., *(Werke* 3:18).

6. *Werke,* 20:266, my translation.

7. Jürgen Habermas, *Der philosophische Diskurs der Moderne* (Frankfurt am Main: Suhrkamp, 1985), p. 57.

8. Michel Foucault, "Un cours inédit," *Magazine Littéraire* (May 1984): p. 36.

9. Ibid.

10. Jürgen Habermas, "Hegel's Critique of the French Revolution," *Theory and Practice* (London: Heinemann, 1974), p. 121.

11. For a recent discussion of this problematic see Jürgen Habermas, "Moralität und Sittlichkeit. Treffen Hegels Einwände gegen Kant auch auf die Diskursethik zu?," in *Moralität und Sittlichkeit, Das Problem Hegel und die Diskursethik,* ed. Wolfgang Kuhlmann (Frankfurt am Main: Suhrkamp, 1986), pp. 16-38. I have found it impossible to find one English equivalent for the German term *Sittlichkeit.*

12. Hegel, *Phenomenology,* p. 14 *(Werke* 3:28).

13. Habermas, *Der philosophische Diskurs der Moderne,* p. 27.

14. Ibid.

15. Ibid., p. 28.

16. By subjective idealism I mean the philosophies of Kant, Jacobi, and Fichte, which, to simplify drastically, conceive of the absolute from the standpoint of self-consciousness. The Hegelian provenance of the term is not beyond criticism; however, such a critique cannot be attempted here.

17. G. W. F. Hegel, *Faith and Knowledge,* trans. W. Cerf and H. S. Harris (Albany: State University of New York Press, 1977).

18. G. W. F. Hegel, *Early Theological Writings,* ed. T. M. Knox (Chicago: University of Chicago Press, 1948), p. 73 *(Werke* 1:110).

19. Taylor, *Hegel,* ch. 1.

20. G. W. F. Hegel, *Three Essays, 1793-1795,* ed. and trans., P. Fuss and J. Dobbins (Notre Dame, Ind.: University of Notre Dame Press, 1984), p. 49 *(Werke* 1:33).

21. By rational religion I mean a conception of the religious that is founded not on any notion of revelation but on immanently ethical principles.

22. By private religion I mean a definition of the religious that centers on the question of individual faith rather than the question of a civic ethos as is, in part, the case with the public religions of antiquity.

23. Hegel, *Three Essays*, p. 51 (*Werke* 1:36).

24. Ibid., pp. 57-8 (*Werke* 1:44).

25. Ibid., p. 59 (*Werke* 1:47).

26. Ibid., p. 59 (*Werke* 1:48).

27. Ibid., p. 63 (*Werke* 1:52).

28. Ibid., pp. 64-5 (*Werke* 1:53-4).

29. However, one could also argue that it is precisely the parasite that makes communication possible. For such a concept of communication, see Michel Serres, *Le parasite* (Paris: Grasset, 1980).

30. Hegel, *Three Essays*, p. 88 (*Werke* 1:82-3).

31. Ibid., pp. 101-3 (*Werke*, 1:99-101).

32. Hegel, *Early Theological Writings*, pp. 81-2, 151 (*Werke* 1:119-120, 202).

33. Ibid., p. 154 (*Werke* 1:204-5).

34. Ibid., p. 214 (*Werke* 1:326).

35. Ibid., p. 244 (*Werke* 1:359-60).

36. *Werke* 1:394.

37. Habermas, *Der philosophische Diskurs der Moderne*, p. 14.

38. Ibid.

39. *Werke* 18:441. As I have found the English translation unsatisfactory, all translations from the Socrates' chapter of Hegel's *Vorlesungen über die Geschichte der Philosophie* are mine.

40. G. W. F Hegel, Introduction, in *Lectures on the History of Philosophy*, trans. T. M. Knox and A. V. Miller (Oxford: Clarendon Press, 1985), p. 9.

41. *Werke* 18:441.

42. *Werke* 18:442.

43. For a more precise discussion of the significance of the concepts of *nomos* and *physis* in antiquity, see Cornelius Castoriadis, *Les carrefours du labyrinthe* (Paris: Seuil, 1978), pp. 269-78.

44. *Werke* 18:445.

45. *Werke* 18:445.

46. *Werke* 18:468.

47. In his discussion of the Kantian philosophy, Hegel argues explicitly that Kant returns to a Socratic standpoint (*Werke*, 19:329).

48. Hegel, Introduction, in *Lectures*, pp. 49-50.

49. See Herbert Schnädelbach, *Philosophy in Germany*, 1831-1933 (Cambridge: Cambridge University Press, 1984).

50. Hegel, Introduction, in *Lectures*, p. 50.

51. See Cornelius Castoriadis, "La *polis* grecque et la création de la démocratie," in *Domaines de l'homme: Les Carrefours du labyrinthe II* (Paris: Seuil, 1986), pp. 261-307, on the inextricability of the birth of philosophy and freedom.

52. Hegel, Introduction, in *Lectures*, pp. 181-2.

53. Once again, the plausibility of this nonassimilation is grounded in Hegel's historiosophical seperation of the Greek from the Germanic world.

54. Hegel, Introduction, in *Lectures*, p. 139.

55. *Werke* 18:449.

56. *Werke* 18:452.

57. *Werke* 18:176.

58. Martin Heidegger, "Hegel und die Griechen," in *Gesamtausgabe, Wegmarken*, vol. 9 (Frankfurt am Main: Vittorio Klostermann, 1976), p. 428.

59. Ibid., pp. 438-39.

60. G. W. F. Hegel, *Aesthetics: Lectures on Fine Art*, trans. T. M. Knox (Oxford: Clarendon Press, 1975), p. 4.

61. Ibid., p. 518.

62. Ibid., p. 436.

63. Ibid.

64. *Werke* 18:453.

65. *Werke* 18:454.

66. *Werke* 18:454.

67. Michel Foucault, *L'usage des plaisirs*, vol. 2 of *Histoire de la sexualité* (Paris: Gallimard, 1984), p. 67.

68. *Werke* 18:454.

69. See Walter Benjamin, "On Some Motifs in Baudelaire," in *Illuminations*, trans. H. Zohn (London: Collins/Fontana, 1973).

70. *Werke* 18:456.

71. *Werke* 18:456.

72. See Karl-Otto Apel, *Sprachanalytik, Semiotik, Hermeneutik*, vol. 1 of *Transformation der Philosophie* (Frankfurt am Main: Suhrkamp, 1973), p. 10. Apel argues that "the institutionalization of impotent philosophy as an island of communication this side of or beyond party political control, which has been at least reasonably successful since Socrates, is both necessary and, in a certain sense, comforting."

73. *Werke* 18:458.

74. *Werke* 18:458.

75. G. W. F. Hegel, *Logic, Being Part One of the Encyclopaedia of the Philosophical Sciences*, trans. W. Wallace (Oxford: Clarendon Press, 1975), p. 115.

76. Ibid., p. 116.

77. Ibid., p. 117.

78. Ibid., p. 118.

79. *Werke* 18:461.

80. *Werke* 18:461.

81. *Werke* 18:460.

82. *Werke* 18:463.

83. *Werke* 18:466.

84. *Werke* 18:467.

85. *Werke* 12:329.

86. *Werke* 18:470.

87. *Werke* 18:470.

88. See G. W. F. Hegel, "Über die wissenshaftlichen Behand-lungsarten des Naturrechtes," in *Werke, Band 2* (Frankfurt am Main: Suhrkamp, 1986; and *System der Sittlichkeit* (Hamburg: Felix Meiner, 1967).

89. See Axel Honneth, "Moralische Entwicklung und sozialer Kampf, Sozialphilosophische Lehren aus dem Frühwerk Hegels," in *Zwischenbetrachtungen im Prozeß der Aufklärung*, ed. A. Honneth et al. (Frankfurt am Main: Suhrkamp, 1989), pp. 549-579; and "Atom-isierung und Sittlichkeit. Zu hegels Kritik der Französischen Revo-lution," in *Die Ideen von 1789 in der deutschen Rezeption*, ed. Forum für Philosophie Bad Homburg (Frankfurt am Main: Suhrkamp, 1989), pp. 174-186.

90. Michel Foucault, *Le souci de soi*, vol. 3 of *Histoire de la sexualité* (Paris: Gallimard, 1984), p. 58.

91. Foucault, *L'usage de plaisirs*, p. 100.

92. *Werke* 18:473.

93. *Werke* 18:475.

94. G. W. F. Hegel, Intoduction, in *Lectures*, p. 169.

95. See Jürgen Habermas, "Labour and Interaction: Remarks on Hegel's *Jena Philosophy of Mind*," in *Theory and Practice*, pp. 142-170.

96. Hegel, Introduction, in *Lectures*, p. 173.

97. *Werke* 18:481.

98. *Werke* 18:491.

99. *Werke* 18:493.

100. *Werke* 18:495.

101. *Werke* 12:326-29.

102. *Werke* 18:512.

103. *Werke* 18:503.

104. *Werke* 18:502.

105. *Werke* 18:505.

106. *Werke* 18:505.

107. *Werke* 18:508.

108. *Werke* 18:509.

109. *Werke* 18:510.

110. Jürgen Habermas, "Moralität und Sittlichkeit. Treffen Hegels Einwände gegen Kant auf die Diskursethik zu?," in *Moralität und Sittlichkeit*, p. 30.

111. Joachim Ritter, "Morality and Ethical Life: Hegel's Controversy with Kantian Ethics," in *Hegel and the French Revolution: Essays on the "Philosophy of Right,"* trans. R. D. Winfield (Cambridge, Mass.: MIT Press, 1984), p. 169 *(Metaphysik und Politik, Studien zu Aristoteles und Hegel* [Frankfurt am Main: Suhrkamp, 1969], p. 300).

112. *Werke* 18:515.

Chapter 2

1. See Alasdair MacIntyre, *After Virtue: A Study in Moral Theory,* 2d ed. (London: Duckworth, 1985), p. 42. For his full interpretation of *Either/Or,* see pp. 39-43.

2. Cornelius Castoriadis, *Domaines de l'homme: Les carrefours du labyrinthe II* (Paris: Seuil, 1986), p. 268.

3. Soren Kierkegaard, *Stages on Life's Way,* trans. W. Lowrie (Princeton: Princeton University Press, 1945), p. 430.

4. See Hubert L. Dreyfus & Jane Rubin, "You Can't Get Something for Nothing: Kierkegaard and Heidegger on How Not to Overcome Nihilism," *Inquiry* 30:1, 2 (March 1987): pp. 33-77.

5. Charles Taylor, *Hegel* (Cambridge: Cambridge University Press, 1975), p. 6.

6. Soren Kierkegaard, *The Sickness Unto Death,* in *Fear and Trembling and the Sickness Unto Death,* trans. W. Lowrie (Princeton: Princeton University Press, 1968), p. 146.

7. Ibid., p. 147.

8. Ibid., p. 146.

9. Dreyfus and Rubin, "You Can't Get Something for Nothing," p. 37.

10. Soren Kierkegaard, *Either/Or*, vol. 2, trans. W. Lowrie (New York: Anchor Books, 1959), pp. 198-9.

11. Kierkegaard, *Stages on Life's Way*, p. 430.

12. Kierkegaard, *Either/Or*, vol. 2, p. 252.

13. Ibid., p. 253.

14. Ibid., p. 256.

15. Ibid., p. 259.

16. Soren Kierkegaard, *Concluding Unscientific Postsript*, trans. David. F. Swenson and Walter Lowrie (Princeton: Princeton University Press, 1968), p. 494.

17. Ibid., p. 478.

18. John Powell Clayton, "Zarathustra and the Stages on Life's Way: A Nietzschean Response to Kierkegaard," in *Nietzsche-Studien*, vol. 14, ed. E. Behler (Berlin and New York: Walter de Gruyler, 1985), p. 192.

19. Mark C. Taylor, *Kierkegaard's Pseudonymous Authorship: A Study of Time and Self* (Princeton: Princeton University Press, 1975), pp. 62-76.

20. Ibid., p. 74.

21. Ibid., pp. 68-69, 74.

22. Soren Kierkegaard, *The Concept of Anxiety: A Simple Psychologically Orienting Deliberation on the Dogmatic Issue of Hereditary Sin*, trans. R. Thomte and A. Anderson (Princeton: Princeton University Press, 1980), pp. 16-17.

23. Kierkegaard, *Concluding Unscientific Postscript*, pp. 184-85.

24. Soren Kierkegaard, *Journals and Papers*, vol. 4, ed. and trans. H. V. Hong and E. H. Hong (Bloomington: Indiana University Press, 1975), p. 677.

25. Martin Heidegger, "La fin de la philosophie et la tâche de la pensée," in *Kierkegaard Vivant*, colloque organisé par l'UNESCO (Paris: Gallimard, 1966), pp. 167-205.

26. Soren Kierkegaard, *Johannes Climacus or De omnibus dubitandum est,* trans. T. H. Croxall, Adam & Charles Black, London, 1958.

27. Soren Kierkegaard, *The Concept of Irony, with Constant Reference to Socrates,* trans. Lee M. Capel (Bloomington: Indiana University Press, 1965), p. 349.

28. Soren Kierkegaard, *Point of View of My Work as an Author* (New York: Harper and Row, 1962).

29. Ibid., p. 40.

30. G. W. F. Hegel, *Phenomenology of Spirit,* trans. A. V. Miller (Oxford: Oxford University Press, 1979), p. 409.

31. Kierkegaard, *The Concept of Irony,* p. 49.

32. Ibid., p. 50.

33. Ibid., p. 64.

34. See Vladimir Jankelevitch, *L'ironie* (Paris: Flammarion, 1964), p. 80.

35. Ibid., p. 81.

36. Kierkegaard, *The Concept of Irony,* p. 73.

37. Ibid.

38. See Jacques Derrida, "From Restricted to General Economy: A Hegelianism without Reserve," in *Writing and Difference* (London: Routledge and Kegan Paul, 1978), pp. 251-78, for the concepts of a general and restricted economy.

39. Kierkegaard, *The Concept of Irony,* p. 113.

40. Ibid., p. 115.

41. Ibid., p. 117.

42. Ibid., p. 144.

43. Ibid., p. 151.

44. Ibid., p. 152.

45. Ibid., pp. 174, 180.

46. Ibid., p. 163.

47. Ibid., pp. 167, 180.

48. Ibid., p. 159.

49. Ibid., p. 202.

50. Ibid., p. 203.

51. Ibid., p. 213.

52. Ibid., p. 217.

53. Ibid., p. 219.

54. Ibid., p. 221.

55. Ibid., p. 224.

56. Ibid., p. 233.

57. Ibid., p. 255.

58. Ibid., pp. 287-88.

59. Ibid., p. 288.

60. Ibid., p. 260.

61. Ibid., p. 290.

62. Ibid., p. 292.

63. It would not be difficult to show the affinities between this type of thought and postmodernism in its Derridean variant in particular, for many of the French followers of Derrida have shown an intense interest in German romanticism. This interest is determined by the obvious philosophical correspondences and not by philological preoccupations. The similarities between Derrida's philosophy and the philosophy of Schelling have been convincingly demonstrated by Manfred Frank in his book *Was ist Neostructuralismus?* (Frankfurt am Main: Suhrkamp, 1983).

64. Ibid., p. 294.

65. Ibid., p. 300.

66. Ibid.

67. Ibid., p. 324.

68. Ibid., p. 325.

69. Ibid., p. 331.

70. Ibid., p. 334.

71. Ibid., p. 338.

72. Soren Kierkegaard, *Philosophical Fragments, or a Fragment of Philosophy*, trans. David F. Swenson and Howard V. Hong (Princeton: Princeton University Press, 1967), p. 139.

73. Kierkegaard, *The Sickness Unto Death*, pp. 220-21.

74. Hannah Arendt, *Willing*, in *The Life of the Mind* (New York: Harcourt Brace Jovanovich, 1981), p. 37.

75. The conflict between the intellect and the will has resonances in the sociological literature; for in Weber's theory of Occidental rationalism, it is an "inner worldly activism," and not the essentially contemplative forms of Greek rationalism, that is the "royal road" to modernity.

76. Kierkegaard, *Philosophical Fragments*, p. 29

77. Ibid., p. 46.

78. Ibid., p. 55.

79. Ibid., p. 61.

80. Ibid., p. 76.

81. Kierkegaard, *Sickness Unto Death*, p. 80.

82. Kierkegaard, Philosophical Fragments, p. 105.

83. Ibid., p. 77.

84. Ibid., p. 152.

85. See the author's dedication in Theodor Adorno, *Minima Moralia: Reflections from Damaged Life*, trans. E. F. N. Jephcott (London: New Left Books, 1974).

86. Kierkegaard, *Concluding Unscientific Postscript*, p. 37-8.

87. Kierkegaard, *The Concept of Anxiety*, p.16.

88. Ibid., p. 70.

89. Kierkegaard, *Concluding Unscientific Postscript*, p. 275.

90. Ibid., p. 68.

91. Ibid., p. 73.

92. Ibid., p. 551.

93. Ibid., p. 74.

94. Ibid., pp. 173-74.

95. Ibid., p. 83.

96. Ibid., p. 85.

97. Kierkegaard, *Either/Or*, vol. 2, p. 298.

98. Kierkegaard, *Journals and Papers*, p. 3617.

99. Kierkegaard, *Concluding Unscientific Postscript*, p. 132.

100. Ibid., p. 180.

101. Ibid.

102. Ibid., p. 182.

103. Jürgen Habermas, "Wahrheitstheorien," in *Vorstudien und Ergänzungen zur Theorie des kommunikativen Handelns* (Frankfurt am Main: Suhrkamp, 1984), p. 138.

104. Jürgen Habermas, "What Is Universal Pragmatics?" in *Communication and the Evolution of Society*, trans. T. McCarthy (Boston: Beacon Press, 1979), p. 68.

105. Kierkegaard, *Concluding Unscientific Postscript*, p. 181.

106. Ibid., p. 183; see also p. 185.

107. Ibid., p. 184.

108. Ibid., p. 267.

109. Ibid., p. 269.

110. Ibid., p. 314.

111. Ibid., p. 339.

112. Ibid., p. 449.

113. Ibid.

114. Ibid., p. 446; the phrase is repeated on p. 452.

115. Ibid., p. 502.

116. Soren Kierkegaard, *The Age of Revolution and the Present Age: A Literary Review*, ed. and trans. H. V. Hong and E. H. Hong (Princeton: Princeton University Press, 1978), p. 68.

117. Ibid., p. 81.

118. Kierkegaard, *Journals and Papers*, p. 222.

Chapter 3

1. G. W. F. Hegel, *The Philosophy of Right*, trans. T. M. Knox (Oxford: Clarendon Press, 1952), pp. 10-12 (*Werke* 7:26-27).

2. Friedrich Nietzsche, *The Will To Power*, trans. W. Kaufmann and R. J. Hollingdale (New York: Vintage Books, 1968), p. 3.

3. Ibid., p. 17.

4. Ibid., p. 3.

5. Ibid., p. 9.

6. Ibid., p. 13.

7. Ibid., p. 14.

8. Ibid.

9. Ibid., p. 35.

10. Ibid., p. 36.

11. Ibid., p. 14.

12. Ibid., p. 270.

13. Ibid., p. 270.

14. Jürgen Habermas, *Der philosophische Diskurs der Moderne* (Frankfurt am Main: Suhrkamp, 1985), p. 27.

15. Reiner Schurmann, *Heidegger on Being and Acting: From Principles to Anarchy*, trans. C. M. Gros (Bloomington: Indiana University Press, 1987), pp. 53-55.

16. Ibid., pp. 46-47.

17. Friedrich Nietzsche, *On the Genealogy of Morals*, in *On the Genealogy of Morals and Ecce Homo*, trans. W. Kaufmann and R. J. Hollingdale (New York: Vintage Books, 1969), p. 121.

18. Ibid. p. 70.

19. Nitzsche, *The Will to Power*, p. 291.

20. See Karl Löwith's chapter entitled "Der antichristliche Wiederholung der Antike," *Nietzsches Philosophie der ewigen Wiederkehr des Gleichen, Sämtliche Schriften,* vol. 6 (Stuttgart: Metzler, 1979), pp. 238-56.

21. Walter Burkert, *Greek Religion, Archaic and Classical,* trans. J. Raffan (Oxford: Basil Blackwell, 1985), p. 162.

22. On the concept of *anaisthetos* see Aristotle's *Nichomachean Ethics,* in *The Ethics of Aristotle* (Harmondsworth: Penguin, 1976), p. 247.

23. Euripides, *The Bacchae,* in *The Bacchae and other Plays,* trans. P. Vellacott (Harmondsworth: Penguin, 1954), p. 201.

24. Nietzsche, *The Will To Power,* p. 322 *(Der Wille Zur Macht Versuch einer Umwertung aller Werte, Sämtliche Werke in zwölf Bänden* (Stuttgart: Alfred Kröner Verlag, 1964), pp. 408-9).

25. Friedrich Nietzsche, *The Twilight of the Idols,* in *Twilight of the Idols and the Anti-Christ,* trans. R. J. Hollingdale (Harmondsworth: Penguin, 1968), pp. 40-41.

26. Nietzsche, *Genealogy of Morals,* p. 20.

27. Friedrich Nietzsche, *Human, All Too Human: A Book for Free Spirits,* trans. R. J. Hollingdale (Cambridge: Cambridge University Press, 1986), p. 37.

28. Nietzsche, *Genealogy of Morals,* pp. 31, 37-38.

29. Ibid., pp. 62-63.

30. Ibid., p. 92.

31. Ibid., p. 57.

32. Ibid., p. 309.

33. Nietzsche, *Human, All Too Human,* p. 51.

34. Friedrich Nietzsche, *Daybreak: Thoughts on the Prejudices of Morality,* trans. R. J. Hollingdale (Cambridge: Cambridge University Press, 1982), p. 10.

35. Ibid., p. 11.

36. Friedrich Nietzsche, "On the Uses and Disadvantages of History for Life," in *Untimely Meditations,* trans. R. J. Hollingdale (Cambridge: Cambridge University Press, 1983), p. 62.

37. Ibid., p. 79.

38. Ibid.

39. Ibid., p. 120.

40. Ibid.

41. Ibid., p. 123.

42. See Löwith, "Der antichristliche Wiederholung der Antike," pp. 125-27. Werner J. Dannhauser in *Nietzsche's View of Socrates* ([Ithaca: Cornell University Press, 1974], pp. 19-20) also takes this view, as does Walter Kaufmann in *Nietsche: Philosopher, Psychologist, Antichrist* (Princeton: Princeton University Press, 1974). Kaufmann, however, prefers to operate more with the contrast between an early and late period.

43. Friedrich Nietzsche, *Sämtliche Werke*, vol. 11 of *Kritische Studienausgabe in 15 Bänden*, ed. Giorgio Colli and Mazzino Montinari (Munich and New York: Deutscher Taschenbuch Verlag und de Gruyter, 1980), pp. 159-60. References to this German edition of Nietzsche's works are cited as follows: *KSA* 11:159-60. When references to this edition are unaccompanied by an English reference, then all translations are mine.

44. *KSA* 12:123-24.

45. Dannhauser, *Nietzsche's View of Socrates,* pp. 140-74.

46. *KSA* 9:363.

47. Nietzsche, *Human, All Too Human*, p. 328.

48. Ibid., p. 332.

49. Ibid.

50. Nietzsche, *Genealogy of Morals*, p. 113.

51. Hans Blumenberg, *Das Lachen der Thrakerin, Eine Urgeschichte der Theorie* (Frankfurt am Main: Suhrkamp, 1987).

52. *KSA* 1:808-9.

53. *KSA* 1:810. This does not mean that philosophy should be an apologist for the state. Nietzsche argues that it is only modern philosophy, regulated as it is by all sorts of institutions, that performs this role. If you want to philosophize, Nietzsche argues, then first of

all you have to ban philosophy. The idea that philosophy itself is a hinderance to thinking is a major motif in certain streams of modern philosophy.

54. *KSA* 1:869.

55. *Werke* 18:124.

56. *KSA* 1:880-81. Nietzschean critique of truth and his consequent emphasis on interpretation has been the subject of a great deal of academic discussion over the past decade due, partly, to the influence of deconstruction and its critique of the ontotheological nature of western metaphysics. See, for example, Alexander Nehamas' "Untruth as a Condition of Life," chapter 2 of *Nietzsche, Life As Literature* ([Cambridge, Mass.: Harvard University Press, 1985], pp. 42-74), which rejects the pragmatist account of Nietzsche's theory of interpretation for a more textualist account of Nietzsche's thoughts about the relationship between knowledge and the world. For a more recent discussion, see Part 3 of Alan D. Schrift's *Nietzsche and the Question of Interpretation: Between Hermeneutics and Deconstruction* ([New York: Routledge, 1990], pp. 123-99), where Nietzsche's theory of interpretation is seen as an empirical epistemology. There have also been more hermeneutic attempts at an ontological construction of Nietzsche's theory of interpretation. See Johann Figl, *Interpretation als philosophisches Prinzip, Friedrich Nietzsches universale Theorie der Auslegung im späten Nachlaß*, Monographien und Texte zur Nietzsche-Forschung, vol. 7 (Berlin and New York: Walter de Gruyter, 1982.

57. *KSA* 1:883.

58. *KSA* 1:889.

59. Friedrich Nietzsche, *The Birth of Tragedy*, in *The Birth of Tragedy and the Case of Wagner*, trans. W. Kaufmann (New York: Vintage Books, 1967), p. 110.

60. *KSA* 8:97.

61. Nietzsche, *The Birth of Tragedy*, p. 35 (*KSA* 1:27).

62. Peter Bürger, *Zur Kritik der idealistischen Äesthetik* (Frankfurt am Main: Suhrkamp, 1983), pp. 71-74.

63. Nietzsche, *The Birth Of Tragedy*, p. 37.

64. Ibid., p. 40.

65. Ibid., pp. 44-45.

66. Ibid., p. 45.

67. Ibid., p. 50.

68. Ibid., p. 52. Bracketed comment mine.

69. Ibid., p. 52.

70. Ibid.

71. Ibid., p. 59.

72. Ibid., pp. 64-65.

73. Ibid., p. 74.

74. Ibid.

75. See Burkert, *Greek Religion*, on this point.

76. Nietzsche, *The Birth of Tragedy*, p. 81.

77. See Joachim Ritter, *Metaphysik und Politik, Studien zu Aristoteles und Hegel* (Frankfurt am Main: Suhrkamp, 1969), p. 14.

78. Nietzsche, *The Birth of Tragedy*, p. 84.

79. *KSA* 7:41.

80. Nietzsche, *The Birth of Tragedy*, p. 94.

81. Ibid., pp. 95-96 (*KSA* 1:99).

82. Ibid., p. 96.

83. *KSA* 7:133.

84. *KSA* 7:133.

85. *KSA* 7:134.

86. Nietzsche, *The Birth of Tragedy*, p. 97.

87. Ibid., p. 98.

88. *KSA* 7:193.

89. *KSA* 7:203.

90. *KSA* 7:203.

91. Nietzsche, *The Birth of Tragedy*, p. 86.

92. *KSA* 7:21.

93. *KSA* 7:17.

94. Nietzsche, *The Birth of Tragedy*, p. 85.

95. Ibid., p. 87.

96. *KSA* 7:157.

97. *KSA* 7:179.

98. *KSA* 7:544.

99. *KSA* 7:544.

100. *KSA* 7:545.

101. *KSA* 7:555.

102. *KSA* 7:548.

103. *KSA* 8:98.

104. *KSA* 8:104.

105. *KSA* 8:105.

106. *KSA* 8:104.

107. *KSA* 8:107.

108. *KSA* 8:102.

109. *KSA* 8:108.

110. *KSA* 9:386.

111. *KSA* 9:363.

112. *KSA* 8:97.

113. Friedrich Nietzsche, *The Gay Science, with a Prelude in Rhyme and an Appendix of Songs*, trans. W. Kaufmann (New York: Vintage Books, 1974), p. 272.

114. Ibid.

115. Georges Dumézil, "Divertissement sur les dernières paroles de Socrate," in ". . . *Le moyne noir en gris dedans Varennes*," in *Sotie nostradamique suivie d'un divertissement sur les derniéres paroles de Socrate* (Paris: Gallimard, 1984), pp. 151-52.

116. *KSA* 10:248-49.

117. *KSA* 10:257.

118. *KSA* 10:257; 11:16.

119. *KSA* 11:37.

120. *KSA,* 11:68.

121. Nietzsche, *The Will to Power*, p. 420. See also Martin Heidegger, *Nietzsche*, vol. 1 (Pfullingen: Neske, 1961), pp. 117-18 on this point.

122. Nietzsche, *Twilight of the Idols*, p. 73.

123. Ibid., p. 110.

124. Nietzsche, *The Will to Power*, pp. 420-21.

125. Ibid., p. 420.

126. *KSA* 11:87; similar thought, 11:226.

127. *KSA* 11:87.

128. *KSA* 11:554.

129. *KSA* 11:87.

130. *KSA* 11:435.

131. *KSA* 11:440.

132. *KSA* 11:446.

133. *KSA* 11:431.

134. *KSA* 11:244.

135. Friedrich Nietzsche, *Beyond Good and Evil: Prelude to a Philosophy of the Future*, trans. R. J. Hollingdale (Harmondsworth: Penguin, 1973), p. 14.

136. Nietzsche, *On the Genealogy of Morals*, p. 152.

137. Ibid., pp. 152-53.

138. See Herbert Schnädelbach, *Philosophy in Germany, 1831-1933* ([Cambridge: Cambridge University Press, 1984], p. 190) on this point.

139. Nietzsche, *Beyond Good and Evil*, pp. 95-96.

140. Ibid., pp. 124-25.

141. *KSA* 13:289.

142. Nietzsche, *The Will to Power*, p. 156 (*KSA* 12:429).

143. *KSA* 12:303.

144. Schnädelbach, *Philosophy in Germany*, p. 161.

145. Nietzsche, *Twilight of the Idols*, p. 55 (*KSA* 6:98).

146. *KSA* 13:330-31.

147. *KSA* 13:330.

148. Nietzsche, *Twilight of the Idols*, p. 21.

149. *KSA* 13:268.

150. Nietzsche, *Twilight of the Idols*, p. 31.

151. Ibid., p. 108.

152. Ibid., pp. 32-33.

153. Ibid., p. 33.

154. Ibid., p. 34.

155. *KSA* 13:270.

156. *KSA* 13:403.

157. Nietzsche, *Twilight of the Idols*, p. 32.

158. Nietzsche, *The Will to Power*, p. 237 (*KSA* 13:270).

159. Ibid., p. 237 (*KSA* 13:270).

160. *KSA* 13: 270.

161. See Nietzsche, *The Anti-Christ*, in *Twilight of the Idols and the Anti-Christ*, pp. 145, 164.

Conclusion

1. See Agnes Heller, "*Ecce Homo*: Socrates and Jesus," in *Renaissance Man*, trans. R. E. Allen (New York: Schocken Books, 1978), pp. 139-47.

2. See Claude Mossé, *Le procès de Socrate* (Paris: Editions complexe, 1987), pp. 139-45.

3. See Jürgen Habermas, *Der philosophische Diskurs der Moderne* (Frankfurt am Main: Suhrkamp, 1985) for these concepts.

4. See Jürgen Habermas, *Reason and the Rationalization of Society,* vol. 1 of *The Theory of Communicative Action,* trans. T. McCarthy (Boston: Beacon Press, 1984), p. 249.

5. See Georges Gusdorf, *Naissance de la conscience romantique au XVIII* (Paris: Payot, 1976).

6. Alexandre Koyré, *From the Closed World to the Infinite Universe* (Baltimore: John Hopkins University Press, 1968), p. 2.

7. Ibid., p. 276.

8. See Hauke Brunkhorst, "Romanticism and Cultural Criticism," *Praxis International* 6:4 (January 1987): p. 409. By expressivism, I mean in this context an intellectual attitude that arises out of romanticism and that privileges the authenticity or sincerity of action as gesture over and above either traditional warrants or the discursive testing of the norms and values that underpin action.

9. Friedrich Nietzsche, *Thus Spake Zarathustra: A Book for Everyone and No One,* trans. R. J. Hollingdale (Harmondsworth: Penguin, 1969), p. 55 (*KSA* 4:30).

10. Ibid., (*KSA* 4:31).

11. Soren Kierkegaard, *Either/Or,* vol. 1, trans. D. F. and L. M. Swenson (Princeton: Princeton University Press, 1971), p. 290.

12. Soren Kierkegaard, *Journals and Papers,* vol. 8, trans. H. V. and E. H. Hong (Bloomington: Indiana University Press, 1975), p. 82.

13. What follows has been reworked from the author's "Writing and Discourse: The Problem of Socrates in Deconstruction and Discourse Theory," in A. Milner and C. Worth (eds.), *Discourse and Difference: Post-Structuralism, Feminism and the Moment of History* (Melbourne: Centre for General and Comparative Literature, 1990).

14. Jacques Derrida, "Différance," in *Margins of Philosophy* (Chicago: University of Chicago Press, 1982), p. 11.

15. Ibid., p. 12.

16. Manfred Frank, *Was ist Neostructuralismus?* (Frankfurt am Main: Suhrkamp, 1983), pp. 316-76. See also Rudolphe Gasché, *The Tain of the Mirror: Derrida and the Philosophy of Reflection* (Cambridge, Mass.: Harvard University Press, 1986) for a similar argument. I also try to bring out the Judaic provenance of Derrida's notion of interpretation, which is a perspective first developed by Susan A. Han-

delman in *The Slayers of Moses: The Emergence of Rabbinic Interpretation in Modern Literary Theory* (Albany: State University of New York Press, 1982), particularly "Reb Derrida's Scripture," pp. 163-79. I am more sympathetic, however, to Habermas's more critical account of this influence, and I shall try to show the problems it causes for his account of Socrates. See Habermas, *Der philosophische der Moderne*, particularly pp. 211-18

17. Jacques Derrida, "Différance," p. 15.

18. Richard Rorty, *Contingency, Irony, and Solidarity* (Cambridge: Cambridge University Press, 1989).

19. See Jacques Derrida, "Privilège. Titre justicatif et remarques introductives," in *Du droit à la philosophie* ([Paris: Galilée, 1990], pp. 9-111), for the concept of *démocratie*; and "Some Statements and Truisms about Neologisms, Postisms, Parasitisms, and Other Small Seisims," in David Carroll (ed.), *The States of "Theory"* ([New York: Columbia University Press, 1990], pp. 63-94) for the concept of *jetty.*

20. See Karl-Otto Apel, "Vorwort," in *Diskurs und Verantwortung, Das Problem des Übergangs zur postkonventionellen Moral* (Frankfurt am Main: Suhrkamp, 1988) pp. 7-14.

21. Ibid., p. 10.

22. Ibid., pp. 104-5.

23. See Jürgen Habermas, "Moralität und Sittlichkeit. Treffen Hegels Einwände gegen Kant auch auf die Diskursethik zu?" in *Moralität und Sittlichkeit*, Wolfgang Kuhlmann (ed.), (Frankfurt am Main: Suhrkamp, 1986), pp. 16-38.

24. Apel, *Diskurs und Verantwortung*, p. 387.

25. Jacques Derrida, Plato's Pharmacy, in *Dissemination* (Chicago: University of Chicago Press, 1981).

26. Martin Heidegger, *Kant and the Problem of Metaphysics* (Bloomington: Indianna University Press, 1962), p. 95.

27. Derrida, *Plato's Pharmacy*, p. 119.

28. Ibid., pp. 126-27.

29. Ibid., p. 124.

30. Ibid., p. 134.

31. Ibid., p. 148.

32. Ibid., p. 158.

33. Ibid., p. 163.

34. Jacques Derrida, *The Post Card: From Socrates to Freud and Beyond* (Chicago: University of Chicago Press, 1987), p. 66.

35. Ibid., p. 65.

36. Ibid., p. 165.

37. Ibid.

38. Ibid., p. 191.

39. Karl-Otto Apel, "The *a priori* of the communication community and the foundations of ethics: The problem of a rational foundation of ethics in the scientific age," in *Towards a Transformation of Philosophy* (London: Routledge and Kegan Paul, 1980), p. 278.

40. Karl-Otto Apel, Introduction, in *Transformation der Philosophie*, vol. 1 (Frankfurt am Main: Suhrkamp, 1984), p. 10.

41. Karl-Otto Apel, Deitrich Böhler, and Gerd Kadelbach, *Funk-Kolleg*, in *Praktische Philosophie/Ethik: Dialoge 1* (Frankfurt am Main: Fischer, 1988), p. 97.

42. Apel, *Diskurs und Verantwortung*, pp. 353-54.

43. Ibid., p. 190.

44. Apel et. al., *Funk-Kolleg*, p. 106.

45. Ibid.

46. See Sarah Kofman's Derridean reading of interpretations of Socrates in *Socrate(s)* (Paris: Galilée, 1989), for the notion of the Socratic novel.

47. For Gilles Deleuze's interpretation of Nietzsche see *Nietzsche and Philosophy* (London: Athlone Press, 1983); and for Michel Foucault's see "Nietzsche, Genealogy, History," in *Language, Counter-Memory, Practice: Selected Interviews and Essays* (Ithaca: Cornell University Press, 1977), pp. 139-65. Foucault's interpretation of Socrates in terms of the problematic of eros in the works of Plato can be found in *L'usage des plaisirs*, vol. 2 of *Historie de la sexualité* (Paris: Gallimard, 1984), pp. 205-71.

48. See Marcel Detienne, "L'espace de la publicité: ses opérateurs intellectuelles dans la cité," in *Les savoirs de l'écriture en Grèce ancienne*, ed., Marcel Detienne (Presses Universitaires de Lille, Lille, n.d.).

49. See Gernot Böhme, *Der Typ Sokrates* (Frankfurt am Main: Suhrkamp, 1988).

Bibliography

Adorno, Theodor W. *Minima Moralia: Reflections from Damaged Life.* Trans. E. F. N. Jephcott. NLB, London, 1974.

———. *Philosophische Frühschriften, Gesammelte Schriften.* Vol. 1. Suhrkamp, Frankfurt am Main, 1973.

Apel, Karl-Otto. *Diskurs und Verantwortung, Das Problem des Übergangs zur postkonventionellen Moral.* Suhrkamp, Frankfurt am Main, 1988.

———. *Towards a Transformation of Philosophy.* Routledge and Kegan Paul, London, 1980.

———. *Transformation der Philosophie.* Vol. 1, *Sprachanalytik, Semiotik, Hermeneutik.* Suhrkamp, Frankfurt am Main, 1973.

Apel, Karl-Otto, Dietrich Böhler, and Gerd Kadelbach. *Praktische Philosophische/Ethik: Dialoge 1.* Fischer, Frankfurt am Main, 1986.

Arendt, Hannah. *The Life of the Mind.* Harcourt Brace Jovanovich, New York, 1981.

Arnason, Johann P. "The Imaginary Constitution of MOdernity." *Revue européenne des sciences sociales* 10 (1989): p. 318ff.

Aristotle. *The Ethics of Aristotle.* Penguin, Harmondsworth, 1976.

Benjamin, Walter. *Illuminations.* Trans. H. Zohn. Collins/Fontana, London, 1973.

Böhme, Gernot. *Der Typ Sokrates.* Suhrkamp, Frankfurt am Main, 1988.

Blumenberg, Hans. *Das Lachen der Thrakerin, Eine Urgeschichte der Theorie.* Suhrkamp, Frankfurt am Main, 1987.

———. *The Legitimacy of the Modern Age.* MIT Press, Cambridge, Mass., 1983.

———. *Work on Myth.* MIT Press, Cambridge, Mass., 1985.

Brunkhorst, Hauke. "Romanticism and Cultural Criticism." *Praxis International* 6:4 (January 1987): p. 409ff.

Bürger, Peter. *Zur Kritik der idealistichen Äesthetik*. Suhrkamp, Frankfurt am Main, 1983.

Burkert, Walter. *Greek Religion, Archaic and Classical*. Trans. J. Raffan. Basil Blackwell, Oxford, 1985.

Carroll, David, ed. *The States of "Theory."* Columbia University Press, New York, 1990.

Castoriadis, Cornelius. *Les carrefours du labyrinthe*. Seuil, Paris, 1978.

―――. *Domaines de l'homme: Les carrefours du labyrinthe II*. Seuil, Paris, 1986.

―――. *L'institution imaginaire de la société*. Seuil, Paris, 1975.

Clayton, John Powell. "Zarathustra and the Stages on Life's Way: A Nietzschean Response to Kierkegaard." In *Nietzsche-Studien*. Vol. 14. Ed. E. Behler. Walter de Gruyter, Berlin and New York, 1985.

Dannhauser, Werner J. *Nietzsche's View of Socrates*. Cornell University Press, Ithaca, 1974.

Deleuze, Gilles, *Nietzsche and Philosophy*. Athlone Press, London, 1983.

Derrida, Jacques. *Dissemination*. University of Chicago Press, Chicago, 1981.

―――. *Du droit à la philosophie*. Galilée, Paris, 1990.

―――. *Margins of Philosophy*. University of Chicago Press, Chicago, 1982.

―――. *The Post Card: From Socrates to Freud and Beyond*. University of Chicago Press, Chicago, 1987.

―――. *Writing and Difference*. Routledge and Kegan Paul, London, 1978.

Detienne, Marcel. *Les savoirs de l'écriture en Grèce ancienne*. Presses Universitaires de Lille, Lille, n.d.

Dreyfus, Hubert L. and Jane Rubin. "You Can't Get Something for Nothing: Kierkegaard and Heidegger on How Not to Overcome Nihilism." *Inquiry* 30: 1, 2 (March 1987): pp. 33-77.

Dumézil, Georges. *". . . Le moyne noir en gris dedans Varennes."* In *Sotie nostradamique suivie d'un divertissement sur les dernières paroles de Socrate.* Gallimard, Paris, 1984.

Euripides. *The Bacchae and Other Plays.* Trans. P. Vellacott. Penguin, Harmondsworth, 1954.

Figl, Johann. *Interpretation als philosophisches Prinzip, Friedrich Nietzsches universale Theorie der Auslegung im späten Nachlaß.* Monographien und Texte zur Nietzsche-Forschung. Vol. 7. Berlin and New York: Walter de Gruyter, 1982.

Forum für Philosophie bad Homburg, ed. *Der Ideen von 1789 in der deutschen Rezeption.* Suhrkamp, Frankfurt am Main, 1989.

Foucault, Michel. *Histoire de la sexualité.* Vol. 2, *L'usage des plaisirs.* Gallimard, Paris, 1984.

———. *Histoire de la sexualité.* Vol. 3, *Le souci de soi.* Gallimard, Paris, 1984.

———. *Language, Counter-Memory, Practice: Selected Essays and Interviews.* Cornell University Press, Ithaca, 1977.

———. *"Un cours inédit." Magazine littéraire* (May 1984): pp. 17-22.

Frank, Manfred. *Was ist Neostructuralismus?* Suhrkamp, Frankfurt am Main, 1983.

Gasché, Rudolph. *The Tain of the Mirror: Derrida and the Philosophy of Reflection.* Harvard University Press, Cambridge, Mass., 1986.

Gusdorf, Georges. *Naissance de la conscience romantique au XVIII.* Seuil, Paris, 1976.

Habermas, Jürgen. *Communication and the Evolution of Society.* Trans. T. McCarthy. Beacon Press, Boston, 1979.

———. *Der philosophische Diskurs der Moderne.* Suhrkamp, Frankfurt am Main, 1985.

———. *Theory and Practice.* Heinemann, London, 1974.

———. *The Theory of Communicative Action.* Vol. 1, *Reason and the Rationalization of Society.* Trans. T. McCarthy. Beacon Press, Boston, 1984.

————. *Vorstudien und Ergänzungen zur Theorie des kommunikativen Handelns.* Suhrkamp, Frankfurt am Main, 1984.

Handelman, Susan A. *The Slayers of Moses: The Emergence of Rabbinic Interpretation in Modern Literary Theory.* SUNY Press, Albany, 1982.

Hegel, G. W. F. *Aesthetics: Lectures on Fine Art.* Trans. T. M. Knox. Clarendon Press, Oxford, 1975.

————. *Early Theological Writings.* Ed. T. M. Knox. University of Chicago Press, Chicago, 1948.

————. *Faith and Knowledge.* Trans. W. Cerf and H. S. Harris. SUNY Press, Albany, 1977.

————. Introduction. *Lectures on the History of Philosophy.* Trans. T. M. Knox and A. V. Miller. Oxford University Press, Oxford, 1985.

————. *Logic, Being Part One of the Philosophical Sciences.* Trans. W. Wallace. Clarendon Press, Oxford, 1975.

————. *Phenomenology of Spirit.* Trans. A. V. Miller. Oxford University Press, Oxford, 1979.

————. *The Philosophy of Right.* Trans. T. M. Knox. Oxford University Press, Oxford, 1952.

————. *Science of Logic.* Trans. A. V. Miller. London, 1969.

————. *System der Sittlichkeit.* Felix Meiner, Hamburg, 1967.

————. *Three Essays, 1793-1795.* Ed. and trans. P. Fuss and J. Dobbins. University of Notre Dame Press, Notre Dame, 1984.

————. *Werke.* Suhrkamp, Frankfurt am Main, 1986.

Heidegger, Martin. *Gasamtausgabe.* Vol. 9, *Wegmarken.* Vittorio Klostermann, Frankfurt am Main, 1976.

————. *Kant and the Problem of Metaphysics.* Indiana University Press, Bloomington, 1962.

————. *Nietzsche.* Neske, Pfullingen, 1961.

Heller, Agnes. *Renaissance Man.* Trans. R. E. Allen. Schocken Books, New York, 1978.

Honneth, Axel and Hans Joas. *Kommunikatives Handeln, Beiträge zu Habermas' "Theorie des kommunikativen Handelns."* Suhrkamp, Frankfurt am Main, 1986.

Honneth, Axel, Thomas Macarthy, and Claus Offe, ed. *Zwischenbetrachtungen im Prozeß der Aufklärung.* Suhrkamp, Frankfurt am Main, 1989.

Jankelevitch, Vladimir. *L'ironie.* Flammarion, Paris, 1964.

Kant, Immanuel. *Critique of Pure Reason.* Trans. N. K. Smith. Macmillan, London, 1933.

Kaufmann, Walter. *Nietzsche: Philosopher, Psychologist, Antichrist.* Princeton University Press, Princeton, 1974.

Kofman, Sarah. *Socrate(s).* Paris, Galilée, 1989.

Kierkegaard Vivant. Colloque organisé par l'UNESCO. Gallimard, Paris, 1966.

Kierkegaard, Soren. *The Age of Revolution and the Present Age: A Literary Review.* Ed. and Trans. H. V. Hong and E. H. Hong. Princeton University Press, Princeton, 1978.

————. *The Concept of Anxiety: A Simple Psychologically Orienting Deliberation on the Dogmatic Issue of Hereditary Sin.* Trans. R. Thomte and A. Anderson. Princeton University Press, Princeton, 1980.

————. *The Concept of Irony, with Constant Reference to Socrates.* Trans. Lee M. Capel. Indiana University Press, Bloomington, 1965.

————. *Concluding Unscientific Postscript.* Trans. David F. Swenson and Walter Lowrie. Princeton University Press, Princeton, 1968.

————. *Either/Or.* Vol. 1. Trans. D. F. and L. M. Swenson. Princeton University Press, Princeton, 1959.

————. *Either/Or.* Vol. 2. Trans. W. Lowrie. Anchor Books, New York, 1959.

————. *Fear and Trembling and the Sickness Unto Death.* Trans. W. Lowrie. Princeton University Press, Princeton, 1968.

————. *Johannes Climacus, or De omnibus dubitandum est.* Trans. T. H. Croxall. Adam and Charles Black, London, 1958.

———. *Journals and Papers*. Eds. H. V. and E. H. Hong. Indiana University Press, Bloomington, 1975.

———. *Philosophical Fragments, or a Fragment of Philosophy*. Trans. David F. Swenson and Howard V. Hong. Princeton University Press, Princeton, 1967.

———. *Point of View of My Work as an Author*. Harper Torchbooks, New York, 1962.

———. *Stages on Life's Way*. Trans. W. Lowrie. Princeton University Press, Princeton, 1945.

Koyre, Alexandre. *From the Closed World to the Infinite Universe*. John Hopkins University Press, Baltimore, 1968.

Kuhlmann, Wolfgang, ed. *Moralität und Sittlichkeit, Das Problem Hegels und die Diskursethik*. Suhrkamp, Frankfurt am Main, 1986.

Löwith, Karl. *From Hegel to Nietzsche: The Revolution in Nineteenth Century Thought*. Constable, London, 1964.

———. *Meaning in History*. University of Chicago Press, Chicago, 1949.

———. *Nietzsches Philosophie der ewigen Wiederkehr des Gleichen*. Vol. 6. Stuttgart, Metzler, 1979.

Lukács, Georg. *The Destruction of Reason*. Trans. P. Palmer. Humanities Press, Atlantic Highlands, N.J., 1981.

———. *The Theory of the Novel*. Trans. A. Bostock. Merlin Press, London, 1971.

MacIntyre, Alasdair. *After Virtue: A Study in Moral Theory*. 2d ed. Duckworth, London, 1985.

Mossé, Claude. *Le procès de Socrate*. Editions Complexe, Paris, 1987.

Nehamas, Alexander. *Nietzsche: Life As Literature*. Harvard University Press, Cambridge, Mass., 1985.

Nietzsche, Friedrich. *Beyond Good and Evil: Prelude to a Philosophy of the Future*. Trans. R. J. Hollingdale. Penguin, Harmondsworth, 1973.

———. *The Birth of Tragedy and the Case of Wagner*. Trans. W. Kaufmann. Vintage Books, New York, 1967.

———. *Daybreak: Thoughts on the Prejudices of Morality*. Trans. R. J. Hollingdale. Cambridge University Press, Cambridge, 1982.

———. *The Gay Science, with a Prelude in Rhyme and an Appendix of Songs*. Trans. W. Kaufmann. Vintage Books, New York, 1974.

———. *Human, All Too Human: A Book for Free Spirits*. Trans. R. J. Hollingdale. Cambirdge University Press, Cambridge, 1986.

———. *On the Genealogy of Morals and Ecce Homo*. Trans. W. Kaufmann and R. J. Hollingdale. Vintage Books, New York, 1969.

———. *Sämtliche Werke, Kritische Studienausgabe in 15 Bänden*. Ed. Giorgio Colli and Mazzino Montinari. Deutscher Taschenbuch Verlag and de Gruyter. Munich and New York, 1980.

———. *Thus Spake Zarathustra: A Book for Everyone and No One*. Trans. R. J. Hollingdale. Penguin, Harmondsworth, 1969.

———. *Twilight of the Idols and the Anti-Christ*. Trans. R. J. Hollingdale. Penguin, Harmondsworth, 1968.

———. *Untimely Meditations*. Trans. R. J. Hollingdale. Cambridge University Press, Cambridge, 1983.

———. *Der Wille Zur Macht, Versuch einer Umwertung aller Werte*. In *Sämtliche Werke in zwölf Bänden*. Vol. 9. Alfred Kröner, Stuttgart, 1964.

———. *The Will to Power*. Trans. W. Kaufmann and R. J. Hollingdale. Vintage Books, New York, 1968.

Ritter, Joachim. *Hegel and the French Revolution: Essays on the "Philosophy of Right."* Trans. R. D. Winfield. MIT Press, Cambridge, Mass., 1984.

———. *Metaphysik und Politik, Studien zu Aristoteles und Hegel*. Suhrkamp, Frankfurt am Main, 1969.

Rorty, Richard. *Contingency, Irony, and Solidarity*. Cambridge University Press, Cambridge, 1989.

Schnädelbach, Herbert. *Philosophy in Germany, 1831-1933*. Cambridge University Press, Cambridge, 1984.

Schrift, Alan D. *Nietzsche and the Question of Interpretation: Between Hermeneutics and Deconstruction*. Routledge, New York, 1990.

Schurmann, Reiner. *Heidegger on Being and Acting: From Principles to Anarchy.* Trans. C. M. Gros. Indiana University Press, Bloomington, 1987.

Serres, Michel. *Le parasite.* Grasset, Paris, 1980.

Taylor, Charles. *Hegel.* Cambridge University Press, Cambridge, 1975.

Taylor, Mark C. *Kierkegaard's Pseudonymous Authorship: A Study of Time and the Self.* Princeton University Press, Princeton, 1975.

Weber, Max. *From Max Weber.* Trans. H. H. Gerth and C. W. Mills. Routledge and Kegan Paul, London, 1970.

——— . *Geammelte Aufsätze zur Wissenschaftslehre.* Ed. J. Wincklemann. J. C. B. Mohr (Paul Siebeck), Tübingen, 1922.

——— . *The Protestant Ethic and the Spirit of Capitalism.* Trans. T. Parsons. George Allen and Unwin, London, 1930.

Index

253